NOTES OF TRAVEL

IN

SOUTH-WESTERN AFRICA.

BY

C. J. ANDERSSON,

AUTHOR OF "LAKE NGAMI," "THE OKAVANGO RIVER," ETC., ETC.

NEW YORK:
G. P. PUTNAM'S SONS,
FOURTH AVENUE AND TWENTY-THIRD STREET.
1875.

PREFACE.

IN the preface to Andersson's recent work, "The Lion and the Elephant," edited by myself, it was stated that, if well received by the public, I should probably give out other of his Memoranda in my possession, relating to his more recent Travels; and as the above-named work has proved a success, I now proceed to fulfil my promise.

Owing, however, to severe illnesses, brought on by the hardships Andersson underwent during his early travels; to wounds inflicted by wild beasts, and to his broken fortunes, which compelled him to devote the greater part of his time to mercantile, instead of, as heretofore, to scientific pursuits, he was in a great degree prevented from following up his explorations in unknown lands, and hunting the Elephant, and other denizens of the forest, as in by-gone days. Hence the reader of these pages must not expect to find in them quite so many stirring adventures by flood and field, as are recorded in his earlier publications, viz.: "Lake

Ngami," and "The Okavango River." Had he, however, lived to explore the countries to the north of the River Cunené (at present comparatively little known in England), as was his full purpose, he would, no doubt, have had much to narrate of both a new and interesting nature; but, unhappily, on his reaching the banks of that stream the hand of death was upon him, and a few days afterward he ceased to exist.

This volume, nevertheless, contains matter that it is hoped will afford both interest and amusement to the reader. Among the rest, his graphic description of the great battle between the "Namaquas" and the "Damaras," the latter of whom he commanded in person, and in which he was so severely wounded as to be rendered a cripple during the remainder of his life.

Then again, his account of the "Ovambo," a primitive tribe, bordering on the Portuguese settlement of Benguela, is well deserving of perusal.

His remarks, also, on the South Africa Missionaries, whom no traveller had better opportunities of becoming intimately acquainted with than Andersson, will, I feel assured, interest not a few.

The like may be said as to his observations on the so called "*lung-sickness*," which annually carries off so many animals, both wild and tame, in South Africa; (this the rather, as he himself was not only possessed of vast herds of horned cattle, but was a great sufferer by the epidemic in question—having lost two thousand head—and, in consequence, his remarks will carry due weight with them), for as this disorder may not improbably bear some affinity to the " Rinderpest," which of late years has so ravaged England and other European countries, it is very possible some useful hints, as to the proper treatment of the latter, may be gained from learning the *remedies* usually had recourse to for the "lung-sickness" in Damaraland and adjacent regions.

The chapter on "Game Birds" of the country will also probably prove acceptable to the reader, of such, at least, as are either sportsmen or naturalists. Of other African birds I have not ventured to speak, for the reason, that Mr. John Henry Gurney has recently published an abridgment of Andersson's great projected work—the " Avi Fauna of South Africa "—under the title of " The Birds of Damaraland," to which valuable publication I beg to refer the ornithologist for information respecting the rest of the feathered tribe.

In conclusion, I would add that, among numerous other papers, Andersson left behind him " Notices of several of the Quadrupeds indigenous to Damaraland and neighboring countries." These "Notices" it was my intention, at first, to insert when opportunity offered in present work; but on reflection it struck me that such constant references to matters relating to Natural History would greatly have tended to distract the attention of the reader from the Narrative itself, and I have therefore thought it best—with the exception of a single chapter on the Leopard and its congeners— to exclude them (the " Notices ") altogether; though not without hopes, at some future time, of submitting them to the public.

THE EDITOR.

CONTENTS.

CHAPTER I.

CHAPTER II.

CHAPTER III.

CHAPTER IV.

CHAPTER IX.

CHAPTER X.

CHAPTER XI.

CHAPTER XII.

CHAPTER XIII.

CHAPTER XIV.

CHAPTER XV.

CHAPTER XVI.

CHAPTER XVII.

CHAPTER XVIII.

CHAPTER XIX.

NOTES OF TRAVEL.

CHAPTER I.

The explorer transformed into the proprietor of a large trading establishment—Important journey—Wilhelm Zwartbooi—David Christian—Alarm caused by lung-disease in cattle—Disputed right of way—Damaraland traders—Stopped on our journey by Namaquas—Courage and determination of my wife—Cattle-lifting—Pursuit of the robbers—Caught in a trap—F. Green's coolness in danger—Insolent messages—Sale of my cattle.

WHEN I last appeared before the public in my narrative entitled "The River Okavango," I had become a complete invalid through many months of distressing illness, and consequently quite unfit for any serious exertions. The spirit for exploration and discovery, nevertheless, was far from extinguished in me, but the power to execute failed me, and I determined to await events quietly until such time that my health was restored.

About this period the Walwich Bay Mining Company, whose operations in this country I had at one time conducted, finding that they were carrying on an unprofitable business, determined to wind up their affairs, and to offer their large establishment for sale. They not unnaturally turned to me as a probable purchaser. It is true I had neither the inclination nor the means to work the mines, but it struck me that their head-quarters, Otjimbingue—a place so often mentioned in my former works—might be most advantageously turned to account as a trading station, being very centrally and conveniently situated for such a purpose. Moreover, the company possessed a large number of cattle, chiefly well-trained wagon-oxen, a most essential item toward the success of such a venture as I contemplated. Finally, I thought this kind of life, which, while in a great measure sedentary, had a good deal of desultory activity attached to it, would suit me while recruiting my shattered constitution. But the risk was very great. In the first instance I was aware that Jonker Afrikaner looked upon the company's property with a covetous eye—in fact he had openly declared that they had no right to part with what he considered his own! And I am sorry to say he was backed in this unrighteous assertion by more than one European, who thus thought to serve their own ends. Secondly, that most fearful scourge, the "lung-sickness" (of which more hereafter), had just made its appearance in Damaraland, and was playing sad havoc among the live stock of the inhabitants. But notwithstanding all these serious drawbacks, I began to entertain the project; and quickly making my calculations, I came to the conclusion that, even under very unfavorable circumstances, I could hardly fall to do well. Accordingly I closed with the company's offer, and thus somewhat unexpectedly found myself the proprietor of a large establishment—in short, I, who had recently been an explorer, became converted into a merchant. The step proved ultimately my ruin, though brought about in a way little anticipated, and without any particular fault on my part; but I will not anticipate. Nor will I try the reader's patience by asking him to follow me through all the vicissitudes of a trader's experience in a barbarous country, but I will select such episodes of my life at this period as I think may fairly challenge the interest and attention of an indulgent public.

I had been settled about a year, not unprofitably, at Otjimbingue, when I found it necessary to try to dispose of some of the live stock acquired by my original purchase, as well as that afterward obtained in exchange. Unfortunately the "lung-sickness" had by this time acquired a wonderful repute among the tribes bordering on Damaraland to the south, which had as yet been spared this curse; and it was currently believed that no person coming from my part of Africa would be permitted to pass through their territories with live stock, for fear of having their own also affected. However, as there had always been an acknowledged highway from time immemorial, and as the country was large enough to admit of a free passage to traders and travellers, without any particular danger or inconvenience to any one concerned; and, above all, as the Europeans settled in Damaraland could not exist without a market for their produce, which consisted almost solely of cattle and sheep, I felt it necessary to have the matter at once and forever decided; and as I dared trust no one with this important mission, I determined to undertake the journey in person.

At this time I was on a very friendly footing—in

fact had always been so—with our nearest neighbors to the southward, a tribe of Namaquas under the chief Wilhelm Zwartbooi. I anticipated consequently little or no opposition in this quarter, a view which proved correct; for after due representations had been made to my friends, and I have very little doubt also through the kind interposition of my esteemed friend their venerable missionary, the late Reverend Henry Kleinschmidt, permission to pass through their country was granted with promptitude and consideration. The real obstacle was a long way ahead of us, and lay principally with the people under the chief, David Christian, whose head-quarters were Bethany—a long-established missionary post.

My arrangements for the journey being completed, I set out with a fine troop of cattle and sheep, and proceeded for a considerable distance without any interference or molestation. At last, having passed the boundaries of my friends, we met with other people, who, though civil enough in their way, one and all gave us to understand that much further progress was out of the question, and advised us strongly to retrace our steps. Several traders, with cattle, on the path which we were pursuing, having heard an exaggerated account of the state of health of our own herds, fled precipitately, thus making matters worse for us. When still several days' journey distant from the obnoxious chief, I determined to proceed ahead of my party, with a view of having our fears confirmed, or our hopes verified. I had apparently nothing to dread for my own cattle; for though I certainly had had several cases of death occasioned by "lung-sickness," all symptoms of this disease had long since disappeared. But even had my cattle continued affected, I did not think that the chief could have any right to stop my progress on a road, the use of which was sanctioned by immemorial custom.

I met the chief, and after I told him my story, permission to proceed was readily granted to me. I returned to my people in good spirits, thinking that all our difficulties were now happily at an end, but I had sadly reckoned without my host, as the sequel will shortly prove. In my company were several other traders from Damaraland, and of course in the same situation as myself, who usually journeyed a little ahead of me. One day, it seems, a large party of Namaquas on horseback, headed by David Christian in person, made their appearance, and peremptorily forbade their further progress; they even went so far as to order some cattle to be slaughtered for their inspection. This proved nothing against my fellow-travellers, but a good feast to our foes—and probably it was meant to be so from the first; but the enemy had evidently predetermined to stop us. When my turn came, I at first tried every argument that reason could suggest, and finding these unavailing, I told the chief plainly that nothing but his superior force should stop me. "Indeed," I fearlessly added, "were I but strong enough, I would try a conclusion with you that might prove unpalatable enough;" at the same time laying my hand firmly on the handle of my revolver. The chief became exceedingly fierce and indignant at my resolute conduct, but I quietly assured him that to get into a passion with me was useless, as I did not care one straw for him and his myrmidons, and that they failed utterly to intimidate me. Of course, should he persist in refusing me a passage, circumstanced as I was, there was no alternative but to send back my cattle; but as for myself, I would go forward, and return next season strong enough, I hoped, to defy him and any force that he could oppose to me. At this his wrath knew apparently no bounds; he swore, he stamped, he suddenly rose from his seat, and as suddenly re-seated himself, trembling all the while like an aspen leaf with anger and excitement. But under all this frothy outburst of passion and assumed indignation, it was easy to see that my firm behavior had considerably intimidated him: for he knew enough of me to feel certain that I would carry my threats into execution if within the range of possibilities. Indeed, he honestly acknowledged to poor Jonathan (of whom more presently) that he was in a "funk." "I thought at one time," he said, "that Mr. Andersson would have shot me!" Thus ended our last inauspicious interview.

I reached the Cape in safety, after a long and harassing journey, and lost no time in maturing my plans. I had fully made up mind to fight it out with the obnoxious chief, if necessary, and took measures accordingly. Among other things, I supplied myself with two small but handsome and serviceable brass field-pieces—not so much for the sake of the execution I meant to do with them, as for the moral effect they were likely to produce on a semi-barbarous people, who had probably an exaggerated opinion of cannon. Some of my friends, it is true, thought this a most imprudent step, as it might tend to make the natives more obstinate and unaccommodating; but I had fully calculated all the consequences, and the result justified the measure.

On my return to Damaraland, I found a number of my hunting friends and acquaintances congregated at Otjimbingue, partly awaiting my own return, and partly recruiting themselves for fresh exertions against the elephants. On hearing of my determination to force my way to the colony through the Namaquas, they came forward in a body to offer me their escort, deeming my own servants much too small a party for undertaking so dangerous an enterprise. I was somewhat reluctant to avail myself of their valuable services, inasmuch as their absence from their usual occupations would, in all probability, involve the loss of a whole season—to most of them an object of the utmost importance. At the same time, they were entirely dependent on me for their necessary supplies and creature comforts, and were fully aware that, unless I could bring my cattle speedily and safely to a market, they themselves would stand no chance of having their wants provided for. Their offer of assistance, therefore, though certainly most kind and considerate, was not altogether disinterested, and after due consideration I accepted their proffered help. But even with this opportune, and altogether unexpected, addition to my party, we mustered hardly twenty really serviceable guns, a mere cipher as compared with the many hundreds that were likely to be raised against us, should it be found necessary to have recourse to force, in order to open up the disputed passage. But I correctly estimated my own strength, and that of my apparently formidable enemy. Thus I felt certain that, when once fairly *en route*, many-tongued rumor would vastly exaggerate our real strength; the names of some of my party were in themselves a host; and lastly, not the least, I felt sure that my noisy *brass* friends could not fail to inspire a certain respect, if not awe—in short I felt pretty sure of success.

Everything being finally settled for our adventurous journey, we set out in high spirits. Each man was provided with a double-barrelled gun or rifle, a Colt's revolver, a pistol, and a stout hunting-knife. Most of the party had adopted a kind of uniform—scarlet and drab—and being all pretty well mounted, my escort made both a picturesque and martial appearance.

Apprehending considerable trouble and danger, I had decided on leaving my wife and child—then a mere infant—behind me at Otjimbingue; but my wife having accompanied me a few days' journey on the way, we found each other's society so pleasant that, as the time for leave-taking approached, my brave little helpmate was determined to share with me every danger and trial. Having hastily consulted my companions upon the advisability of the step, she was allowed to have her own way, and we were thus spared a painful and long separation. The result justified our decision, and thus I had the inestimable boon of the company of my family during this long, dangerous, and harassing journey, extending, as it did, over a distance of upward of a thousand miles, through regions the most bleak and barren.

As on a former occasion, all went on smoothly for some days, only one incident occurring worthy of being here recorded. We had just arrived at a Mr. S——'s house (the last European habitation we were likely to meet with for some months to come), and were enjoying ourselves so far as liberty, good cheer, fine weather, and happy spirits would allow, having in fact selected for our motto "Sufficient for the day is the evil thereof." In the midst of our rejoicings, the astounding news reached us that a considerable number of cattle belonging to our hospitable host had been carried off by a set of rascals living at no great distance, and who belonged to a tribe of Hottentots called Topnaars, the fellows in question acknowledging Jonker Afrikaner as their chief; but only nominally, for they did very much as they pleased, laying friend and foe alike under occasional contribution. In fact the tribe was enlarged and strengthened by a conglomeration of the most villainous and wretched scoundrels in the country. Any man outlawed from his own tribe was sure to meet with a hearty welcome from the Topnaars, who with their lawless associates were truly a savage crew.

Neither deeming it safe to absent myself from my own property and people, nor indeed essential to the success of the enterprise, I left it to my escort to pursue, and, if possible, recapture the lost cattle. But the undertaking proved a far more serious one than was at first anticipated, and might have resulted in the most serious consequences to myself and chattels, had there been less presence of mind and pluck among my brave volunteers.

The stolen stock was duly traced, but on account of the rocky and embarrassing nature of the ground traversed by the thieves, it was only late on the second day after the departure of my friends that they found themselves approaching the place to which the booty had been conveyed. They were quietly following on the spoor, when, suddenly turning the angle of a rock in an intricate passage along which they had been for some time unsuspiciously winding their way, they found themselves in full view of a wretched village, and were at the same moment challenged by at least fifty rascals completely hidden from view. Only a few women and children were visible about the huts, but, on looking toward the surrounding rocks whence the challenge had proceeded, they found them literally bristling with fire-arms, while they were unable to distinguish the form even of one of those in whose hands they were. On finding themselves thus fearfully entrapped—for even their retreat was cut off—my friends honestly confessed that they experienced a feeling of horror, and had it been practicable would probably have beat a precipitate retreat; but though they might have done so with honor, the muzzles of guns threateningly pointed at them from every nook and corner prevented them from attempting it with safety. The hesitation and trepidation, however, were only momentary, for finding escape impossible, the leader of the devoted little band, my brave friend F. Green, ordered his followers to dismount, and pulling out his pipe, coolly proceeded to fill and light it. This presence of mind in the face of imminent danger had the desired effect, and in a few minutes every volunteer was sending forth volumes of smoke from his clay bowl, thus hiding the temporary dismay by which they had been struck, and utterly dumbfounding the enemy by their temerity.

Repeating their challenge not to proceed, the villains insolently demanded the cause of the presence of the strangers. This was explained, and intimation was at the same time conveyed that they were determined not to stir from the spot until the stolen cattle were given up. A terrible hubbub then ensued, and a few of the men appeared in view, brandishing their arms threateningly and gesticulating wildly; but the greater number of their guns remained pointed toward them, and in unpleasantly close proximity. The moments that followed were intensely exciting, my friends not knowing but that every second might be their last on earth; they were so utterly helpless, a single false movement and they would inevitably have been ushered into eternity. Whatever courage they might have possessed, and there was no lack of that manly quality, availed them nothing, as their enemies remained concealed from view during the whole of a somewhat protracted parley. But to make a long story short, after endless questions, accompanied with menacing gesticulations and angry threats, the foe gave in, and not only restored the cattle they had purloined, but entertained their unwelcome visitors hospitably! In journeying homeward in safety, with the recovered stock, there was not one among my escort who did not feel sincerely thankful for his narrow escape from destruction, at one time so imminent.

After this adventure nothing occurred for some time to disturb our peace, except when we encountered any of the friendly or neutral Namaquas, who jeered us on account of our determination to proceed, assuring us that David Christian with the whole of his tribe was waiting to dispute our passage at a certain intricate and dangerous point of the road. At last we actually met messengers sent by the chief in question to forbid peremptorily our further progress. We received from time to time several of these haughty and insolent messages, to all of which we quietly answered, "We are friendly disposed, and only require a road for our cattle now and henceforth, grant our reasonable demand and you will insure our gratitude," all the while steadily pursuing our course. At last a neutral chief, one of some note, came as ambassador to us on behalf of himself and his brother chief, through whose territories we desired to pass. Fortunately he was not only friendly disposed toward us and our cause, but a sensible man, who, after listening to our arguments, suddenly declared that he had been authorized by David Christian to grant our request in full should he deem it reasonable, and he would do so. I need not say that this happy termination of our troubles was hailed with the utmost satisfaction and joy by every one of my party, more particularly as it was in a great measure unexpected. It was certainly more favorable than any of us had dared to anticipate.

I have been thus minute in the particulars of my life at this period, not out of a vain bravado, I hope, but as an encouragement to future travellers. My own experience proves that a person similarly situated need never despair, and that, with judicious determination, great ends may be accomplished with very small means. It would have been my utter ruin had the natives been able to stop my progress; but, as it was, I was the means of obtaining immense benefits for all those who were interested in my expedition, since not only was the road opened on the present occasion, but every one obtained full liberty to use it for the future as he thought fit.

Shortly after this happy termination of our troubles, we said farewell to our gallant escort who were now able to return to their usual occupation, having still the best part of the season left for hunting the elephant. I proceeded to the south, and they turned to the north. How they fared, I may perhaps tell in a future chapter, as for myself and my loving and courageous wife, we got over the rest of the journey in safety. On my arrival at the Cape, not reached without great trouble and hardship, I made a famous sale of my cattle, winning golden opinions from all for my beef and mutton

CHAPTER II.

Jonker Afrikaner—Visit to David Christian—Arrogant conduct of a Hottentot—Ruffianly attack—Fatal error committed by my opponent—Tragical incident—In the presence of death—My wife's courage—Reputation of the author in Africa—Daniel Cloete—Inquiry into the death of my Hottentot assailant—Decision—Return to Otjimbingue.

SHORTLY after my return to my residence in Damaraland, I resolved upon paying a visit to the then paramount chief of the country. Jonker Afrikaner had now been dead some time, and it was impossible to deny that his death was a misfortune to the country at large; for though he had slain and plundered on a large scale, he possessed certain qualities that made him at least feared both by friend and foe. He had been succeeded in the chieftainship by his eldest son, Christian, a weak, easy man, not badly disposed, but utterly unfit for his high, important, and difficult station. It was this man I proposed to visit, for I knew he both wished and expected to see me. I was also desirous of showing my wife a little more of the country, and no season could have been more propitious, the weather being moderately warm, and the earth revelling in her richest and most profuse spring dress, as the season had been very favorable for the vegetation.

We set out, and had accomplished rather more than one half of the journey, when we reached the small werft of a Hottentot distinguished for his insolence, brutality, and lawlessness. Christian Afrikaner was his chief, but in the conversation, or rather quarrel, that took place between us, he laughed at the idea of this being the case, maintaining that he himself was the captain, and Christian only his servant!—monstrous arrogance! On several occasions he had levied black-mail on travellers and traders, even ill-treating them personally. Nevertheless, I never dreamt of his daring to interfere with me, more particularly as I was on a visit to the chief. But it proved otherwise, for we had hardly "out-spanned" and kindled a fire preparatory to our frugal meal, when the individual in question, a big, surly fellow, with the visage of a scoundrel, made his appearance.

On seeing me he grunted forth a few words—they might have meant a curse for aught we knew, then leaning forward against his long stick, so indispensable to every Hottentot of consideration, he eyed me for awhile with lowering looks, and suddenly demanded my name, which in fact he knew as well as I did myself, having learned it from his numerous attendants.

"Oh," I replied, "my name? There can be no occasion to give you *that*, since I must be well known to you by report, if not by sight. I just heard one of your people repeat it to you."

"Yes, but I want your name."

"Very well, Andersson then it is."

"Oh! Andersson, Andersson is it? The savage Andersson. Ah, we shall see to-day who is master, you or I."

This was most provoking language, but I rejoined good-humoredly that I could have no wish to be his master; and as for him ever becoming mine, I thought it a most unlikely event. He next demanded our coffee-kettle, dresses for his women, the wagon-chests, etc., indeed I verily believe everything he *saw*, or could *think* of, whether I had it or not! I began to feel a little riled, as a Yankee would say, at the fellow's impertinence, no native having ever dared to go thus far; and if, unhappily, any of them had forgotten what was due to me, they had always received suitable chastisement. It was evident that the scoundrel had made up his mind beforehand to be troublesome, perhaps violent, reckoning no doubt, upon his former successes in that line; for he now burst forth in a torrent of abuse of the most scurrilous kind, and certainly utterly uncalled for, as this, to the best of my belief, was the very first time that we had met, and though I had frequently heard of his villainy, I had never injured him either in deed or word.

Seating myself on the pole of the wagon, I folded my arms, quietly allowing the fellow to exhaust, if possible, his vocabulary of scurrilous language, which was translated to me word for word; I, merely remarking in a undertone to my wife, "I will have that fellow on his knees if he continues much longer his unwarrantable conduct." Finding me determinedly silent, he came close up to me, shaking his clenched fist in my teeth, and hissing forth between his teeth:

"You cannot pass on your way, span in and go back the way you came," at the same time pointing toward Otjimbingue, thus trying to give further effect to his words. It was now high time to undeceive the brutal scoundrel, and I sprang to my feet, and thus slowly addressed him:

"Look here. I have, out of respect to your chief, borne with your insolence thus far. I am, as I have already told you, on my way to visit him, and unless he should order me to go back, neither you nor any one else shall turn me from my purpose, as long as there is breath in my body; if you attempt to stop me, be the consequences on your own head." Suiting my action to my words, I called for the trek-oxen to be caught and yoked. While my boys carried out my orders, I went a few paces on the other side of the wagon to fetch my horse. While I was stooping to undo the knee-halter, with which he was secured, I saw my enemy deliberately walk up to where my saddle and gun were lying on the ground, and possess himself of the bridle. This was a climax to his insolence which I could not endure; but still keeping my temper, I went quietly up to the fellow and said: "Come, give me that bridle," at the same time laying my hand on his shoulder, while with the left I seized the reins. To avoid losing his hold, he stepped rather suddenly back, and coming in violent contact with our cooking utensils, he rolled over on his back. But unwieldy as his carcass appeared to be, he was on his legs in a moment, striking me at the same time a fearful blow in the face just about my eyes, with some hard and angular substance, whether it was the bit of the bridle, or a stone, I never knew. Be that as it may, I felt my face suffused with blood, and I was half-stunned with the violence of the blow. Almost simultaneously I was laid hold of by three or four sturdy ruffians, his servants and backers no doubt in many a similar outrageous affray; but having always possessed an extremely agile and somewhat muscular though slight frame, and having a hazy notion that I was in a somewhat desperate situation, I, with a violent and sudden effort, shook off both drowsiness and assailants, flinging the latter to some distance, and retreated precipitately toward my gun. My enemy perceived in a moment his fatal error, and now realized fully the nature of the man he had to deal with, and whom he had so grossly provoked and so unjustly assaulted. He again rushed upon me wildly, his face contorted frightfully with passion, and with such a fiend-like expression in his eyes as I had never seen before. But quick as he was, he was too late to prevent me from accomplishing the object I had in view. I seized the gun, and in fewer moments than it would take to describe the horrible scene, the unfortunate man lay a corpse at my feet, never more to disturb or annoy inoffensive travellers.

The scene that now ensued baffles all description; the women and children screamed and gesticulated wildly, some of the men rushed to arms, while others ran off furiously in various directions, evidently with the intention of circulating the news and summoning further aid.

It has been my lot in life to witness many an appalling sight, and to find myself involved in many a trying situation, but none more trying than this; for had I not a helpless wife and infant to care for as well as myself? It was dreadful; and the mere narration of the incident, after the lapse of many years, still excites my deepest feelings. My case now appeared utterly hopeless, for the instant they saw my enemy fall dead, my few native servants, mere boys as already said, fled precipitately, leaving me to my fate. Nevertheless, I did not lose my presence of mind for a moment, but shouting to my run-away people, entreated them to stop, not with a view or hope for personal protection, but to collect and attend to the dispersed trek-oxen. I also requested my wife, who was in the wagon with the child, to put my spare rifle in a convenient and accessible position, and then folding my arms, I faced the foe and boldly defied them to do their worst. The sight that then met my eyes was not calculated to re-assure me, or to give me any hope of escape from the trap into which I had fallen. My eyes fell on three men, in a kneeling posture within a distance of one hundred yards, taking each a deliberate aim at my exposed person, so deliberate, indeed, that in order to insure perfect accuracy in their aim, they were resting their guns against the ramrods stuck upright in the earth for that purpose. Expecting nothing short of instant death, I was now only anxious to shield my poor wife and offspring as much as possible from bodily harm, and accordingly just moved sufficiently on one side to allow the balls to pass them harmlessly should the villains confine their fire to me alone. At this moment I heard one of the Damara lads, who had returned to the vicinity at my earnest solicitations, call out, "Oh! master, get behind the wagon, the Hottentots are about to fire on you." Though duly appreciating the poor fellow's anxiety for my safety, I of course did not leave my exposed situation, well knowing that my *only* chance of safety lay in putting a bold face on the matter, as retreat at that moment would have been a sure signal for the cowards to fire. Besides, how could I think of sheltering myself behind the wagon, which at that moment contained all that I held dearest on earth?

After enduring several minutes—to me an age—of the most intense mental anguish, for the muzzles of the guns were constantly pointed at my breast. I saw, to my astonishment and inexpressible relief, the fellows rise from their threatening attitudes and make off! Of course I did not flatter myself that the danger was over, but it gave me breathing time; and now that the enemy was out of sight, I was enabled to recall my panic-stricken servants, and to collect the scattered trek-cattle, etc., which were now inspanned, with the utmost despatch, and we proceeded on the journey.

I cannot here refrain from paying a fitting tribute of thanks and praise to my dear wife, who, during the whole of this trying scene never uttered one word of alarm, or in the slightest way interfered with my movements. Had it been otherwise, how easily might I have been unnerved! She proved herself a true traveller's wife, and gained by her singularly calm and collected conduct a great deal of well-merited applause.

I had now the alternative of proceeding on my journey or retracing my steps—the latter of course being the most tempting, as the road was comparatively free of danger, while an onward movement would certainly entail on us fresh perils, if not utter destruction. I chose notwithstanding to incur these rather than be branded with cowardice. Moreover, I felt convinced that a retrograde movement would have been construed into a sign of guilt, which no after-conduct of mine could rectify or obliterate. After a hurried consultation with my heroic wife, who saw the matter in the same light as myself, I resolved on prosecuting our journey, with the intention of boldly laying my case before the chief whose subject I had slain, but who had given me such ample cause for the deed.

There will be those of my readers, I fear, who will censure me for my proceedings, and brand the act as one of unnecessary precipitation ; but difficult as it may appear to exculpate myself, it would be somewhat unfair to judge my conduct on this occasion by the ordinary standard of right or wrong—only those who have been in a similar position can form a fair judgment on my conduct. Had I been opposed to a single foe, or even had my opponents been three or four men only, I might have been spared the dreadful alternative ; but the odds against me were at least ten to one, an overwhelming majority it must be confessed. In a country utterly devoid of all laws, the only chance of safety to the poor traveller lies in his own power of defence, and in the fear with which he is able to inspire his foes. When a savage semi-civilized man ceases to fear, he becomes overbearing and insolent, from which it is but one step to personal violence, and probably ultimate destruction. At this period, not one of the numerous Europeans gaining their living, either by trade or hunting, had escaped insults and deadly threats, nay, mostly all had been robbed, flogged, and otherwise brutally ill-treated. Hitherto I had escaped personal violence, but I could hardly expect to remain forever unmolested among such a set of ruffians. The Namaquas, with a few exceptions, hated me, and simply for possessing the very qualities they themselves were destitute of, viz., courage, and a true estimate of the sanctity of a man's word. The terms the "proud," the "devil"—the latter equivocal appellation being a compliment to my supposed hardihood in penetrating to distant and little known, or altogether unknown regions—were indifferently applied to me. Knowing therefore that loss of prestige would soon be followed by loss of property, perhaps of life itself, I had made a vow to kill the first savage who attempted to lay violent hands on my person, and I had now fulfilled it. Far be it from me, however, to glory in the deed—on the contrary, I shall always regret having shed human blood; but it was an act of necessity, and I feel I acted for the best.

But to return to my story. I had but too justly estimated the precariousness of our situation. As soon as everything was ready, I ordered the wagon to proceed, following at a short distance on horseback, the post of danger, I conceived, in this instance. Scarcely had we got a mile or two on our way, before I saw a Namaqua—an old friend and acquaintance—running up to us in breathless haste, exclaiming in Dutch: "Oh, Mr. Andersson, for God's sake hurry on to Barmen," (the nearest missionary station), "for the sons of the man you have killed are coming on with a strong party to murder you. I have come away from them, at the risk of my life, to warn you." Poor fellow, he was hardly able to articulate for fear and trepidation, and evidently felt a most sincere anxiety for my safety, and I was much touched with the interest he evinced on my behalf. Bidding him a hurried farewell, and telling him to be of good cheer—how my heart belied the encouragement!—we steadily pursued our journey, but without any unseemly hurry, which in fact would not have availed us, as ere long we must have been overtaken by our relentless foe. Scarcely had my kind-hearted well-wisher departed, when the report of a gun was heard, and at the same time a ball whistled unpleasantly near us. But there was nothing for us to do but quietly to await the deadly encounter, which I no longer doubted would take place ere many minutes had elapsed. Nothing more, however, was seen or heard until we arrived at a narrow part of the road, where we had the misfortune to get our wagon almost helplessly jammed in mud against half-buried rocks. Night was coming on, and with it a drizzling rain—a cheerless and gloomy prospect with a revengeful foe at our backs. At this moment at least fifty armed men came up to us, but instead of massacring us on the spot, they merely stopped to glare and scowl at us for a few minutes, and then passed on. This reprieve, however, had in nowise diminished the danger; it merely changed our relative positions, our savage foes were now in front of us, instead of behind, and likely to increase in numbers at every step they made in advance.

Night had now closed in, and with it the rain increased, so that ere long our garments were saturated. I had made up my mind to stay with the wagon and defend it and myself to the last. Just then, however, we were joined by Daniel Coëte, the catechist at Barmen, who told us he had been informed by the rascals of our forlorn condition, and of their determination to put me to death, asking him at the same time to turn back with them, and see the cruel deed executed. But happily he possessed some influence with them, partly through his inoffensive conduct, and partly because he was himself a half Namaqua by birth, and at his earnest entreaties, therefore, they agreed to bring their complaint before the chief, and to do nothing rashly of their own accord. Thus, under God, this good man was probably the means of saving our lives—mine at least. That night we slept under Daniel's hospitable roof, or rather rested, for it can hardly be supposed that I was able to sleep after a day of such fearful peril and excitement, and with our fate still undecided.

I no longer considered my life in immediate danger; for though now more than ever at the mercy of my enemies, I felt pretty certain that, if I could but see and speak to the chief personally, I should be able to clear myself satisfactorily. I knew, moreover, that the dead man was far from being liked by the tribe, whom his reckless, cruel, and lawless conduct had gone far to disgrace, and that, therefore, his death, in reality, would be regarded as a boon rather than a loss to them. Still he was a Namaqua, and I a white man; more than enough to prejudice better-disposed people against me than those ruled by an Afrikaner, even though I had always been on a good understanding with him.

That same night a messenger was despatched to the chief, informing him of the unlucky deed, and requesting his presence forthwith with a view of investigating the case. The next day his eldest brother John arrived, he whom most people thought best suited for wielding the chieftain's staff. John Afrikaner possessed as much cunning, shrewdness, and determination as the deceased father, and was more free in the expression of his feelings. Moreover, he was the only one of a numerous progeny that was at all liked by the enslaved and much abused Damaras; for though he could not be said to treat them exactly well, yet he was the only one who would occasionally speak in their behalf, and sometimes reprove and restrain the unbridled license and cruelties of his fellows. He was rather liked also by the European settlers in this country. This same John, who was at this time my stanch friend, became afterward my mortal enemy, and, as the sequel will show, we managed to ruin each other in the deadly contest that not long after took place.

John was instructed by the chief, his brother, to escort me and my party to his residence, Schmelen's Hope, of which place frequent mention has been made in my former narratives, and where I spent some very happy days at one period of my erratic life.

I was in great hopes that the chief would at once have entered into the consideration of my situation, but though he received me very kindly and hospitably, he declared that nothing could be done with my case until his uncles and other important personages had arrived—a delay of some time, and quite unexpected, realizing the old saw, "hope deferred maketh the heart sick." But everything has an end, and thus it was with my anxiety. After a week, during which period numerous *raads* or consultations were held about me, I was told that I might return home in peace with an unstained character; that it would perhaps have been better (?) if I had left it to them to punish the guilty man, than to take the law in my own hands, but as the

2

provocation had been very great they did not see that I was seriously to blame. The deceased, they acknowledged, had all his life been a villain, and consequently richly deserved his fate, and letters would be written forthwith to the neighboring tribes, explaining the matter and exonerating me from blame. Thus ended this most tragical affair, which, so far from lowering me in the estimation of the Namaqua nation, not only preserved my prestige among them, but was a warning to them not to interfere with me when peaceably occupied. It is true some were inspired with a deadly hatred toward me, particularly the relatives of the deceased; and Christian Afrikaner confessed secretly as much. In fact, though he had succeeded in clearing my conduct with the tribe at large, he acknowledged he could not answer for my safety when once I left his werft. My friend, Daniel, indorsed the chief's statement, and assured me that, though no open danger was any longer to be apprehended, I stood every chance of having my brains blown out from behind some rock or bush!

I must not here omit to mention that on the news of my unpleasant situation reaching Otjimbingue, several of my acquaintances, who were living on the place at the time, hastened promptly to my assistance. I need not say that I felt much pleasure at this proof of sympathy, which was further heightened on my reaching home by finding nearly two hundred Damaras assembled to greet my safe return. Like a wise general, who leaves nothing to chance, I had, immediately on my arrival at Barmen, secretly sent orders to my manager at Otjimbingue to collect what men he could, to be ready at a moment's warning to hasten to my assistance should judgment go against me, as it was of course impossible to trust implicitly to a favorable verdict from the Namaquas, who, I thought, in such a case would be sure to be more or less prejudiced against me.

CHAPTER III.

Game birds of South Africa—The Kori bustard—Rufous-crested bustard—Rupell's bustard—Cape Knorhaan bustard—Cape guinea-fowls—Great travellers—The chasse—Swainson's Francolin—Double-banded sand-grouse—Variegated sand-grouse—Harlequin quail—Little quail—Painted snipe—Common snipe—Jack snipe and woodcock.

MY business left me but little time for either study, amusement, or recreation, my duties were so multifarious. It is true I kept a clerk and storekeeper, but I always made a point of checking all my books and accounts personally, and as business often called me away for weeks, nay, months, to distant posts and parts, I was not unfrequently greatly in arrears. Thus I remember once returning home with several months' extra work accumulated on my hands; indeed, I had to work by nights to enable me to get through all. This was very harassing and fatiguing, the more so as for more than one-half of the year my labors were performed in a sweltering atmosphere. But whenever I could snatch a moment from my onerous duties it was to study the fauna of the country, which afforded me inexhaustible delight and amusement.

In this chapter, however, I will only speak of the "game birds" found in the vicinity of Otjimbingue and elsewhere in Damaraland and the adjacent regions, feeling assured that some notice of them will prove more or less interesting, both to the sportsman and the naturalist.

I will commence with the bustards, of which there are at least ten species, some of them beautifully plumaged, indigenous to Southern Africa, and of these, five are natives of Damara and Great Namaqua Lands, viz.: The Kori bustard (*Eupodotis Kori*, Burch), usually called the "*wilde pauw*," or wild peacock, a name, however, very wrongly applied; the rather as it also attaches to the *Balearica Negulorum*, or southern-crowned crane.

The splendid bustard in question is thus described by Doctor Burchell, from a fine specimen shot by his party: "The under part of the body was white, but the upper part was covered with fine lines of black on a light chestnut-colored ground. The tail and quill-feathers partook of the general coloring of the back. The shoulders were marked with large blotches of black and white, and the top of the head was black The feathers on the occiput were elongated into a crest. Those of the neck were also elongated, loose, narrow and pointed, and were of a whitish color, marked with numerous transverse lines of black. The irides were of a beautiful pellucid, changeable, silvery ferruginous color."

Personally, I have never known this bird to exceed thirty pounds in weight, but I have been assured on good authority that, in parts of the free states and the Transvaal districts, individuals are sometimes killed very considerably larger.* Usually, however, it does not weigh more than fifteen or twenty pounds. The

* A bird of this species was shot by Mr. E. C. Buxton (a relative of mine, who recently visited the eastern coast of Africa), near the Labourbo mountains to the north of Natal, "weighing," he says, "near forty pounds!"—Ed.

spread of its wings is about eight feet four inches. Its flight is heavy, but nevertheless very rapid; and at night, when changing its feeding-ground, it may be seen flying at a very great height.

It is found throughout the year, in both Damara and Great Namaqualand; and is common, indeed, as far as Ondonga, but is partially migratory. On extended plains, its usual resorts, one often sees it strutting about with its head erect, and looking in size very much like a young ostrich.

Its food consists of insects, berries, etc., and it is very partial to the sweet, gummy exudations of the low mimosa thorn, so abundant in Damaraland. The flesh is very tender and palatable, and, to my notion, about the best of all the South African game birds.

In my time I have killed many of these noble birds. Not, however, with small shot, for even the highest numbers make little impression, owing to their bodies being so thickly protected by feathers, but with a rifle; though even with that weapon, from their extreme shyness and difficulty of approach, it is is considered rather a dexterous exploit to bag one of them.

The rufous-crested bustard (*Eupodotis ruficrista*, Smith).

*Measurement of a Male.**

	In.	Lines.
Entire length	17	9
Length of folded wing	10	8
Length of tarsus	3	2
Length of middle toe	1	9
Length of tail	6	6
Length of bill	1	11

* Naturalists vary somewhat as to the size of this bird. Andersson, as seen above, gives its length as 17 inches 9 lines, breadth of wing 10

Top of head, neck, and upper part of chest, bluish-ash, darkest on the head ; ground color of black, deep rufous mottled with deep brown and black ; the prevailing markings on this part are of a rufous color > shaped, with a black centre—chin and sides of head, dirty white ; head crested ; crest, deep ferruginous, under parts all black. The irides are grayish-brown, with a whitish-yellow ring next the pupil—this ring is sometimes tinged with orange.

I have met with this species pretty often in Great Namaqualand, and also, but less frequently, in Southern Damaraland. It is usually found on open ground thinly-covered with dwarf bush.*

Rupell's bustard (*Eupodotis Rüppellii*, Wahl).

	In.	Lines.
Entire length about	20	0
Bill from forehead	1	5

inches 8 lines, and tail 6 inches 9 lines ; whereas Dr. Smith, a very high authority, makes out its length to be 22 inches, wing 10¾ inches, and tail 5½ inches. Much, however, I should remark, depends on the locality where the bird from whom the measurement is taken was killed, as in certain districts of the eastern coast of Africa, for instance, the Kori bustard, and probably others of that species, attain by all accounts to a greater size than in Damaraland and adjacent parts.—Ed.

* Mr. Buxton, whom I have just quoted, says of this bird, "It is common over Bomba, that is between Transvaal and the coast, and arises from the ground like gray-hen. I could not believe it was anything else till I had it in my hand."

And Ayres, "They appear to be solitary in their habits, lie close, and rise very silently, in the evening they utter a melancholy note 'goo, goo,' often and slowly repeated. When I first heard their note I thought it must be that of an owl."

Dr. Smith further informs us that "Insects, small lizards, and scolopendra seem to constitute its favorite food."—Ed.

	In.	Lines.
Wing from carp joint	12	3
Tail	6	0
Tarsus	2	9
Mid. toe with claw	1½	0

General color of the upper parts (including wings and tail), pale fulvous, tranversely vermiculated with numerous irregular and very narrrow black markings, the fulvous color intermixed with bluish-gray on the crown of the head and the back of the neck, the first four primaries brownish black, except at the base, where they are yellowish-white.

A black streak running from the bill above the eye and down the nape of the neck, a narrower white streak above this, immediately over the eye. A white mark round the eye, cheeks resembling the crown of the head, ear coverts blackish, between the ear coverts and the black-marked stripe, a white band reaching in one direction to the back of the neck, and on the other to below the lower mandible. Skin, throat, and part of neck black, edged with white on the sides. Breast and belly dirty white, under tail-coverts pale brown, legs and toes pale yellow. Bill brown.

The Cape Knorhaan bustard (*Eupodotis Afra*, Gmel.) is in length nineteen inches, the wing twelve inches, and the tail five inches. The top of head, back, part of wings and tail brown-black varying in intensity, and crossed with irregular streaks of rufous, paling into white. Stripe over the eyes reaching to the back of the head. Ear coverts, half collar on back of neck and part of wings pure white, the rest of the plumage deep black, legs bright yellow. The female differs from the male in having the whole of the head, neck, and breast of the same color and markings as the back.

This species is plentiful in Great Namaqualand, and is not uncommon in some of the more open parts of Southern Damaraland. I have also frequently met with it to the south of the Orange river, though at no great distance from it, but never to the north of that stream. It is partial to slightly undulating ground abounding in bowlders and loose stones, and is usually found in pairs. When disturbed, it utters a succession of quick harsh notes, and crows not unlike a corn-crake on taking wing, but in a much lower strain. The eggs of this bustard are of a dark greenish drab, more or less profusely spotted and blotched with brown.

The black and white-winged bustard (*Eupodotis Afroides*, Smith) resembles the preceding in every respect except the great distinguishing mark, viz., on opening the wings the quill-feathers of this species will be found with a large blaze of white on them, while those of the *E. Afra* are entirely black.

Its size is "about that of an old cock grouse," its neck and legs long, like those of the ostrich, and its wings, as the name of the bird denotes, black and white. On taking wing the male becomes outrageously noisy, flying over the plain in circles, much after the manner of the green plover, or pewit, uttering the while a harsh grating cry, and at times rising vertically to a considerable height, often descending as abruptly. It is a great nuisance to the hunter, who is frequently done out of his quarry by its sudden and noisy apparition. Two nests of this bustard found by me at Omapigu, in January 1867, contained each two eggs.

The wild guinea-fowl, commonly called by the colonists the pintado (*Numida cornuta*, Finsch and Hartl.), which probably derives its name from an allied species, having been first met with on the coast of Guinea, and which differs but little from the domestic race, though perhaps somewhat larger, was another of our game birds. It abounds both in Damara and Great Namaqualand, as also from the Orange river in the south to Okavango in the north, and is common, moreover, in the Lake regions.

It is a highly gregarious bird, especially during the dry season, when it is not unfrequently met with in flocks of several hundreds. On a certain occasion, indeed, I saw upward of a thousand collected in one spot, which was one of the prettiest sights I have had the good fortune to witness.

These wonderful congregations usually occur in the immediate neighborhood of waters of small extent. It is quite evident that were such a mass of birds to make a simultaneous rush at the precious liquid, there would be much confusion, and comparatively few would be enabled to satisfy their thirst; but on the contrary, they go to work most systematically, and it is very interesting to watch their proceedings. The first comers enter the well, or hole, as the case may be, and having rapidly and dexterously taken their fill, they make their exit in a different direction, if possible, from that by which they came. In the meantime the outsiders gradually and surely approach, and the ring is thus narrowed by a steady progressive movement of the whole. A batch of fresh comers never attempt to force their way among those which are present, but remain quietly on the outside of the ring until it is their turn.

These birds are great travellers, often going over fifteen or twenty miles in the course of the day, but always returning, if possible, to the water at night; so that by judiciously dogging their steps, the thirsty traveller may often find the desired pool; though implicit reliance should never be placed on this mode of obtaining water. They usually rest for awhile about noon under some mimosa trees, resuming the journey when the greatest heat is over.

A flock of guinea-fowl is in general discovered by their sharp, discordant, and metallic cries, something like a rapid succession of blows struck upon iron. They have many enemies, and seek security at night by roosting in tall mimosa trees.

They feed on grasses, seeds, and insects; but chiefly on small bulbs, which are also eagerly sought for by all gallinaceous birds, and which grow very abundantly throughout the country.

The nests of these birds, which may be found from the end of December to May, consist merely of a slight rounded depression in the ground. It usually contains from fifteen to twenty eggs of a pale buff color, sometimes speckled with pale gray.

These are not unfrequently placed by the colonists and others under domestic fowl, and the young are not difficult to rear; but as they grow up, their propensity to roosting in high trees is rapidly developed, much to the distress of their foster-mother, who is unable to follow them to their lofty perch.

I have also known chicks of this bird, captured in a

wild state, to be reared; but in no one instance, so far as I am aware, have these chicks, when arrived at maturity, brought up families of their own.

The flesh of the young wild guinea-fowl is very white, tender, and well-flavored; but that of the old one is far from tempting.

This bird not only furnished me with many a meal, but excellent sport. With management, indeed, any number may be shot in a day. To give some idea of this, I may mention that one evening we had started an immense flock near the water, and thinking it a favorable opportunity of replenishing our exhausted larder, I slung a double shot-gun over my shoulder and started in pursuit. But though I soon found the quarry, they were so wild that for a long time I could not get within range. At last, and after having chased them about the rocks till I was nearly tired, they scattered themselves among the stones, and lay so close that, unless I almost trod on them, they would not rise. With a steady pointer, it is my belief the whole flock might have been killed. As it was, I made a very large bag.

We had another fine game-bird, the francolin, a kind of grouse (called by the colonists and others, the pheasant), that frequently afforded me, not only capital shooting, but a delicacy for the table. There are several species of this bird, of which the following came under my notice; viz.:

Swainson's francolin (*Pternises Swainsonii*, Smith). In travelling northward I first met with this powerful and somewhat coarse francolin, at the southern extremity of Omuveroom, where it occurred sparingly, but became more common as I proceeded further north, till, on the banks of the Okavango river I found it quite abundant. It frequents grassy localities, sprinkled with brush-wood, generally, but not always, selecting the neighborhood of springs, streams, or marshes. It feeds in open spots, but retires to the jungle on the first approach of danger, chiefly trusting to its legs to effect a retreat. It always roosts in trees, and occasionally perches on them by day; in the early morning and evening it utters frequent harsh cries. The young of this francolin are strong on the wing about the month of May.

The iris of this species is dark brown; the loose and bare skin around the eyes and on the chin and throat, pale red, and the same color tinges the lower mandible of the bill and the base of the upper: the remainder of the latter being a dark horn color, lightest at the tip.

The Orange river francolin (*Scleroptera gariepensis*, Smith). This beautiful francolin was only met by me on the high table-land of Great Namaqua and Damara Lands, where it is frequently very abundant. The covey usually consists of six or eight individuals, though sometimes as few as three, but at others of as many as fourteen.

These francolins invariably frequent glassy slopes sprinkled with dwarf bush. They lie very close, and after having been once or twice flushed, are not easily found again, even with the assistance of dogs.

The iris is brown; the bill horn-color, except near the base, where it is yellowish.

Dr. Smith's figure of the female of this species, it is to be remarked, is altogether too dull; for although the tints in the female are not so deep as in the male, they are still exceedingly rich and bright.

The Cogui francolin (*Scleroptera subtorquata,* Smith). I only met with this bird in the neighborhood of the Okavango river, where it is found in coveys, on grassy plains interspersed with large trees and brushwood. As with the last named, it is difficult to get on the wing unless with the assistance of a dog, and even then it is not always easy. It roosts on the ground, and utters a shrill, but not unpleasant call-note in the early morning and also toward evening.

The iris is reddish-brown; the bill dark horn-color; angle of the mouth lemon-colored, which is also the color of the tarsus.

The pileated francolin (*Scleroptera Pileata,* Smith). It was when travelling northward I first met with this francolin, on the stony and wooded slopes above Okambute, in northern Damaraland, but subsequently I observed it to the north of that locality. It occurs in coveys, and its flesh it very palatable.

The iris is brownish.

The red-billed francolin (*Scleroptera adspersa,* Waterhouse). This, the most common and abundant francolin in Damara and Great Namaqua Lands, is usually met with in coveys, which, in favorable seasons, not uncommonly consist of from ten to fourteen individuals. This species is seldom found at any considerable distance from perodical streams, and on the least approach to danger, seeks shelter in the trees and bushes with which their banks are generally studded. It, indeed, lives much in trees, roosting among the branches by night, and resting there during the heat of the day.

These francolins run with extraordinary swiftness, and will not use their wings unless very hard pressed; and when they do fly, it is with the view of concealing themselves among the thickest branches of some convenient tree, where they remain perfectly motionless, and should it be a full foliaged tree in which they have taken refuge, it requires a good and practised eye to detect them; but when the danger is over, they generally again seek the ground.

The feeding time of these birds is the early morning and the cool of the evening. Their food, as with the other francolins, consists of small bulbs, seeds, berries, insects, etc.

Their notes are harsh, and so loud that they may be heard at a great distance; they resemble a succession of hysterical laughs, at first slow, but increasing in rapidity and strength till they suddenly cease.

The female is smaller than the male; she deposits her eggs in a hollow in the ground without any lining.

The iris is dark brown; the bare skin round the eye pale yellow; the bill and legs in the adult bird are a rich warm red; the toes and spurs of the male are purple. In very young birds the bill is dark purple, and the color of the legs is much paler than in the adult.

Numberless francolins, more especially of the last-named species, fell to my gun in Africa, and for the most part to a splendid pea-rifle by Purdy. On one occasion, indeed, I bagged with it thirty-three of these birds without missing a single shot. They were "treed," it is true; but I still thought it rather a feat, as from the habit of concealing themselves behind the stem and branches, little more than the head or tail was often to be seen, and as a consequence, the position of their bodies was only to be guessed at.

Francolins would seem to be equally as numerous in Caffraria as in Great Namaqua and Damara Lands; for Delegorgue tells us (though without naming the particular species) "that with a few charges of small shot he could always obtain a sufficient number of these birds for the wants of himself and party; and that had ammunition been more abundant, and had he felt interest in the sport, two hundred might easily have been killed in a day."

The sand-grouse, commonly called the Namaqua partridge, was another of our game birds, but not being, to my taste, particularly good eating, it was but seldom that I went in pursuit of it. There are several species of this bird in Southern Africa. of which three were well-known to me, viz.:

The double-banded sand-grouse (*Pterocles bicinctus*, Tem.), the most common, perhaps, in Damara and Great Namaqua Land.

The eggs of this species are from two to three in number, laid upon the bare sand, and of a pinkish-yellow color, spotted with gray and reddish-brown.

The iris is deep red; the skin round the eye chrome-yellow; the bill yellowish-brown; the legs and toes pale dull yellow.

The variegated sand-grouse (*Pterocles variegatus*, Burch). This species is not uncommon in the northern and middle parts of Damaraland, as well as in the Lake regions; but I do not recollect having met with it further to the south.

The Namaqua sand-grouse (*Pteroclurus Namaqua*,

Gmel.), is very abundant in some parts of Damaraland.

Its eggs are deposited on the sand, and are of a drabbish color, closely spotted with gray and brown; they are oval, and less elongated than those of the *P. bicinctus*.

The iris is very dark brown; the skin round the eye is a somewhat pale yellow; the bill is bluish, tinged with white on the lower mandible.

Measurement of a Female.

	In.	Lines.
Entire length	11	0
Length of folded wing	6	5
Length of tarsus	0	11
Length of middle toe	0	9
Length of tail	3	6
Length of bill	0	7

Ordinarily, the several species of sand-grouse spoken of are met with in pairs, or two or three together, dispersed over sandy plains, where they seek their sustenance; but in the dry season, when the rain-pools are exhausted, they, morning and evening, resort in large flocks to permanent waters to quench their thirst, announcing their arrival and departure by incessant sharp cries. They usually make their appearance at about eight or nine o'clock in the morning, circling round the fountain at a considerable height before they descend, and adding to their number at almost every turn they take. Frequently they make no attempt at alighting, until directly over the spot they intend to visit, when they descend with great velocity, at the same time describing more or less of a semicircle before they alight. And when thus congregated at the water, they conduct themselves in a like orderly manner as the guinea-fowl spoken of a few pages back, viz., they do not rush simultaneously to the pool, but each one waits its turn, the first comers having the precedence. And as with the guinea-fowl, the traveller, by watching the flight of these birds at morn or even, is often guided to the water.

Their food consists of seeds, berries, and small bulbs, with which they mingle considerable quantities of sand to assist digestion.

When the sand-grouse are collected at their drinking-places, any numbers may be shot. I have heard indeed of fifteen or twenty being slaughtered at a single discharge.

The European quail (*Coturnix communis*, Bonn), is not uncommon in middle and southern Damaraland. During the year 1865, countless numbers of these birds arrived in the neighborhood of Cape Town, while much of the rest of the colony, which had suffered severely from drought, was nearly denuded of them.

The Harlequin quail (*CoturnixDelegorgues*, Deleg.), was killed by me for the first time on the 30th of March, 1867. Mr. Chapman also obtained it at Lake Ngami.

The iris of this species is the color of new leather when well browned by exposure; the bill nearly black, but the point of the upper mandible is light horn-color; the legs and toes are dusky.

The Little quail (*Kurichane Hemipode*) is not uncommon in Great Namaqualand during the rainy season; but I have never found many of these birds together, and it is rarely that more than one of them is flushed at a time. Their favorite resorts are rank grassy spots in the neighborhood of temporary rain pools and periodical water-courses; here they run about with great celerity, and hard pressed, lie so close as almost to allow themselves to be trodden on before they take wing, after which it is nearly impossible to flush them a second time. They feed on insects and seeds.

The iris is lemon-colored, the bill blue, with the tip of the mandible dark horn-color; the tarsi and feet flesh-colored white.

	In.	Lines.
Entire length	5	8
Length of folded wing	2	10
Length of tarsus	0	10
Length of middle toe	0	6
Length of tail	1	5
Length of bill	0	8

The snipes were also among our game birds. At least the African painted snipe (*Rynchœa Capensis*, Linn.).

Measurement of a Male.

	In.	Lines.
Entire length	9	2
Length of folded wing	4	9
Length of tarsus	1	9
Length of middle toe	1	5
Length of tail	1	9
Length of bill	1	10

The head of this bird is brown, slightly variegated with white, a yellow stripe passes from the base of the bill over the centre of the head to the back of the neck, a similar stripe rises immediately in front of each eye, passing to the back of the head, two similar stripes, bordered by black, extend from the shoulders down the back to the root of the tail; neck grayish-brown, barred finely on the back portion with dark brown, on the anterior portion more coarsely with the same color: it is likewise bisected by a white collar; under parts all white, back beautifully marked with transverse black, white, and gray bars, the wings with numerous semi-ocelli, which are yellow edged with black; when extended they expose numerous yellow or white ocelli, also edged with black, and also numerous black wavy transverse bars, chiefly on a slate-colored ground, the tail being similarly marked.

The female, eye stripe pure white, chin dirty white, neck and breast deep dull rufous, succeeded by a broad black collar, and pure white on the under part, broken only by a patch of black on each side; the plumage of the back is much darker than on the male, and the wings, when closed, instead of having the black and yellow markings of the male, are a shining green, transversely and minutely barred with black, all lustrously with metallic green, legs green, bill red at the tip, iris hazel.

This bird, though only found sparingly in Great Namaqua, was common in Damaraland, a pair or two being always met with wherever the ground was swampy; it is also pretty common in all the water-sheds to the north and east on the last-named country; as also in Ondonga, where it breeds.

Though partial to marshy ground, this species is also found on the side of little rills and running springs, it lies close like common snipe, but its flight is very different, being heavy and comparatively slow, and when flushed it flies but short distances before again alighting. It lives singly or in pairs ; but a dozen may sometimes be found scattered over a small marsh within a short distance of each other. It would seem to feed chiefly on insects ; the flesh is very palatable.

The painted snipe makes no nests ; the female deposits her eggs—three to four in number, and of a very dark color, freely blotched with black—near to the water.

Though the double or solitary snipe (*Gallinago major*, Gmel.) is a regular migrator to Natal and the Transvaal Republic (arriving in the former country in September or October, and leaving again in January or February) I am very doubtful if it be indigenous, or even a visitor to Great Namaqua or Damaraland, as I never met with or even heard speak of it in either of those countries. The only specimen of this bird, indeed, that came into my possession while in Southern Africa, was at Ondonga (Ovampo Land) in 1867.

I have very great doubts, moreover, of the common snipe (*G. Scolopacena*) being a native of, or even a migrate of Damaraland and the adjacent regions. At one time, it is true, I was of a different opinion ; this was when encamped at Omonbonde, waiting for the rains to enable me to penetrate into the far interior. In the extensive marsh at that place both ducks and snipes were pretty plentiful, and afforded me many a good meal. At that time, however, I was simple enough to imagine the snipes I then shot were of the common kind, and therefore neglected to preserve specimens ; but since then I have had reason to believe that I was mistaken, and that they might have been examples of the South African snipe (*G. nigrepennes*), which bears a very considerable resemblance to the *G. Scolopacena*.

Neither the jack snipe (*G. Gallinula*), nor its congener, the woodcock, I may add, ever came under my notice either in Damaraland or elsewhere in Southern Africa.

CHAPTER IV.

Vultures—Power of scenting their prey at a distance—Sir Samuel Baker's theory—Extraordinary field of vision—Waterton's theory—Andersson's theory—The Marabou stork—The ostrich—New species—Chase of ostriches by Namaquas—Pursuit of ostriches on horseback—Hottentot expedient for carrying off ostrich eggs.

SPEAKING of birds, I would say a few words regarding the vulture, or rather on the much vexed question as to whether it is directed to its food by scent or sight, regarding which various opinions have been hazarded. M. ——, for instance, as will be seen, advocates the former. He writes as follows:

"One day when standing outside a farm-house in company with my friend, Charles Bainbridge, as I was casually casting my eyes heavenward, I perceived little specks in the sky, which gradually became larger and larger. Drawing my host's attention to these objects, and asking for explanation, he quietly remarked, 'they are vultures, evidently scenting some carcass; let us go in the direction they are hovering over and descending.' After a short walk we came upon two sick sheep. 'These,' remarked my friend, 'are what the birds are looking for.' It seemed to me incredible that a bird at that enormous height should be able to distinguish anything, and much more between an animal lying down, and one in the same situation, but sick. Nevertheless, the farmer, accustomed to these sights, was right, for on removing the suffering brutes to the homestead, the vultures gradually began to rise, and as quickly disappeared as they had appeared.

Sir Samuel Baker, on the contrary, though admitting that scent often aids the vulture, would seem to be clearly of opinion that it is chiefly by sight that it is guided to the carcass; he says:

"A question has been frequently discussed whether the vulture is directed to his prey by the sense of smell or by keenness of vision. I have paid much attention to their habits, and, although there can be no question that their power of scent is great, I feel convinced that all birds of prey are attracted to their food principally by their acuteness of sight. If a vulture were blind it would starve; but were the nostrils plugged up with some foreign substance to destroy the power of smell, it would not materially interfere with its usual mode of hunting; scent is always stronger near the surface of the ground; thus hyenas, lions, and other beasts of prey, will scent a carcass for a long distance, provided they are to leeward, but the same animals would be unaware of the presence of the body if they were but a short distance to windward.

"If birds of prey trusted to their nostrils, they would keep as near to the ground as possible, like the carrion crow, which, I believe, is the exception that proves the rule. It is an astonishing sight to witness the sudden arrival of vultures at the death of an animal, when a few moments before not a bird has been in sight in the cloudless sky. I have frequently lain down beneath a bush, after having shot an animal, to watch the arrival of the various species of birds in regular succession. They invariably appear in the following order:

"No. 1. The black and white crow; this knowing individual is most industrious in seeking for his food, and is generally to be seen either perched upon rocks or upon trees. I believe he trusts much to his sense of smell, as he is never far from the ground, while at the same time he keeps a vigilant look-out with a very sharp pair of eyes.

"No. 2 is the common buzzard; this bird, so well-known for its extreme daring, is omnipresent, and trusts generally to sight, as it will stop at a piece of red cloth in mistake for flesh; thus proving that it depends more upon vision than smell.

"No. 3 is the red-faced small vulture.

"No. 4 the large bare-throated vulture.

"No. 5 the Marabou stork, sometimes accompanied by the adjutant.

"When employed in watching the habits of these birds, it is interesting to make the experiment of concealing a dead animal beneath a dense bush. This I have frequently done, in which case the vultures never find it unless they have witnessed its death; if so, they will already have pounced in their descent while you have been engaged in concealing the body; they will then, upon near approach, discover it by the smell. But if an animal is killed in thick grass eight or ten feet high, the vultures will seldom discover it. I have frequently known the bodies of large animals, such as elephants and buffaloes, to lie for days together beneath the shade of the dense nabbuk bushes, unattended by a single vulture; whereas, if visible, they would have been visited by these birds in thousands.

"Vultures and the Marabou stork fly at enormous altitudes. I believe that every species keeps to its own particular elevation, and that the atmosphere contains regular strata of birds of prey, who, invisible to the human eye at their enormous height, are constantly resting upon their wide-spread wings, and soaring in circles, watching with telescopic sight the world beneath. At that great elevation they are in an exceedingly cool temperature, and therefore require no water; but some birds that make long flights over arid deserts, such as the Marabou stork and the buzzard, are provided with water-sacks; the former in an external bag a little below the throat, the latter in an internal sack, both of which carry a large supply. As the birds of prey that I have enumerated invariably appear at a carcass in their regular succession, I can only suggest that they travel from different distances or altitudes. Thus the Marabou stork would be the farthest from the earth, the large bare-necked vulture would be the next below him, followed by the red-faced vulture, the buzzard, and the crow that is generally about the surface. From their immense elevation, the birds of prey possess an extraordinary field of vision, and although they are invisible from the earth, there can be no doubt that they are perpetually hunting in circles within sight of each other. Thus, should one vulture discover some object upon the surface of the earth below, his sudden pounce would be at once observed and imitated by every other in succession. Should the one vulture nearest the earth perceive a body, or even should he notice the buzzards collecting at a given point, he would forthwith become aware of a prey, and his rush toward the spot would act like a telegraphic signal to others that would be rapidly communicated to every vulture at successive airy stations.

"If an animal be skinned, the red surface will attract the vultures in an instant. This proves that their sight, and not their scent, has been attracted by an object that suggests blood. I have frequently watched them when I have shot an animal, and my people have commenced the process of skinning. At first, not a bird has been in sight, as I have lain on my back and gazed into the spotless blue sky, but hardly has the skin been half-withdrawn when specks rapidly moving have appeared in the heavens, 'caw! caw!' has been heard several times from the neighboring bushes, the buzzards have swept down close to my people, and have snatched a morsel of clotted blood from the ground. The specks have increased to winged creatures, at the great height resembling flies, when presently a rushing sound behind me, like a whirlwind, has been followed by the pounce of a red-faced vulture that has fallen from the heavens in haste, with closed wings, to the bloody feast, followed quickly by many of his brethren. The sky has become alive with black specks in the far-distant blue, and with wings hurrying from all quarters. At length a coronet of steady, soaring vultures forms a wide circle far above, as they hesitate to descend, but continue to revolve around the object of attraction. The great bare-necked vulture suddenly appears. The animal shot has been skinned, and the required flesh secured by the men. We withdraw a hundred paces from the scene. A general rush and descent takes place; hundreds of hungry beaks are tearing at the offal. The great bare-necked vulture claims respect among the crowd. But another form has appeared in the blue sky, and rapidly descends; a pair of long, ungainly legs hanging down beneath the enormous wings, now touch the ground, and *Abou Seen* (the father of the teeth and beak, the Arab name for the Marabou) has arrived from the higher regions, and stalks proudly toward the crowd, pecking his way with his long beak through the struggling vultures that had preceded him, and swallowing the lion's share of the repast. This bird is very numerous throughout the Nile tributaries of Abyssinia, and may generally be seen perched upon the rocks on the water-side, watching for small fish and reptiles that may chance to come within his reach."

Waterton would seem to take a different view of the subject in question, from Sir Samuel Baker; he says:

"Vultures, as far as I have been able to observe, do not keep together in a large flock when they are soaring up and down, apparently in quest of a tainted current. Now suppose a mule has just expired behind a high wall under the denser foliage of evergreen tropical trees; fifty vultures, we will say, roost on a tree a mile from the dead mule. When morning comes, off they go in quest of food. Ten fly by mere chance to the wood where the mule lies, and manage to spy it out through the trees; the rest go in quite a different direction. How are the last mentioned birds to find the mule? Every minutes carries them farther from it.

Now reverse the statement, and instead of a mule newly dead, let us suppose a mule in an offensive state of decomposition. I would stake my life upon it that, not only the fifty vultures would be at the carcass next morning, but also that every other vulture in the adjacent forest would manage to get there in time to partake of the repast."

The much mooted question as to whether the vulture hunts by sight or scent, has also occupied much of my attention, and what came under my observation on a certain occasion goes far to convince me the bird employs both the one and the other of these senses in finding its prey.

Early one morning I was toiling up the ascent of a somewhat elevated range of hills, with the view of obtaining bearings for my travelling map. Before arriving at the summit, however, I observed several vultures descending the declivity; but thinking I had merely disturbed them from the lofty perch where they passed the night, I did not at first take particular notice of them. On gaining the summit of the hill, nevertheless, I found that the birds in question had not come from the high ground, but from an independent distance on the other side of the hill. This circumstance, coupled with the recollection that I had wounded a zebra on the preceding day in the same direction as the vultures were proceeding, and fancying that this animal might be their object, I paid more attention to their movements. Beyond the hill in question, the flight of the birds was at least five hundred or a thousand feet beneath me, but when they approached the base of the hill, and, at times so far apart that the next comer was not visible to the naked eye, they abruptly rose, and without deviating from it in the slightest degree, followed the course pursued by their companions. They were a very numerous company.

Having completed my observations, I descended the hill, and proceeded in the direction taken by the vultures; and after about an hour's rapid walking I found, as I had anticipated, the carcass of the zebra mentioned, with a numerous company busily employed in discussing it.

The other vultures discovered the zebra in the first instance, though whether by sight or scent I know not, is certain; but that those met with by me on the hill, so far from having been directed to the carcass by scent, were merely following by sight those who preceded them, I fell satisfied.

Both in my own works and in those of other sportsmen and travellers, I would observe, mention is frequently made of the swarms of vultures that usually congregate about the carcass of a dead animal; nevertheless, but few probably form to themselves an idea of the number as estimated by Delegorgue, who, after telling us that "on his return to a buffalo shot by him some little time previously," says:

"Notwithstanding our near proximity to the spot, the vultures came from all quarters, and disputed furiously with each other for the best places; the last comers descending from the air, resting their feet on the bodies of the first, whom they constrained by their weight to give place to them. Many sharp blows with their beak were exchanged, of which, however, such was their ardor, even the wounded seemed to take no notice. Their number probably exceeded five hundred. The carcass of the buffalo was completely hidden from sight by them, and on all sides round about were many others attempting to drive away those who were already gorging themselves.

"Though all were equally greedy, yet doubtless there was among this great mass of sharp beaks and upraised tails more than one unjust oppressor. Observing this, the idea came into my head to keep some kind of order among them. My gun was pointed into the midst of this mountain of vultures, distant one hundred and ten paces. The explosion ensued, and seven of the number remained on the spot, either killed or helplessly wounded by a single ball! Certainly a justifiable motive was wanting to induce me so to act, because the innocent as well as the guilty equally suffered; but to speak the truth, my real object was to ascertain the effect my bullet would have on a great gathering of individuals of this species. It was, however, a destruction not only useless, but blamable, because the vultures render these countries a signal service in rapidly absorbing quantities of offal that would otherwise contaminate the air with deleterious miasma."

Of the ostrich I have also a word to say, not, however, as regards its natural history, etc., of which, in my former works I entered into rather full particulars, both in consequence of having recently discovered what, from an early period of my wanderings, I had suspected, viz., that another species of that bird, one quite new to science, exists in Southern Africa, a fact that may interest many.

In the common species the male is black, with white

tail and wings, while the female is of a grayish color. Of the new species I have not an entire specimen so as to be enabled to give an accurate description of the entire bird; still I possess sufficient data to enable me to vouch for the correctness of my statement, having three pieces or portions of skin of two males, one female, and a young one, apparently about half grown.

The male bird would seem to differ but little from the well-known African species, except in size, it being somewhat larger; the great and specific difference lies with the female and the young. The former is jet black in the body, like the male. The young is of a sooty-brown, and the feathers, which are narrow, and come to an acute point, are tipped with light brown; the tail similar, but interspersed with a few gray or grayish-white feathers; the wings similar to the tail, but of a softer texture; the thighs and neck white. The egg of this species is said to be larger than that of the common ostrich. The bird in question seems to be pretty commonly distributed over the boundless wastes and plains of both Great Namaqua and Damaraland, and herds with the ordinary species.

Many of the natives, hunters also, speak of a third species of ostrich, which they characterize by some very marked distinctions; thus, for instance, I am assured that it has a narrow but conspicuous bar across the back or rump, and a double row of quills on each wing; also, that the color is brownish gray in both sexes; nevertheless, I mention it here more for the purpose of drawing the attention of naturalists to the subject, than from any personal belief in its existence as a third distinct South African species.

Though, as recently observed, I have in my former works gone much into detail in regard to the ostrich, the following means of effecting its capture, as pursued by the Namaquas with considerable success, were not then described.

A troop of ostriches having been espied, a number of men set about surrounding them, but at a great distance; and in the first instance, therefore, the hunters stand far apart from each other. When a sufficient time has elapsed for the completion of the circle, they all move forward simultaneously, keeping the while as much out of sight of the birds as possible, and taking care at the same time not to appear to direct their attention to the quarry, but merely to show themselves in such a manner as to cause the birds to "give way," or move off in a different direction, where they are pretty certain to meet an enemy and to be turned back again. For a time the ostriches are thus kept quietly moving within the circle, but when at length this becomes compressed, and the hunters see that the chances of the birds escaping are but small, they keep them moving at a rapid pace, shouting, yelling, and gesticulating violently at the same time; so that the poor creatures soon become utterly exhausted, and an end is presently put to the exciting scene by the slaughter of the whole or greater part of them. With experienced hunters, this plan of capture seldom fails of insuring success.

The same people resort to another, and even more destructive way, of capturing the ostrich than that just described. At times indeed, a whole tribe, many of the men being mounted, take part in it. The locality for the hunt having been determined on, a body of horsemen station themselves at intervals across a defile, on the narrow portion of a plain where the quarry is likely to pass, while others, also mounted, are despatched in search of the birds. These, when on the way, leave at convenient distances one or other of their number to act, not only as sentinels, but for a purpose that will presently be shown. Having found the destined victims, with whose favorite haunts they are pretty well acquainted, the remainder of the party begin gradually and cautiously to drive the unsuspecting birds before them, and in the direction of their comrades, who are lying in wait.

This purpose effected, they urge the poor creatures forward at a telling pace, and on coming to the men, stationed as sentinels, they themselves drop behind, leaving the latter to continue the pursuit in their stead. After breathing their horses they draw up in line, thereby forming a barrier, so to say, should the quarry head back or attempt to escape in that direction. Thus the ostriches have not a moment's respite given them in their headlong flight, and it consequently not unfrequently happens that by the time they reach the horseman waiting for them, they are so exhausted as to come to a dead stand-still—or even to fall helplessly to the ground. The captures on these occasions are often very considerable. At times, indeed, greater than the hunters require for food, and in which case they will allow such of the birds as they stand not in need of, after first despoiling them of their valuable wing and tail feathers, to depart without further injury.

In concluding these few observations on the chase of the ostrich, I would here add the result of not only my own trifling experience, but that of others, of late years; viz., that these birds are easier of approach when congregated in numbers,* than when there are only two or three together; and that in pursuing them on horseback considerable experience is requisite to insure success. Thus, to ride steadily after them without distressing your steed; but so soon as they evince signs of being desirous of halting, give them another start by pushing your horse suddenly forward, and thus continue until such time as they begin to wave their wings heavily, a sure sign of partial exhaustion. This is the moment to urge your steed to the utmost; but never attempt to ride down the ostrich unless the sun be scorching hot.

Speaking of this bird reminds me of a somewhat singular expedient the Hottentots are accustomed to resort to when chance leads them to its nest. After divesting themselves of their trousers, and tying up the lower ends thereof, they securely pack the eggs within them, and when thus converted into a kind of saddle-bags, they either throw them over their shoulders, or, if mounted, across the backs of their steeds, and thus convey the prizes to their homes.

* Though I myself have never seen any very great number of ostriches together, yet other travellers have been more fortunate, Lechtensten, for instance, after describing a spirited chase after these birds, goes no to say, "The number we saw could scarcely have been less than three hundred."

CHAPTER V.

Harassing period of my life—Kamaherero and his tribe—Power of the Namaquas—Wretched condition of the enslaved tribe—Rising of the Damaras—Visit of Philippus, son of a Damara chief—Upright conduct of the Damaras—Rumors—Treachery of the Namaquas—Alarm at Otjimbingue—Battle and victory of the Damaras—Death of Rev. Mr. Kleinschmidt.

I NOW approach a period of my life at once the most painful, the most harassing, and the most fatal—fatal to my worldly and hard-earned possessions in the most complete sense, and all but fatal to my life. As it was, it left me a poor useless cripple for the remainder of my existence. But it is a long story and one difficult to tell.

Those who have perused the pages of "Lake Ngami" may remember the name of Katchamaha, as one of the four great chiefs whom Mr. Galton and myself found on our arrival in Damaraland The old man was dead, but Kamaherero, the eldest surviving son—for several had been killed in the civil wars of the country and by the Namaquas—finding his people diminishing fast, and dreading, I presume, the ultimate destruction of himself and the tribe—he, together with the latter, suddenly threw himself on Jonker's mercy and protection. The refugees were well received by the politic chief, and located, as it would seem, at no great distance from his own werft, where for a time they were treated with consideration, in fact, the Damara chieftain's power, though broken, was still so formidable that Jonker somewhat dreaded him. Moreover, such an ally would prove of inestimable service to him in his numerous predatory excursions against such of the Damaras as still retained their independence, and a bulwark against enemies in general. For some time, therefore, Kamaherero was left unmolested, with the exception of occasional demands upon his purse *i. e.* his cattle. But the Namaquas, long accustomed to power, and to have their slightest whim obeyed by a people who seem naturally to have fallen into serfdom, soon acquired unlimited sway over their *soi-disant* friends and allies, who at length became little bettei than slaves and minions of their unscrupulous protectors.

Things had for some years thus gone on from bad to worse; for not content with keeping them in abject submission, and plundering them of their possessions, the Namaquas proceeded to personal violence, the Damara chief himself not being exempt from insult and degradation. The natural weakness and apathy of the Damara character made them bear their lot patiently, though not contentedly; in fact the tribe had gradually grown strong again, partly by the infusion of the remnants of other tribes, who like themselves, had sought safety with their enemies, and partly by their own natural increase. Moreover, a great portion had become tolerably conversant with the sight and use of fire-arms, as well as with their once equally dreaded enemy, the horse. Lastly, and not the least important circumstance, they began to feel their own physical superiority. It was impossible for them to be blind to the difference between themselves and the Namaquas, the diminutive, slight, and frail figure of the latter, when compared with their own tall and well-made frames. Even Jonker himself was not slow to perceive this defect in his people; but as a set-off, the Damaras were studiously prevented from acquiring any quantity of guns or ammunition. About this time, too, I believe, the Damaras had been secretly invited by another tribe of Namaquas—the sworn enemies of Jonker and his people—to join them openly against their oppressors or, at all events, hints had been broadly given that certain advantages would be insured to them if they only would hold themselves neutral should a rupture take place. Jonker was hated by most of the Namaquas, with whom he had either fought and plundered in former years, or who were jealous of his ever-increasing power and wealth. But so long as he had the main body of the Damaras on his side they hesitated to show their enmity very openly.

Thus fear and suspicions against their friends, which had probably never been altogether absent from minds so debased and naturally prone to distrust as those of the Namaquas, who, moreover, could not altogether shut their eyes to the deadly injuries they themselves inflicted on their allies, began both directly and indirectly to appear in their conduct. Indeed, when "deep in their cups," that is when wildly intoxicated by the brandy of the country, the Namaquas but too frequently gave the Damaras cause for the worst fears, their language then breathing nothing but death and destruction. Kamaherero, therefore, with all his natural weakness and apathy, could not altogether remain indifferent to his precarious position, and he must have felt that he was daily, nay hourly, treading on a slumbering volcano, which a spark would be sufficient to ignite and overwhelm him with ruin. Indeed many of his friends and acquaintances had already been murdered either openly or in secret.

But this state of things could not last forever, and the storm which had been brewing, shortly afterward burst forth in all its fury, confounding in its violence alike the guilty and the innocent, and carrying desolation to many a peaceful home, and ruin to hundreds. At the same time it was fortunately not without its beneficial consequences, humbling and impoverishing, as it ultimately did, the tyrants who had become wealthy through their iniquity, and bringing liberty and competence to many of the oppressed and the poor.

A short time before this general outbreak occurred, and not very long after the tragical incident related in the foregoing pages, Kamaherero came to pay me a visit at Otjimbingue. I entertained him hospitably for a few days, bestowing on him a few trifling presents, and when he was ready to depart, I casually alluded to his position, inquiring whether there was any prospect of improvement.

" None," he dejectedly replied, " I am, as you well know, treated like a dog, and tremble constantly for my life ; for if not openly taken away I am sure to lose it on some dark night. I asked Jonker, and since his death, his sons and others, for a place for my people where we could live by ourselves, and do a little gardening, etc. But I never can get an answer, and it is clear they do not mean to grant my poor request; on the contrary they seem half afraid of us, and would fain take away all our lives."

"And knowing all this," I rejoined, "is it still your resolve to do nothing?"

"Yes, I would like to get away, it is true, but how can I? We are watched night and day," adding, however, abruptly, "Would you let me live at Otjimbingue if I came there?"

"Certainly," I answered, "and simply because I cannot prevent you if I would, for I count only the buildings on the place my own, with sufficient ground for garden purposes, and right to the necessary grazing for my cattle, etc. Whoever remains master of the country at large, remains also master of the land hereabout."

This was all that ever passed between us on this or any other occasion when we met, at least as regards any allusion to the Damaras trying to obtain their liberty. I am so particular in stating this much, because it has been imputed to me that I had urged the Damaras to free themselves. I shall readily be believed, however, when I state that beyond a desire to see the oppressed righted, I had no earthly interest in the Damaras obtaining their liberty, or rather my interest, in a commercial point of view, lay all the other way, since the Damaras were very poor, and the little they did possess they parted with most unwillingly. In fact, being less civilized than the Namaquas, they had naturally fewer wants, and consequently fewer motives to seek the trader.

Not long after Kamaherero's return to his people, then living on intimate terms with their Hottentot protectors, there were rumors of a rising among the Damaras, who it was said had suddenly made their escapė to some neighboring rocks where they received daily additions to their numbers, and were now trying to obtain permission to live in friendship with their hard and cruel masters on terms more favorable than had hitherto been granted to them. They offered to give up all the cattle they had charge of, provided they were allowed to depart peaceably. But though the Afrikaners were quite unprepared for the emergency, they had been so accustomed to look upon the Damaras as little better than dogs, that they were unwilling to believe that their late slaves had been guilty of the presumption of rising against them, and therefore refused to listen to any proposals whatever. When this news reached us we were equally incredulous; but a friendly Griqua, coming from the scene of disturbance, fully corroborated the common report.

At this period there was living at Otjimbingue, at least that part of it belonging to the Rhenish Missionary Society, a Christian Damara of the name of Philippus. He had been brought up by the Rev. Mr. Hahn, and in addition to the polish thus obtained, possessed shrewdness, intelligence, and much good sense. Philippus was the son of a deceased chief of some importance, and related to Kamaherero somewhat closely. Very shortly after the news of the Damara rising had been confirmed, he came to inform me that he was about to join his kinsman, and inquired whether I would in any way assist him or Kamaherero?

"Certainly not," I replied, "I have no wish to get involved in an affair that I but too clearly foresee must ultimately ruin my business, if not bring about worse consequences. But I will allow the Damaras to supply their wants at my store, provided they honestly pay for what they obtain."

With this understanding we parted, and from that day small parties of Damaras were frequently passing my place, all wearing on their countenances a determined air as if bent on accomplishing some fixed purpose, On inquiring their destination, they replied they were on their way to join their countrymen, who, they were told, had risen against their oppressors, and had asked their help. I never encouraged them by word or deed, though I considered their conduct very natural. I did not even wish them God speed, and yet I have been blamed for backing them in their rebellion.

A week had now elapsed, during which time the most contradictory reports had reached us, and we were thus kept in considerable suspense as to the issue of this sudden rupture. At one time we heard that a battle had been fought in which the Damaras had come off victorious, then the report was the reverse. The first reliable news we had was from Kamaherero himself, who one day suddenly presented himself before me, informing me that he and his people had made their escape in safety, and wished to settle down at Otjimbingue. They had likewise brought with them large numbers of cattle, and though most of these had been purloined from the Damaras at various times, they offered them to me with a request that I would return them forthwith to the Namaquas. This, under the circumstances, was utterly impossible, but I told my new acquaintances that I would write and tell Christian Afrikaner of their wishes and intentions, begging him to send a few trustworthy men to receive the cattle, and guaranteeing the safety of his men with my own life. I had myself already received a letter from this chief, informing me of the *émeute* of the Damaras, and insolently forbidding me to give them protection, or to sell them necessaries. I took this opportunity to tell him respectfully, but firmly, that I acknowledged no chief in my private transactions; that I was a neutral party, wishing to earn my bread without fear or favor, and that I would most assuredly sell the Damaras whatever I chose, provided they were able honestly to pay for what they required. I further earnestly entreated the chief to grant the Damaras their liberty, and to come himself, or to send some men of consideration, to talk matters over quietly. "Attempt nothing by force," I concluded, "for I cannot then answer for the result."

After some delay an answer arrived, but couched in most equivocal terms. The letter reached us on a Sunday, just as we were coming out of the Missionary church, and was dated two long days' journey off, informing us that the Namaquas would be at Otjimbingue in two or three days' time, and that their intentions were peaceable. We knew enough of the Namaquas' character not to put too implicit faith in their promises; and we were strengthened in our suspicions by the messengers, who declared that, so far from their intentions being friendly, they had uttered the most deadly threats, and would only be satisfied when they had slain every man of the Damaras, and razed Otjimbingue to the ground! If this was really true, it involved myself and my property in the general ruin contemplated. Still I would do nothing to compromise myself, but wait for ocular demonstrations of their hostility, before I took up arms in my own defence.

On the Monday morning following, having risen pretty early, as was my custom, I was passing from my house to the store, when, happening to cast my eyes in the direction in which we might expect to see the enemy in the course of another day or so, I was startled by observing an immense cloud of dust extending over several miles of road, and almost simultaneously I was surprised by the wild and fearful cry, "The Hottentots, the Hottentots are coming! to arms, to arms!" The scene that followed baffles all attempts at description. Notwithstanding the warning that had been received, it was apparent that nothing was ready; and we had clearly been surprised. In five minutes every nook and corner of the accessible parts of my house was crowded by terror-stricken women and screaming children. Truly it was a pitiful sight! Nevertheless, I drove them pell-mell into the yard, which afforded them ample protection, being surrounded on all sides by thick walls. The concealment, however, was premature; but, in any case, to have allowed them to keep possession of the house would have been unwise, as their presence would have hampered our movements, had it been found necessary to convert it into a temporary "fortress." The whole establishment, however, was very favorable for defence, being built in the form of a square, consisting in a great measure of substantial ball-proof buildings, capable of sheltering hundreds, nay thousands of human beings if requisite.

Hastily preparing ourselves for defence, should the Hottentots have the temerity to attack the place itself, we proceeded quietly (my brave wife and other women belonging to the establishment accompanying us) to view the battle which had already begun, and of which we commanded at every point a full view.

What with the intended surprise and the cowed nature of the Damaras, the Hottentots, it seems, had confidently reckoned on an easy victory. Accordingly, a strong party of horsemen made a bold push for the missionary station, which had to be passed before they could reach my own place, and for a few minutes it really appeared as if their anticipations were about to be realized. The firing was very close and regular, and for some minutes so dense were the volumes of smoke that the whole scene was hidden from our view. When at last it began to clear away a little, we saw, to our horror, that the Damaras were giving way on every side, and the battle seemed on the point of being lost, but somehow they rallied, and the contest became more fierce and deadly. Meanwhile, the rest of the enemy, several hundreds strong, extended themselves in a long line to the right and left, and the left wing, which had got opposite to my premises was within long rifle-range. They had advanced so far without any serious resistance, and I began to have some doubts as to the issue of this day's doings. That portion of the Damaras who could be most depended on, lived at a considerable distance, and had not yet arrived, and I much feared that all might be lost ere they could reach the scene of action. The appearance of the Hottentots had been so sudden, and the fight had begun so soon after, that there had been no time for sending them word. Our only hopes rested on the chance of their hearing the firing, and in this we were not deceived; for just at this critical moment, when the Namaquas were evidently carrying all before them, a small but gallant body of men were seen emerging from the bush on the flank of the enemy, whom they charged at their utmost speed, throwing them into considerable confusion. The victorious band was greeted by a yell of triumph, swelled by the joyful acclamations of the women, who had come forth in great numbers from their hiding-places to view the battle like ourselves.

The Damaras were shortly after joined by a strong detachment, the last, and the most reliable of all. I now began to breathe with considerably more ease, especially as the Damaras held their own for upward of two hours, and were slowly but steadily gaining upon their opponents, who were giving way in more than one quarter. The Damaras displayed on that day a wonderful facility for insinuating themselves into places in which I should hardly have deemed a child could have been concealed—in fact, for awhile, we, the spectators, commanding as we did a full view of the animating scene of struggle, had for a time lost sight of many of the combatants. At last, however, was heard the exultant cry, "They are running! they are running!" and at the same instant, as if by magic, every bush, rock, and hollow seemed alive with swarthy human beings. A grand but appalling scene now followed. Fully fifteen hundred Damaras set off in hot pursuit of the flying Namaquas, who now only thought how they might best use their legs; it was, however, short work, as the broad assegai of the Damaras made terrible havoc in the ranks of their opponents, ten or a dozen dead bodies being frequently found heaped on one another in one spot, testifying to the dreadful character of the weapon when used at close quarters, and the unsparing hands of those who dealt the deadly thrusts. Quarter that day was rarely asked, and certainly never given, if demanded. The carnage was fearful, as I can personally testify to, having ridden over the battle-field while the action was still far from ended; indeed, at one time, I found myself quite surrounded by combatants. I had followed out of curiosity; and though terribly exciting, I cannot say that it was an edifying sight. It was my first battle-field, but alas! not the last I had to witness.

Had every Damara present that day done his duty, not one Hottentot ought to have survived, as they might have been cut off to a man with the greatest ease. But, until the pursuit began, there were not certainly three hundred actually engaged, and instead of pursuing the enemy in earnest, most of them fell to plundering; and hundreds of Damaras might have been seen carrying off booty, or stripping the slain. It was not unusual to see a fellow hastily covered with the torn garments of some slaughtered foe, still reeking with gore. As it was, the Damaras had gained a complete victory, and they were justly proud of the exploit—the more remarkable as it was won under the most unfavorable circumstances. Their spirit had been completely broken by years of slavery; they were indifferently supplied with fire-arms, and many who did possess guns knew not the proper use of them; ammunition failed to numbers almost at the commencement of the action; they possessed no leader, no union of purpose; and, as we have already seen, they had been taken by surprise.

I never could correctly ascertain the number of slain; but upward of one hundred and fifty Hottentots, including the chief, Christian Afrikaner, were counted by myself and my people within a few miles of Otjimbingue, and the total number must have exceeded two hundred, to say nothing of those who escaped wounded. For days, nay, weeks after the fight, men were picked up dead and dying, having hidden themselves in cavities of rocks, or in the dense bush which skirted the river on both sides, along which a running fight had been kept up for some time after the general flight and pursuit had commenced. The losses of the Damaras must also have been considerable; I ascertained the names of fifty who it was said had been killed, and many were wounded more or less severely. But I marvelled that the number was not greater, considering the deliberate firing on the part of the enemy, who were mostly all fair marksmen.

Several of the Hottentots died game, and I could mention some curious scenes which occurred. Some Damaras who were one day out "looting," seeing a gun barrel partially protruding from a bush, one of the party went to draw it out, when lo! it exploded, killing the fellow on the spot. Another and another were shot before the men could recover from their consternation and storm the place. When at last they did so, they found a man with both his legs shot off! The poor fellow, it seems, had during the nights managed to drag himself about in search of water and food. A few shells of snails, scattered about his place of concealment, testified to the means employed for eking out the mutilated wretch's miserable existence. Of course the Damaras at once put him out of his misery.

The Hottentots were said to have always professed a certain respect for missionaries and their property, but if any such consideration really existed, it did not show itself during the aforesaid fight, for poor Mr. Kleinschmidt's house was made a regular target of: numerous bullets were lodged in the walls, and more than one penetrated to the interior. Fortunately the family had taken shelter in the back premises, where they were comparatively safe as long as the Hottentots were kept at bay. At one time during the fight the enemy were heard to shout to one another to throw fire on the thatch. I need hardly add that it proved a most anxious day to my esteemed and venerable friend, who was only temporarily residing at Otjimbingue, Rehoboth being his proper quarters. I regret to say that, having returned there with his family at a later period, he was exposed to even greater danger than those he had just passed through, and in consequence of the fearful privations and hardships then endured, added to mental anxiety, the poor man lost his life, to the universal regret of every acquaintance and friend; even some of the Hottentots seeming to have been touched with regret at his untimely death.

CHAPTER VI.

Flight of the Namaquas—Alarming rumors—Frederick Green—Plan to surprise the Hottentot head-quarters—A treacherous European—Spoil taken from the Namaquas—Return of the victors to Otjimbingue—Thrown into arrears—Attack of ophthalmia—Dangerous trust—Sad calamity—The cry of vengeance—Victoria Falls.

THEIR late defeat had terribly scared the Hottentots, but those who were best acquainted with their revengeful and proud nature, well knew that they would sooner or later make renewed efforts to recover their lost ground. To be beaten by the Damaras, their dogs, as they called them, was a thing they could not understand, and which they could neither forget nor forgive. They admitted they had been terribly thrashed, but many unexpected causes, they said, had contributed to this result. Thus, the Damaras had been secretly sheltered and abetted by Europeans, while they were openly assisted by the Œrlams (people born or bred in the colony, or in a wider sense, simply brought up by white men), and who had from time to time become domiciled in Damaraland. The first of these insinuations was quite false, while, though the latter statement was correct, it scarcely justified the stress they laid upon it, as not more than half-a-dozen individuals had assisted the Damaras. These assertions were simply made in order to hide their shame.

The Namaquas, very soon after the events here

narrated, abandoned Schmelen's Hope, hitherto their head-quarters, as no longer tenable, and fled to Eikhams, formerly their chief residence. This place was better capable of defence, more distant from their enemies, and indeed, taken all in all, it was the finest place in the whole of Damaraland.

Scarcely a day now passed without rumors that a commando of Hottentots was *en route* to attack Otjimbingue; and it was no longer doubted, or denied, that they intended to involve me in the general destruction contemplated. Accordingly, anxious as I really was to keep neutral, I made up my mind to fight them should they again appear in the place. But with the exception of myself, and servants, and my stanch and attached friend Frederick Green, all the Europeans kept aloof. And I regret to say that there were even some among them that would not have cared to see me ruined, if not destroyed. And yet, with but one or two exceptions, these were all dependent on me, not only for articles of exchange, but for their very bread. Indeed, many a time have I stinted myself in order to supply their wants. I had no wish to see them actually engaged in war, but I did expect, under the circumstances, to have had their sympathy at least. As it was, this was entirely with the Hottentots. I speak this advisedly, for among the booty captured in the recent fight, there were found several letters from many of these men, addressed to Christian Afrikaner, expressing but too clearly their inimical feelings toward me. These letters are still in my possession, and can be produced at any time to corroborate my statement.

At last these repeated threats of the Hottentots

became insupportable, and it was determined to attack the enemy before he could carry his own plans into execution. We were perfectly aware that they were in even greater terror of a surprise than the Damaras, and it was calculated that a blow directed at their head-quarters, if successful, would doubly intimidate them. A plan was accordingly made to surprise Eikhams; and Mr. Green, having, by unanimous consent, been elected leader of the expedition, he in a few days set out at the head of a most respectable force, which, before it reached its destination, was said to have increased to fully 1500 men. But even if this could be proved correct, not one-half of the number could have been relied on in the event of any serious resistance. The plans were devised and executed with all possible secrecy and expedition, and had it not been for a certain European who rode express to give the Namaquas warning of our approach, they must have been surprised and consequently taken at great disadvantage. As it was, they had not only time for preparation, but had actually removed their camp to some distance. But they were promptly followed up, and at noon, a few days afterward, my friend encountered them drawn up in battle-array, infantry and ox-riders being stationed in the centre, with a considerable body of horse on each flank. The Damaras at once made a dash at them, notwithstanding the exposed nature of the ground, the Namaquas having extended themselves along a level ridge, up the bare sides of which it was absolutely necessary to advance. It was gallantly done, and after only waiting to exchange a volley or two, the Namaquas fled helter-skelter, the Damaras pursuing hotly.

Mr. Green, with a small party, was in a short time accidentally separated from the main body of his men, and he assured me that it was fully two hours before he was able to discover the position of his followers. He was finally led to them by the sound of the firing, which had become desultory, and evidently extended over a great extent of country. It would seem that the Namaquas possessed more than one camp, for the Damaras stormed and captured several positions occupied by wagons. Upward of thirty of these were destroyed, only a couple being reserved for carrying the wounded, booty, etc.

A running fight had been kept up for several hours, during which time the Namaquas had been chased eight or ten miles, and night was gathering its shadows over the fierce scene, when at last they came to bay, having taken refuge on a hill of a rather formidable nature. Large droves of cattle and sheep were observed near the summit, and several individuals greatly distinguished themselves in attempting to carry off some of these, and in more than one instance they proved successful. Mr. Green himself felt sorely tempted to encamp at the foot of the hill, and recommence the fighting early next morning. But on more mature reflection, and remembering the peculiar and doubtful character of those whom he commanded, he deemed it more prudent to retire at once with the booty already secured, and the victory thus far gained. This was accordingly done, and the Damaras bivouacked that night at one of the chief wagon camps captured in the course of the fight. The retreat was continued on the following morning, in good order and without molestation from the enemy, a solitary horseman merely showing himself occasionally at a respectful distance during that day. It is said, however, with what truth I cannot tell, that a small party of Damaras, greedier than the rest, who had remained behind for further feasting and plunder, were surprised in their "revels" and killed. But of those who had been actually engaged, or who retreated in time, only one or two were slain, while very few were wounded. What loss the Namaquas sustained was not well ascertained, but it may be presumed to have been trivial, since they never allowed any one to approach at all close to them. Unfortunately some Namaqua women lost their lives in the general *mêlée*, but whether designedly or accidentally killed will probably never be known.

But if the killed were comparatively few, the booty was very great; as is usual, however, in all savage warfare, there was a great deal of waste. Fifty head of cattle were daily slaughtered for food for the army. The original capture, therefore, must have been immense. I, whom the captors requested to act as umpire in the division of the spoil, had some difficulty in satisfying the many hundred claimants that appeared for a share. But I did my best, nor did I reserve a single head for my own personal benefit, though I had suffered much indirectly.

The return of the victors to Otjimbingue presented a most animated spectacle, and would have afforded a capital subject for the lively and clever pencil of my friend Baines. The Reverend Mr. Schröder, however, who happened to be present, did his best to reproduce the scene by means of the camera. Unfortunately his negatives proved insufficient to bring out clearly the many characteristics of the barbaric scene and the portraits of the principal leaders.

For several preceding seasons the elephant-hunters, through a variety of causes, had been very unsuccessful in their efforts to obtain ivory. But their wants, so far from decreasing with their diminished good fortune, seemed rather on the increase, and they had drawn heavily on me for supplies. The consequence of this was that I also fell into considerable arrears with my supporters at the Cape. The only property available for immediate realization was my cattle, and of which I certainly (though it can hardly be said fortunately) possessed a goodly number. But the danger of getting them safely to the Cape market was immense, nay, friend and foe pronounced it an impossibility; the latter had been stung to madness by their losses and reverses, and cared but little whom they made to suffer, could they but revenge themselves in some way. Indeed, they had openly declared that they would make me pay for their ill-luck, should they have the chance of falling in with my cattle. Nevertheless I had no choice, for ruin and bankruptcy were the certain consequences were I unable to carry out my intentions.

Mr. Green having kindly offered to undertake the dangerous trust, and knowing that I could pretty well rely on most of my servants, my resolution was taken to risk all. I was myself incapacitated from accompanying the cattle, in consequence of a terrible attack of ophthalmia, which had for a long time quite blinded me, threatening to deprive me ultimately of sight altogether! I was, moreover, anxious to remove my family and the most valuable portion of my movable property to a place of safety, and had accordingly arranged to proceed to Walwich Bay as soon as my friend should have taken his departure, with a view of trying to obtain a vessel to convey us to the Cape, where I had appointed to meet my cattle, etc. But short-sighted man proposes, and God, in his infinite wisdom, disposes; and never was the saying more truly verified than in the present case. I had reached the sea-shore in safety with my wife and family, a vessel had been secured, our effects shipped, and only a day remained before our embarkation, when, oh, horrors! Green and Haybrittel made their sudden appearance. I was suffering most acutely, but though I could not see the former, I recognized but too well his familiar voice and step. No words were needed to tell me the cause of his untimely presence, and I grasped his proffered hand, fervently exclaiming, "Thank God, *you* at least are safe! Of course my cattle and other property are gone; but tell me the worst in as few words as possible."

"Alas, Andersson!" my friend sorrowfully rejoined, "not only are your cattle and effects lost, but several of your people are killed, and I myself and H—— here, escaped the general destruction by a miracle. We had just got nicely over what we considered the most dangerous part of the road, having arrived within an hour's ride on horseback of Rehoboth, and the chief Wilhelm Zwartbooi had received us most kindly, giving us a fine place to graze and rest the cattle on. We never dreamt of any immediate danger. But we had sadly miscalculated our safety, for on the following morning after our arrival, when a move had been decided on with a view of driving the cattle still nearer to the head-quarters of your friends, we were treacherously attacked by overwhelming numbers, just as the 'trek' had got into a narrow part of the road, and in five minutes poor Jonathan, his wife, two children, woman servant, and several men were killed. N—— and H——'s brother here at first made their escape, but were finally captured, and, for aught we know, may be dead by this time. As for myself and H——, we had ridden somewhat in advance, our presence at Rehoboth having been requested, with a view of consulting us about some important news just received, concerning ourselves and our kind host's safety. And thus, my dear Andersson, were we mercifully preserved. But we were far from safe, as you will presently hear.

"It appears that the Hottentots had received notice of our progress by one, if not more, of our *soi-disant* European friends—out upon the traitors!—and had thus been enabled to take steps for our destruction. We had been surrounded, unobserved, during the early part of the night preceding the eventful morning in question; they had allowed myself and H—— to pass unmolested, not from any good-will toward us, but probably out of sheer cowardice, well knowing that we would sell our lives dearly in defence of our property (Green and H—— had a direct interest in the cattle), if not, perhaps frustrate their villainous designs. Poor Jonathan! he died as he had lived—a brave man; but there was not the slightest chance given him for preserving his life, for after the terrible volley poured in upon him and his poor inoffensive family, he had only just time to fire his rifle once, when he received a bullet in the neck, causing him to fall heavily forward. 'God help you, wife; I can do no more for you!' was all that he could say, and then expired. We heard this and many other details of the sad scene from Netty, the Damara woman who accompanied Jonathan's family, and who was brought to the station in the course of the day in a dying state, from a wound in the breast.

"It is my firm conviction," my friend continued, "that the cattle, etc., might have been retaken had our friends, the Rehobothians, at once accompanied me in pursuit of the marauders, as I requested. At the same time it is impossible to blame them much for their hesitation, as the events that quickly followed will show. The news received, about which we had been called to Rehoboth, amounted to this; a second, if not a third, commando, headed by Henric Sex or 'Nanile,' the greatest rogue of all the rogues in this land of scoundrelism, had been seen in the neighborhood, and it was ascertained beyond a doubt that the villains who had attacked us were to join this party or parties in a combined movement against the station itself, not only because the people had tried to befriend me and the Damara cause in general, but on the score of private grievances. And the inhabitants had hardly time to make a few hurried preparations for defence when the combined force appeared, fully 700 hundred strong, and at once surrounded the place within rifle range. The greater portion of the enemy were mounted, and all well-armed, and against this truly formidable host, the Rehobothians could hardly oppose one hundred men, not one half of whom, moreover, were efficiently armed. But notwithstanding these disadvantages our friends showed a determined front, and steadily refused to listen to the demands of the enemy, who ordered the Rehobothians to give up instantly myself and any other white man to whom they might have afforded protection, as also to abandon for once and forever the Damara cause. But though our stanch friends steadily refused to listen to such conditions, they knew they they were in reality incompetent to give us the necessary protection, should the place be carried by general assault, and of which there really seemed to be every probability. Of course there was nothing for us to do but to decamp. H——'s brother and N—— unfortunately lurched and dodged so long about the neighborhood that they were ultimately captured, and heaven only knows whether they are dead or alive by this time; poor fellows! As for myself and H——, we were considerately furnished with horses and guides, and by these means we have succeeded in arriving here in safety; but we are sadly knocked about, what with frightful roads, constant travel, little or no clothing, and still less food. And now what's to be done, Andersson? I am quite ready for anything and every thing. Point but the way to enable us to revenge ourselves upon our treacherous foe!"

Grasping my friend's hand once more, and with my teeth hard set, I exclaimed, "There is but one thing to do, we must punish the scoundrels; they made a sad mistake in allowing you and me to escape, as they will soon know to their cost. Go back to see what the Damaras will do for us. I have indirectly been the means of attaining for them their liberty; if there be a spark of gratitude in them they will now stand by us in our hour of need; go and collect such as are willing to act with us, and I will follow as soon as my eyesight is a little improved."

Thus was crushed at one fell blow all hopes of happiness and prosperity! Many a man, I venture to say, far more determined than myself, might have felt his spirit cowed, and pursued a less bold course than that which I adopted. Some friends (?) indeed, were good enough to hint that I ought to have rested content with my losses, and that I should only bring additional troubles and calamities on my head by any further movements in this sad affair. But I neither could nor would argue thus. I could not conscientiously consider the lost property as my own, so long as I still remained a debtor. But even could I have afforded the loss—and it was not a trifle, amounting, as it did, at the lowest estimate to upward of £3,000, there being 1,600 head of large horned cattle alone—would it have been fair to have left the fate of my poor murdered people unpunished? Would not those very friends have been foremost in branding my conduct as pusillanimous and cowardly had I not tried to strike one blow for the dead? God forbid that I should have ever been such a coward! Even had I been fully aware of the terrible consequences of the step I was about to take—and maybe I was—I would still have acted as I did. Even my loving wife felt the necessity of the act, terrible as the alternative must have appeared to her at this critical juncture, when everything was prepared for our departure from a land and a people who had combined to prove so destructive to our peace and our prosperity. Without a murmur, without one word of complaint, she sanctioned, by her quiet submission to fate, my irrevocable decision, and thus I was spared the painful necessity of acting in opposition to her will. God, it is true, has said: "Vengeance is mine!" But I think there are and must be occasions when we may be allowed to take it into our own hands, and if so, surely mine was one.

But before closing this chapter, I must not omit to mention that Mr. Thomas Baines, the artist, was staying with me at this period, for the purpose of illustrating certain birds, etc., intended for a work on Natural History that I was then preparing for the press. This gentleman was the companion of Livingstone for a time, and subsequently with Mr. James Chapman. By the published narrative of the latter, the reader is probably aware that they had to some extent failed in their attempt at exploring the famous Zambezi river; but, as a set-off, they had visited the glorious and wonderful "Victoria Falls," an event enough to satisfy any ordinary ambition. Mr. Baines kindly presented me and my wife with one of his pictures, representing one of the most charming views of these stupendous Falls—said to far exceed in grandeur and general interest those of Niagara! And I secured a few more at a moderate price. I also induced my friend to paint a picture on the same subject for the King of Sweden, who, I knew, was a lover of the art, and no mean artist himself, and it would perhaps afford me the opportunity in this humble manner of showing my duty and respect to my sovereign, to whom I was personally known, and whose royal father had thought me worthy of a gold medal for meritorious services in the field of exploration and discovery. His Majesty graciously accepted the gift, acknowledging it by a letter in his own hand, and the picture now adorns the chambers of the Royal Palace at Stockholm, so famed for its architectural grandeur. Thus I had the double pleasure of having been able to please my sovereign and serve my friend's interest by exhibiting one of his efforts in so conspicuous and honorable a position. Mr. Baines afterward published a series of chromo-lithographic views of the Victoria Falls, executed in the most finished style. Bnt not content with serving me with his pencil, he spontaneously offered to accompany me to Otjimbingue, and to take charge of the place during my absence against the Namaquas, and to defend it if necessary. He had seen something of military movements during one of the Caffre wars. This experience and his various and versatile talents peculiarly fitted him for the task; and I mention this disinterested act of my friend with more pleasure as, with very few exceptions, I had been abandoned to my fate by the white population of Damaraland. With some this had, perhaps, been an act of necessity, but with others it arose from indifference or cowardice, while many kept aloof out of sheer enmity.

CHAPTER VII.

An Irish Munchausen—Rehoboth—Preparations for our expedition against the Namaquas—Wilhelm Zwartbooi—Conflicting accounts of the position of the enemy—Last acts before the fight—A disappointment—Severe example—Daring act committed by Hottentots—Successful flank movement—Severely wounded—Precarious position.

NEARLY three weeks had now elapsed since my wife took her departure for the Cape, and my eyesight was slowly but steadily improving: but no news had yet reached me of Mr. Green. It was, therefore, with considerable anxiety that I awaited the result of his mission; first, because he had to pass through a Namaqua tribe under Jacobus Boyce, who, though they professed friendship for us, were not altogether to be trusted, as their chief was known to be exasperated in consequence of the untimely death of his daughter, the wife of Jan Jonker, whom I have spoken of as having been unfortunately killed in the engagement headed by Mr. Green; secondly, the Damaras *might* refuse to listen to his representations, or at least throw obstacles in his way. But at last a letter arrived, informing me of his safe arrival at Otjimbingue, and of the readiness of the Damaras to give me the necessary assistance, urging me at the same time to make all possible haste, as things did not progress very briskly. Thus far well.

A day sufficed to make the needful arrangements,

and I and Mr. Baines set out for Otjimbingue, which we reached after a quick and safe journey. And here an unexpected pleasure awaited me; for not only had B——, the missing white man, turned up safe and sound, but H——'s brother and N—— had been restored to liberty; and be it said to the honor of these men, they were ready once more to risk their lives in my service. This time, perhaps, their determination, as was natural, was spiced with a strong feeling of revenge; for it appears that they had suffered dreadfully during their captivity, being not only exposed to great indignities, but made to suffer the very extremes of hunger, thirst, and cold. Thus, when caught, they had been stripped of all their clothes, except their shirt and trousers, and, thus exposed, had been made to walk bare-footed and bare-headed in a broiling sun; at night—and the weather was piercingly cold—sleeping without any covering. And, to cap all this misery, their captors were in the habit of telling them to prepare for death, as their execution had been decided on, and could no longer be delayed. It may well be imagined what sort of life the poor fellows led in consequence. The only man who showed any approach to compassion for their forlorn condition, was the chief himself, and it was to him they ultimately owed their liberty, though it cannot be said to have been a disinterested action, since he demanded a considerable ransom for the privilege.

As for B——, according to his own account, his adventures by the way had been truly marvellous, proving him a very Goliath—or rather a David—for numbers of valiant men fell before his magic strength. And the picture he drew of the hunger, thirst, and other privations that he had suffered, and of the unconquerable spirit with which he supported them, was enough to have drawn tears of compassion from the eyes of his listeners, only they did not altogether believe him, most unkindly hinting that he claimed some relationship to Munchausen of immortal fame. In short, he was a highly imaginative native of the Emerald Isle.

I stayed but one day; and having appointed a rendezvous for the meeting of the men who were to join me, I moved on to it. After a delay here of three days, I found myself at the head of 2,000 men, a number which ultimately swelled to 3,000—a force which, if truly effective, would have enabled me to pass quickly from one end of Great Namaqualand to the other, without much difficulty. But, alas! there were really comparatively few fighting men; the greater part was a mere rabble, come solely for the purpose of rapine and plunder, at once the curses and the vultures of an army. Moreover, we mustered only about five hundred guns, half of which were utterly useless, many actually wanting a cock, a pan, a mainspring, or other equally important part. Nevertheless, there is something cheering in numbers, especially when contending with a savage and undisciplined enemy, whom they serve to intimidate.

I therefore looked forward with some confidence to a successful issue of the expedition, the more so as I expected a strong reinforcement from Wilhelm Zwartbooi's tribe, who had expressly requested to be allowed to join us in any attempt to be made against the common enemy. The Damaras, indeed, grumbled at this, deeming themselves quite strong enough to punish the hostile tribe ; moreover, urging that it would cause too much delay to wait for them, and enable the enemy both to prepare against surprise and for defence. But I had made up my mind that our allies should share alike with us success or defeat, as the case might turn out, and thus matters were allowed to take their course.

After about a week's journeying we found ourselves in the neighborhood of Rehoboth, but though I had sent more than one express to inform our friends of our approach, no such tidings had reached them, and the very first intimation they had of us, was from my own man whom I had now despatched on horseback. Nevertheless, having themselves been kept in a kind of siege, as it were—that is, expecting such an event daily—they were soon ready, and being supplied with such ammunition as I could spare, they joined my standard about fifty strong. The Namaquas are in general bad soldiers, except when brought to bay behind stone walls, when, like the Turks, nothing short of a bayonet or assegai charge will dislodge them. And knowing that an enemy would never attempt to meet us in an open field, but would take refuge in rocks and precipices, I hailed the addition to our party with considerable satisfaction.

No one exactly knew the whereabouts of the Namaquas, nor could we obtain any reliable information on the subject. Some said we should find them one or two days' journey off at the utmost, while others doubled, and even trebled the distance. It was of course very difficult to act under such conflicting accounts, and the utmost caution was necessary in so steering our course as to avoid being ourselves entrapped. But, at last, after many a false alarm, and one slight skirmish, in which several of the enemy were killed, and more than one of our party had narrow escapes, one man being shot through the arm and shoulder of his jacket, and after we had advanced much farther that was anticipated, we made sure of having discovered the enemy's stronghold. Some Berg Damaras whom we had captured, declared that we should find them in a range of hills no great way off, and which we could distinctly see from our camp.

All was now intense eagerness. We carefully concealed ourselves in an extensive hollow during the day, while several scouts were sent during the following night to reconnoitre the supposed enemy's position. Our object was considerably facilitated by a conspicuous hill lying half way, and commanding a full view of the aforesaid range. The spies fully corroborated the story of the Berg Damaras, and preparations were quietly made for a determined assault on the ensuing night.

I felt the critical moment had now arrived, and made all the dispositions that I thought necessary when about to engage a numerous, determined, and probably strongly fortified enemy, at a time when my hours on earth might be numbered. My last act, as may well be supposed, was a long and affectionate letter to my poor wife, expressing my deep regret at the destitute circumstances in which I must unavoidably leave her, but at the same time relying implicitly on an all-merciful Providence, who had thus far so marvellously preserved me, and who was never known to abandon those who placed their faith and trust in His mercy and immeasurable love. "Tell my poor father," I concluded, "that if I fall in to-morrow's fight, I shall die as a Christian and a soldier."

As soon as darkness had sufficiently set in, so as to hide our operations, a forward movement was made, keeping the hill above-mentioned well between us and the supposed whereabouts of the enemy. Having reached its base, we halted to make the final preparations, and to ascertain that they had not decamped, an event we had greatly dreaded throughout our toilsome and cautious march. Judging from the fires seen from this point on the opposite range, the enemy was intrenched in three great parties, a considerable way up the face of the rock. To meet the emergency, I divided my men into as many divisions, appointing Mr. Green to that destined for the attack on the left, placing Haybrittel with a second on my right, while I myself led the centre in person against what appeared to be the largest of their strongholds. Our plan was to make the attack at break of day, but, the intervening distance not being very great, the final movement was delayed till about three o'clock in the morning, when I ordered a simultaneous advance of all the divisions, the distance that each had to go being nearly the same. I had the greatest difficulty in restraining my men from getting ahead too quickly, they seemed so eager for the pending fray. Now I was at the left wing, then on the right, and presently back to the centre, begging and commanding alternately. It was a cold moonlit night, and as objects were discernible a long way off, I feared every moment to see our movements betrayed. Indeed,

I had no doubt about it, as the fires were suddenly stirred into a blaze, while the men were heard calling to one another, having evidently been aroused by the violent barking of the dogs. We were now at the foot of the hill, and so near as to be able to distinguish every word that was spoken. Ordering the men to lie down, I listened eagerly for further signs to determine my movements, when, after awhile, I was glad to find all becoming once more quiet. As there was no longer any time to be lost, we rose and began the ascent, which in a very short time became exceedingly steep and laborious, considerably decreasing the eagerness of my followers. The goal, however, was reached without any accident or molestation just as the first streak of dawn appeared, though from the shadows thrown by the hill, objects could be discerned but dimly. I was the first man to leap into the werft, where, to my disgust, instead of a numerous enemy, I found only some poor Berg Damaras. I paused in sheer astonishment, but just at this moment heavy firing began on my right, and feeling certain that my friends had been more fortunate, and in the hope of being able to render them assistance, as also with a view of cutting off the enemy, I continued the ascent, shouting to the men to follow; but with a very few exceptions, they all remained behind to plunder the wretched abodes of the flying inhabitants. In five minutes every hut was in a blaze, and a wild but harassing sight presented itself to my view from my elevated position. Never was enterprise better planned, and in the beginning so successfully executed, followed by such an indifferent result. We had been fairly gulled, and I felt immeasurably disgusted accordingly.

But I will pass quickly over what followed. Suffice it to say that we captured a large number of women and children (Berg Damaras), some sheep and goats, and a few head of cattle. I did so out of compassion for the poor creatures, well knowing the merciless character of my followers. In about an hour or so I was joined by the right division, who had been even less successful than ourselves. As for Mr. Green and his party, they had never encountered an enemy nor captured any booty. While discussing what further to do, one of the Rehobothians brought word that the Afrikaners were on a neighboring hill, and had actually dared us to the attack. After our many and severe disappointments we were unwilling to lend a too ready ear to his tale, and I exclaimed, "If true, it is the best news we have had yet!" As our way lay in the direction indicated, we leisurely followed the man, and did find several large werfts, but all were deserted, a native appearing only here and there in the distance, timidly peeping forth from behind some rock. In one place, however, we met with some success, having captured about seventy or eighty head of cattle, and nine hundred or a thousand sheep and goats, a most opportune supply to our exhausted larder. Indeed, we had been without any animal food for some days, and had been chiefly subsisting on "veldt cost," *i. e.*, on such roots as the soil yielded.

By this time the day was far advanced, and meeting with water we encamped for the night, hoping that on the morrow we should have a nearer acquaintance with the enemy, of whom we were more than ever determined to give a good account. At this time I found it necessary to shoot a man who had in the most reckless and daring manner set my commands at defiance. I had warned the Damaras, at the very outset of the expedition, that I would suffer no disregard of my authority, having been elected commander by their full and free consent. This severe example had a salutary effect on the minds of my cut-throat followers.

While busy making the camp snug and safe for the night, the cry was suddenly raised, "The Hottentots! the Hottentots!" and sure enough a few horsemen were observed on the rising ground above us, less than half a mile off. The next moment they were seen to dismount and deliberately take aim at some object, which we too surely conjectured to be some unfortunate Damara, who, contrary to my orders and warnings, had strayed thus far from the camp in search of food. It was a daring act to do in the face of such numbers, and though they were chased away faster than they came, we had the mortification to know that we had been bearded on our own threshold by a mere handful of men. Deep and long were the imprecations uttered, and the vengeance vowed against the enemy by the Damaras, though for my part I could not help admiring the daring and hardihood of the fellows. And no one but Jan Jonker himself, I felt sure, could have performed so bold and rash an act.

I retired that night to rest, with considerable anxiety for the morrow. We could no longer doubt that we were in the immediate neighborhood of the enemy, and that so far from fleeing from us, they were prepared to give us battle. I was very poorly, and had been so from the commencement of our march; for, in addition to weakness of the eyes, I had had more than one attack of fever, and, latterly, an old, troublesome enemy, the rheumatism, had returned with some severity. Indeed, my right leg was so much affected by it, that I could hardly sit a horse. But I dared not show any weakness to my followers, as it was absolutely necessary to have nothing but cheerful looks and a confident aspect before them. Oh, how often is it thus in life—a smiling face, with an ailing body, and a bruised spirit beneath the surface!

On the following morning we were early astir, and although still uncertain of the enemy's exact whereabouts, we had a shrewd suspicion that they were to be found located in a grim-looking rock a few miles ahead of us. We moved accordingly in something like battle-array, and as we proceeded, fresh cattle and sheep tracks became abundant; but we had actually reached the base of the hill in question, which we now clearly saw was of great extent and of the most formidable character, without observing anything to indicate the presence of a large body of men. But just at this juncture, the advanced scouts waved their hands as a sign for us to hurry on, and putting spurs to my horse, I galloped ahead, followed by about a dozen horsemen, when lo! less than half a mile ahead of us, and in full retreat, were a number of horsemen—probably the identical ones who had shown themselves so boldly on the night before! We chased them at the top of our speed, and so intent were we on the pursuit that we should probably have rushed upon our own destruction in a few minutes more, had not, fortunately, one of the horsemen called out, "Look, there are people on the hill, we are going too far!" We halted accordingly, and now found ourselves on the opposite side of the hill to which we had advanced, and which here presented an equally steep ascent. I saw at a glance, that if the enemy were really ensconced among its passes and precipices—and I could not well doubt that such was the case—we should have tough work to dislodge them. For the first time I began to entertain some doubts of the success of our enterprise, but it was too late to think of this, and I felt certain that, were time given to the Damaras to fully realize the extent of our peril, we must utterly fail.

Hastily scanning the face of the mountain, therefore, I soon perceived that the only tolerably accessible point was from about half-way between where we were now stationed, and the side that we had originally approached from, and I determined to make the first attack here. Seeing the Damaras begin to come up in large numbers, I instructed Green to choose two of the most trustworthy of the leaders and their men, and then I gave the word to storm; and right gallantly it was done. Being quickly joined by others as they were coming on, I had the satisfaction shortly to see the hill side swarming with dusky warriors. This occupied hardly ten minutes, and shots began to be rapidly exchanged. Feeling satisfied that this flank movement was a success, my next step was to order the Rehobothians, and a strong body of Damaras to follow me. My plan was to keep on a course parallel to the mountain, with a view of trying to draw out the enemy's strength and position, and to draw off their attention in a measure from the storming party, and finally to find an accessible point for attack full in front. But from some misconception, or other cause, my orders, in this instance, were not carried out equally satisfactorily, and the consequence was that, after having proceeded for some distance, I found only the friendly Namaquas, Green, and a few others following me, and most of these even were some way behind. I was making for a gap or ravine in the mountain, seen about midway (and in which the horsemen had sought refuge), where I observed a body of men moving about in apparent hurry and confusion. I had thus, somewhat incautiously, approached to within one hundred and fifty paces of the rocks. Indeed, I was unconsciously getting right into the lion's mouth, as it were, and had the enemy been less eager—and perhaps less frightened too—they might have annihilated us to a man, by allowing us quietly to pursue our course. But fortunately just at this time they opened fire, and, as it would almost appear from the result that followed, on me alone, for not another man was hurt. It was an awkward situation, the whole face of the hill for full a quarter of a mile seemed to present one vivid streak of fire, for nearly at the same moment there flashed forth from fully five hundred guns and rifles a perfect hailstorm of bullets, which made me, strange as it perhaps sounds to the reader, exclaim, "By Heavens! balls are here as plentiful as blackberries are in my own native forests." And what was more strange, I was unhurt! But observing my unsupported condition, I was turning to seek some shelter from this unpleasant "hail" storm, when a second volley was poured upon me, and this time with more precision; for I was simultaneously struck by five balls—one grazing my left arm and elbow, a second carrying off the knuckle of the pointer finger on the right hand, a third dinting the stock of the rifle just under the little finger, a fourth carrying off the heel of one of my boots, while the fifth struck the right leg a little below the knee, laying me at once prostrate.

I experienced a singular sensation when I thus found myself a poor, useless cripple—if life itself was not at stake. It was not fear, for as yet nothing of that kind had fortunately troubled me, but the sense of indescribable oppression and faintness about the heart, as if all the joys and pleasures of this world were forever shut out from my existence. I was conscious that a smile once crossed my features, not one of pleasure, certainly, but that melancholy smile that may be seen to flit across a human face when a friend is trying to comfort another under the weight of heavy misfortune, but who, though grateful for the sympathy, finds human comfort of no avail. Bowing my head for a moment against the ground, I sighed forth, "And thus, Oh God! ends my existence—far from those I hold dear; but Thy will be done." I felt much calmer and more resigned after breathing this short prayer, and was looking up to ascertain what my followers were about, when I caught a glimpse of the Rehobothians, making a dash in a stooping position for the rocks, which they must have reached in safety. Turning next to the mountains, I could only perceive one confused mass of combatants, not charging and retreating openly, but executing all their movements in a stealthy hide-and-seek manner. The place was admirably adapted for this kind of warfare, the face of the entire mountain being covered by huge bowlders, each capable of sheltering a dozen men or more.

The firing had now become general, and was very severe. At the lowest estimate, full twelve hundred small arms were then every two or three minutes belching forth smoke and fire, the rocks constantly echoing the reports. Again and again the cowardly villains poured volley after volley upon my devoted body as I was lying helplessly exposed to their fury ; for I had not succeeded in reaching any shelter before I was struck down. Once, indeed, I attempted to drag myself to a bush about fifty paces off, but found advance or retreat alike impossible. The only movement I was capable of was to roll partially over on my back, and it became quite clear to me that both the bones of the leg must be shattered, for, when turning on my back, the foot refused to follow, in fact, remained on the ground at a right angle to the leg. There can be little doubt that I had been recognized by the enemy, who were determined to afford me no chance of life, and it may hardly be credited, but nevertheless it is a fact, that they kept "pelting" me incessantly with bullets for upward of an hour. Consequently, if there was one bullet that day directed against me, there must have been many scores, and the only marvel is that I was not riddled with the shot.

And now a new danger threatened me. Stray bodies of Damaras would from time to time take up a position at my back, but at such a respectful distance that, so far from their missiles doing any harm to the enemy, they would fall far short, in fact, were more likely to hit me where I lay ; and hundreds of bullets, fired by heaven knows whom, did actually strike the ground all around me, and may, for aught I know, have occasionally grazed my body, or clothing at least. Once a ball struck right under my forehead, as I was resting it momentarily on the ground, and for some seconds I verily believed myself mortally hit, for I felt a difficulty in breathing, and a gurgling sensation in my throat as if choking from a flow of blood, but it arose only from the abundance of dirt and dust raised by the violence of the shot. It was high time, however, to try to hide my head at least, which I partly succeeded in doing at the cost of much pain and labor, having scratched a hole with my hands in the sun-baked soil. Had my wound been less dangerous and my position less precarious, it would have afforded me some amusement to listen to the various sounds produced by the bullets, as they sped thick and fast around me, for there was the spent ball, the musket ball, the rifle ball, and a variety of other balls, to which no particular place can be assigned —all with their own peculiar sounds.

But the enemy was at last compelled to desist, having by this time got enough to do in defending themselves, and I was quietly and resignedly contemplating the fierce scene, for, with the exception of the back of the ravine, I commanded a complete view of the whole face of the mountain, where some of the most determined resistance was met with.

Happening to glance sideways, I perceived, to my consternation, a small party of the enemy, who, coming from the mountain on my left, on horseback, passed round at my back, and having arrived within about one hundred and fifty paces, faced full round upon me.

Hitherto I had not faltered, but I honestly confess that I now experienced a feeling amounting to fear. "Ah, no!" I ejaculated loudly, "a thousand times rather death than fall alive into your hands! it would be too horrible a fate!" With that I rolled on my back quietly, and resting the rifle on my left leg, which I partly raised for the purpose, I took a deliberate aim at the breast of the foremost foe. Thus posted, I felt sure of being able to despatch at least two of my opponents, while my revolver would always give me a good chance at closer quarters, should they venture to advance. The moments that followed were full of agony, for it seemed as if they were consulting as to the best way of getting at me. But to my inexpressible relief, after thus remaining fully five minutes, they turned and rode off. Hardly were they out of sight, when another troop passed me even closer, and a third time was I put to torturing suspense, with a similar result. It is quite impossible that they should not have seen me, and the only explanation that now or then occurred to me of their leaving me unmolested, is, that they probably thought me dead or dying, and that they were afraid to approach closely, for fear of exposing themselves to the danger of being fired at by my followers on the mountain, who by this time were occupying the very fortifications originally held by the enemy.

The battle had now raged for several hours, and I watched with intense anxiety for the final issue; for though it was evident that the Damaras, and our allies, the Rehobothians, had to a certain extent gained the day, the enemy was still far from conquered, and was hanging, as it were, in dense masses on the brow of the hill to the left of me, and close to the ravine alluded to; and I saw clearly that, unless attacked from above and in flank, they might succeed in holding their ground, and possibly turn the tables against us. If Green, poor fellow, was but alive and unhurt, though the chance was but small, I reasoned all might yet be well, for he could not help seeing the necessity of such a step, only I was afraid that the Damaras, if once in possession of the booty, would not support him sufficiently.

What with loss of blood, my cramped position, and a scorching sun overhead, I was getting rapidly exhausted, and more than once I thought I must faint; upward of six hours having elapsed since I was first laid prostrate. A drink of water would have been of priceless value to me, but only once, from the time I was struck down to near the close of this day's trying scenes, a human being came sufficiently within sight and hearing to enable me make my wants and situation known. And when at least half-a-dozen Damaras did appear, no entreaties or command would make them stay for one single moment, or render me the slightest help. The cowards! though more than equal in numbers, they were flying like timid deer before one of the party of horsemen above alluded to, and thus I was mercilessly abandoned to my fate by friend and foe. Truly my situation was a painful one, and few would have blamed me, perhaps, had I given way to despair. Thank God! I did not. And ere long such a decided change took place in our prospects, that all apprehension of further immediate danger was past.

A slight curl of smoke was now seen issuing, near the summit of the mountain, from one of the ravines overlooking the enemy, and the next moment there was an explosion, rapidly followed by others. I well knew that none but friends could be there, and so well had I calculated the result of such a manœuvre that on the very first discharge I unhesitatingly gave vent to my pent-up feelings in the exclamation, "Thank God! the victory is at last complete! complete!" And so it proved; for in a few moments the enemy were heard to call out, "We are getting surrounded!" And the cry among them then was something equivalent to "The devil take the hindmost!" In short, they rushed helter-skelter down the steep sides of their late stronghold, and in five minutes more were seen dispersing wildly over the open country.

It was now in the power of the Damaras to have annihilated the enemy almost to a man; for had an assegai charge been made by them at the moment the Namaquas took to the flat, the matter would have been settled forever. But to my utter disgust, not a soul bestirred himself to intercept their flight, and they were allowed to depart peaceably! But so it is invariably in all savage warfare. Honor, safety, and all that a European would hold dear on such an occasion, is at once sacrificed for plunder and rapine, accompanied by the wildest exultation and disorder.

A few moments more and I was surrounded by all my friends, not one familiar face being missed, and my heart was moved with deep gratitude to the Almighty for the mercies vouchsafed to us during this trying day, and I confess it, I wept like a child. But seeing the mournful looks of my sorrowing companions, I dashed the tears from my eyes, and smiling brightly on them, remarked: "Oh, never mind me; I dare say I shall soon be all right;" how my lips belied my heart! "Now, like good fellows, get me some conveyance, and have me removed to a place of safety, where I can rest, for I am well-nigh exhausted." *

* I can quite imagine that the military reader, especially if he himself has taken part in blood and carnage, will smile at Andersson's description of this fight, as well as at the minute details he has given us of his feelings and sufferings when prostrated by a very severe wound, and for a time, as it would seem, serving as a target for the enemy; but to myself these details are highly interesting, as they may also be to others, for though every poor fellow that is laid low on the battle-field must in a lesser or greater degree experience the same sensations, yet I do not remember any one having recorded them.—Ed.

CHAPTER VIII.

After the battle.—Immense capture of sheep and cattle—Folly and incapacity of the Damaras—The Rehobothians—Rev. Mr. Kleinschmidt—Arrival at Barmen missionary station—Rev. Mr. Hahn—Sufferings from my wound—Rev. Mr. Kleinschmidt's change of station—The Rehobothians attacked by the Namaquas—Sufferings of the unfortunate tribe.

AS may be well imagined, sleep did not much court my pillow during the night that followed on the sanguinary scene related in the last chapter. Sleep, indeed, would have been out of the question; for even had my wound been less severe than it was—cause enough to keep me awake—I should have got no rest, for the Damaras kept up the wildest revelry throughout this trying night, quarrelling and shouting vociferously, and expressing their exultation by frequent discharges of musketry. My couch had been spread at the very foot of the rock that had witnessed so much strife, while my followers were camping or nestling on its sides wherever a sufficiently clear spot afforded them room to crouch down, offering at once one of the wildest and most picturesque scenes that I have witnessed. The flashes of several hundred guns, as they struck upon my upward gaze, blinded me by their nearness and vividness, while the frightful yells that accompanied every fresh discharge tended to appal. Indeed the scene bordered on the awfully sublime.

The total quantity of booty that fell into our hands must have been very great indeed, but no one ever knew its extent; for my friend Green, on whom the command now naturally devolved, refused to stir from my bedside oftener or longer than was absolutely necessary, and consequently the Damaras had it all their own way. Thus there was not only a terrible waste, but large droves of cattle and sheep were driven off clandestinely. When, after a day or two, we were able to take an account of our gains, we found they consisted of upward of three thousand sheep and goats, and of about half that number of cattle. Fully the same number of the former had been slaughtered during the night following on the battle, besides abundance of fat oxen, while quite as many were concealed. I estimated, therefore, that the original number could not have fallen much short of ten thousand sheep and goats, and three thousand large horned cattle. Indeed, the enemy had apparently considered their mountain fastness so secure as to deem it unnecessary to drive off their live stock. About forty horses were also captured, a good deal of ammunition, some guns, etc. Finally, we destroyed seven or eight wagons, only retaining one, which I presented to our trusty allies, the Rehobothians, who had done good service to us on the day of the fight.

The actual number of men killed on this occasion was, I believe, quite out of all proportion to the amount of firing, but this may easily be accounted for when the terribly rocky nature of the disputed ground is taken into due consideration. The dead and wounded, on both sides, probably did not exceed one hundred, and perhaps out of this number the better half fell to our share, being the attacking party, and consequently much more exposed. Only one Damara, of any note, however, was counted among the dead, and even he, it was affirmed, had been treacherously dealt with by some relation who coveted his substance and position. It is quite possible that there had been foul play. Some women, I regret to say, were killed in the general *mêlée*, but as they were mixed up with the combatants during much of the time that the fighting was going on, the result could hardly have been otherwise. A larger number were captured, and I need hardly add they were kindly treated, and ultimately restored to liberty.

There being an insufficiency of water on the mountain, we moved our camp on the ensuing morning a short distance. The object of the present expedition was not only to try to recover my lost property, but to crush Jonker, or at least to punish him so severely as to render him unable, for the future, to persevere in his iniquitous proceedings. But, alas! we had allowed the golden opportunity to slip out of our hands. It is true we had inflicted on him a most severe lesson by the various losses recorded; but his allies—for he had called several tribes to his assistance—had suffered little or nothing. Pursuit was not yet altogether hopeless or useless, if only vigorously conducted, for it was evident that a general panic had seized the enemy, as was shown in various ways, their cattle being allowed to roam about unheeded and unherded, their wagons being abandoned, their huts half-finished, etc., etc. But there was no longer any one to lead the Damaras, etc.; Mr.

Green, as I have said, absolutely refusing to leave me, even for a day; and I told them plainly that they were utterly unfit to execute any plan by themselves. Nevertheless, at their urgent solicitations, I delayed our homeward march a week, at the end of which time, as I had predicted, they had accomplished nothing. Indeed, we had, on the whole, been losers by the delay, for though cattle were captured daily, a far larger number of our own were nightly carried off, and though every imaginable precaution was taken to guard the stock, thefts continued unabated. I made the chiefs responsible, but it was of no avail. Indeed it was perfectly ridiculous the way the natives managed when left to their own resources; their incapacity was equalled only by their timidity. An instance in point will suffice to prove their pusillanimity. One evening it was reported to me that a large wagon-camp had been espied; that the white tent coverings of the vehicles could be distinctly perceived, as well as the cattle and people, but they were not strong enough to make the attack on the supposed enemy, but had retired to get the necessary reinforcements, and that to-morrow they would show me what they could do. Well, they went, remained away two days, returning at the end of that time, with the information that the wagons they had seen were nothing more than white stones! Utterly disgusted with such folly, and seeing clearly that nothing could be done, I broke up the camp.

The Damaras, after this, were naturally desirous of returning straight home, not caring much what became of their allies, the Rehobothians; and could I myself have consulted only my own comfort and safety, I would gladly have acceded to their wishes. But our Namaqua friends had now made themselves so obnoxious to their countrymen, that I felt sure the enemy would embrace the first opportunity to wreak their whole vengeance on the poor fellows, and I could not therefore, conscientiously—be my own fate whatever it might—consent to a step at once so thoughtless and so unjust. On the contrary, I determined to give them the benefit of our escort to or near Rehoboth, and when the time came for parting, to detach a party of trusty Damaras, who would help to defend them in case of an attack. It was further agreed between us, that the Rehobothians should at once set about removing themselves and their effects to the neighborhood of Otjimbingue, their own station being deemed no longer tenable or secure if they were left to their own resources.

By this time my wound began to open, and to exhibit something of its true nature. Indeed, though there was originally but one orifice, all at once the flesh began to give way in several places, making nearly the whole surface of the front of the leg—even considerably beyond the knee—present the appearance of one entire ulceration. I began to feel my case somewhat desperate, and not knowing but that I might be called to my last account at any moment, I thought it prudent to request my friend, the Rev. H. Kleinschmidt, to visit me without loss of time. He came with all promptness; and not the most loving son could have hailed his father's presence with a more affectionate regard than I did that of my reverend friend. We had always been intimate, but, what with my present precarious state, and his people's critical situation, our present meeting was unusually cordial. We embraced each other warmly. The late Mr. Kleinschmidt was one of those true and unaffected Christians whom to see is to love and cherish, and who, in his simplicity and earnestness, must have presented a fair specimen of what the first Christian fathers must have been—the immediate followers of a Peter and a Paul. He was still a hearty, sound old man, who might, in the ordinary course of nature, have many years to run here on earth, while my days seemed confined to the shortest span. But, alas! for our own shortsightedness, it was destined, in the inscrutable designs of God, that the good old man was to be called hence shortly, while I, useless and a cripple, was to live on and to mourn his untimely death, my own fate yet undecided! But I must not anticipate events. May it please the Almighty to comfort his kind-hearted, sorrow-stricken widow, herself a daughter of one of the most estimable of missionaries.

When at last Mr. Kleinschmidt proceeded to inspect my wound, and became fully aware of the awful extent of my miseries, he shook his head sadly and doubtingly, remarking: "That leg ought to be taken off, or you will die." But my friend did not offer to perform the operation—probably he did not feel equal to the task—and I was left to my fate. Shortly after this we parted, alas! never to meet again alive; though, as will be presently seen, we once crossed each other's path.

After many days of weary and painful travel, I was carried on a stretcher on men's shoulders, amid the most intense sufferings, at the mere remembrance of which I even now shudder, and arrived in safety at

Barmen, the most northerly missionary station in Damaraland, but in so exhausted a state that, had the journey lasted but another day, I must inevitably have perished. As it was, every one looked upon me as a dead man. An express had been early despatched to the Rev. Mr. Hahn to request his immediate presence for the purpose of administering to me the sacrament, and other rites usual on the approaching dissolution of a man, as also for the purpose of receiving my final instructions about my worldly affairs. Like Mr. Kleinschmidt, my friend responded most promptly to my call, and the day after our arrival, I had the satisfaction of greeting him, besides other friendly faces; among the rest that of Mr. Baines, who henceforth (like Green) scarcely ever left my bedside. But, indeed, all friends and servants alike vied with each other in attending to my wants, and in trying to forestall my slighest wishes. And I must not here omit to notice the affectionate solicitude, anxiety, and care evinced for me by the Rev. H. Brinker and his kind-hearted wife. May God Almighty reward all those who thus watched by me, and who tried in every way to soothe and alleviate my truly dreadful sufferings! May they be spared so sad a fate as mine, but if unfortunately ill should at any time befall them, I devoutly hope and trust that they may have the same advantages as I myself in this hour of need. Only those who have been placed in similar positions can fully appreciate the priceless boon of friendly faces and sympathizing friends. After my experience, I could well realize the affection and devotion gained by the good and amiable Miss Nightingale among the soldiers and others in the hospitals at Scutari during the Crimean war.

But I am not going to impose upon my reader's patience any longer by a recital of all that I suffered at this period. Let it suffice to say, that for several weeks, nay, almost months, my fate remained doubtful, pain of the severest kind never leaving me for a single moment. Nay, there were moments when no human being had courage enough to witness my agonies, and to hear my heart-rending cries. It seemed impossible for the human frame to sustain so much misery. God Almighty! Thou wast pleased to try me severely, but in Thy great mercy Thou didst vouchsafe me also invariably strength and fortitude to bear with patience and humility Thy dread inflictions, and my almost more than human agonies. May I never forget Thy great mercy.

During all this time we had been startled more than once by false reports, that the Philistines were upon us, and at last one day, when there seemed to be sufficient reason for believing the rumors to be true, Mr. Green became urgent for our immediate removal to Otjimbingue, deeming Barmen unsafe, as he considered it untenable in the event of an attack by the Namaquas, the greater portion of the Damaras having now returned to their homes. I dreaded a removal at this critical juncture, and hardly thought it fair to leave our kind host without any protection. But the latter objection my friend met by assuring me that he would be in no danger, inasmuch as having only recently arrived in the country, he had never had anything to do with the present war, adding, "The consequences be on your head if ill comes to us after the timely warning afforded." This argument, though it did not quite satisfy me, settled the point, and another day saw us *en route* to Otjimbingue, my resting place at least for a time, which we reached in safety.

Here the most distressing news awaited us. On parting with the Rev. Mr. Kleinschmidt, I had urged upon him and his people the necessity of an immediate retreat from his station, as there could not be the slightest doubt that our enemies would soon rally and attack them. My friend, well knowing himself the precariousness of their situation, hardly needed my solicitations, and did what he could to hurry their departure. But in moving thus a whole tribe, much time was necessarily required, and the natural indolence and dilatoriness of the Namaquas increased the delay. Unfortunately, after a few days' journeying, the "trek" got irretrievably entangled in mountains of the most formidable and harassing nature, without a vestige of a road, and difficult for a man to traverse even on foot. Their conveyances, at the best but sorry concerns, broke down repeatedly. By keeping the regular wagon-track, all these misfortunes would have been avoided ; and there is every probability that they would have been spared much, if not all, the terrible calamities that shortly after befell them, as they might then have reached Otjimbingue in safety before the enemy could have overtaken them. Their excuse for choosing so apparently impracticable a path was, that they were afraid that their cattle—hitherto in a great measure spared—might be infected by lung-sickness. But it would have been far more prudent to have risked that danger rather than their own lives.

While in this dilemma, that is without a road, with an insufficient supply of water, broken-down wagons, and a variety of other mischances sufficient to make a speedy progress impossible, they were overtaken by the enemy and all but surprised. Fortunately, a little boy, in herding some calves, had perceived their approach, and gave the alarm forthwith. There was but little time afforded them for making any preparations for defence, still they were not taken altogether unawares. Indeed, at the first onset they managed to turn the tables against their adversaries, having had time to place an ambush into which they fell unsuspiciously. Fifteen men were counted dead in one spot on the very first discharge, the consequence of which was a total rout of the advanced party. But being very numerous, and the fugitives being rallied by Jan Jonker, they soon renewed the attack, and though the Rehobothians once more successfully beat off their assailants, it was thought advisable to abandon their camp during the ensuing night, and take up a fresh position more favorable for defence. In the meantime, instant flight had been urged upon poor Kleinschmidt, and though most loath to leave his people, he saw he could do no good by remaining, and in justice to himself and family he set off, but, unfortunately, utterly unprovided with even the merest necessaries. They left, indeed, with only one loaf of bread between a family of seven or eight. Moreover, they were half naked, their greatest hardship, perhaps, being the want of boots and shoes. In this forlorn and wretched condition, they traversed a frightfully hilly and inhospitable country for several consecutive days, exposed to a broiling sun during the day and a biting cold at night. After nearly a week of incessant marching up one mountain and down another, till their eyelids grew dim by very weariness, their feet lacerated and bleeding, almost maddened by hunger and thirst, scorched by day and frozen by night, they reached the neighborhood of Otjimbingue more dead than alive. Indeed, poor Mr. Kleinschmidt was so exhausted as to be unable to walk the last stage, and he was placed in wagon which was sent for him. When he at last arrived, he was compelled at once to take to his bed, whence, alas! he never rose. He had only been a few days in the place when I arrived, and had I for a moment believed that there was any immediate danger, I would most assuredly, weak and suffering as I was, have caused myself to be taken to my friend's bedside. As it was, I just stopped long enough in passing at a short distance from the house, to shake hands with his wife and family and other kind friends and acquaintances, who thronged around my couch to catch a glimpse of my emaciated face and form.

But to return to the Rehobothians. It would appear that the men and children had taken refuge in the sandy bank of a river near the camp, covered thickly with a species of long, wiry grass, which the blood-minded enemy set fire to, by which means, numbers of the unfortunate creatures were destroyed, and others seriously injured. Finding themselves, on the following day, in possession of the hastily abandoned camp, and moreover, having succeeded in capturing considerable numbers of cattle and sheep, the Hottentots rested content with their success. But, at the same time, it was thought more than probable that they would return as soon as they had secured the booty, and the poor Rehobothians were unfortunately utterly unfit to cope with their adversaries in their present crippled condition. Petrus Zwartbooi, the eldest son but one of the chief, came to Otjimbingue shortly after the catastrophe just narrated, to request assistance. As regards myself and Mr. Green we could do nothing, but the Damaras sent a large party, and by these means, after much misery, the half-ruined tribe found themselves ultimately in safety in our neighborhood, where we must leave them for the present.

CHAPTER IX.

Severity of my wound—Arrival of my wife—Long and painful illness at Otjimbingue—Study of ornithology—Relations with Baines—Discovery of a new species of falcon—Description of Andersson's perm—Machærhampus Alcinus——Other specimens—Difference of two species.

SEVERAL months had now elapsed, and by this time the danger to my life was probably past, though my sufferings had been diminished but little. It had been long ascertained that both the bones of the leg had been utterly smashed, though to an unequal extent. A great number of pieces and splinters—ultimately reaching the astonishing number of seventy—had from time to time been extracted, some being of considerable magnitude. This fact will at once show the reader what a desperate wound it must have been, and every one that witnessed it, took it for granted that it would be impossible for me ever to walk, or even to stand again on the limb. Three to three and a-half inches of the large bone had, in fact, come completely away, and what was to fill up this immense vacuum? It was quite clear that no bone would ever grow there, since the two extremities were entirely unconnected. But Nature, when left to herself, often works out cures which wê little expect or understand. And this was strikingly exemplified in my own case. Thus one day when examining the wound, I was surprised to find that the two ends were perceptibly nearer each other than before, and henceforth a steady forward movement was distinctly visible. My delight at this discovery was at first very great, for, in my ignorance, I conjectured that some connecting link had been left between the stumps, and that fresh bone was thus thrown out from the remnant. But I was wrong, for in proportion as the distance between the broken bones became less, in the same proportion the leg itself became *shorter*. In fact, it was contracting or shrinking together.

Hitherto the leg had been carefully supported by splints, but the moment the shattered extremities met, from some unaccountable cause, I could not bear the pressure any longer. But knowing the great importance of keeping the leg straight at this critical period, the more so as it became apparent that the small bone at the back of the leg had not been disturbed to the same extent, and consequently was pushing the leg, as it were, forward and inward, I made several determined efforts to retain the supports, but each time signally failed; for inflammation of the severest kind set in upon every fresh attempt, causing me the most violent pain, which neither ether nor chloroform was able for a moment to assuage.

Just as affairs had taken this turn, my brave and loving wife joined me. Oh, how my heart had yearned for this meeting—at one time so little expected or hoped for. For months I had expected her, but it appeared that the several letters which I had caused to be dictated and forwarded to her at different times had never reached her, until all at once, shortly before her arrival, when she lost no time in speeding to my sick-couch. I was very thankful that she had been thus spared all the misery and suspense that must naturally have been her lot had my first letter found its way as it was expected and intended. As it was, she received at one and the same time the distressing news of my being desperately wounded, and the more cheering intelligence of an improvement of my health. It is true, rumors had reached Cape Town of the fatal engagement, by the overland route, but as such reports are so often false, or, at the best, exaggerated, my wife's relatives and friends managed to keep the melancholy tidings from her. And truly grateful I felt to the Almighty for the inestimable blessing bestowed upon me in permitting me once more to embrace her and the children.

For nine months I never moved out of a horizontal position, and it may therefore be readily conceived that I suffered no small inconvenience from such a prolonged uniform posture; nay, it was accompanied by real pain, for at one time my back was full of ugly bed sores, which I had the greatest difficulty in getting rid of. Add to this, that the lower half of my body was always more or less immersed in the water constantly applied to my hurts, and which, in consequence of my horizontal position would often find its way up to my very neck, a circumstance both trying and uncomfortable. But bad as this was, it was as nothing compared with the annoyance and pain I suffered from the presence of maggots, which, strange to relate, notwithstanding the utmost care, were produced in the wounds in myriads, even in the short space of twenty-four hours, and frequently of an enormous size. A most disgusting sight presented itself as the bandages and splints were removed at every fresh dressing; and the sensation created by these monsters as they wriggled their way between the flesh and the bandages was indescribable, and at times quite maddening. The very best proof of the agonies caused by these worms was found in the fact that the wounded natives, who also suffered from them, found it impossible to endure the sensation, though otherwise so patient of suffering, and apparently indifferent to the most acute pain. They might be seen frantically trying to tear off the bandages from their wounds as soon as the maggots began their erratic wanderings. It may interest the reader to know that nothing but cold applications were ever used for my wounds, with an occasional drop of arnica, but even this was found of too quickly healing a property to be long continued.

On the tenth month I made the first attempt to change my confined and painful position, by trying to turn a little on my right side. I was now also lifted out of bed for the first time on to a sofa; but it was long before I gained strength enough to support my novel position for more than five minutes together.

During my long and painful illness at Otjimbingue, I, at an early period, had recourse to my favorite pursuit, viz., the study of the feathered tribes, etc., of Damaraland, and by this means I often succeeded in beguiling many a weary hour, as well as in diverting and soothing the anguish of mind and body. I employed several native lads, besides my European servant, to collect specimens. Baines now also entered on his appointed task of depicting the birds. My first step was to measure them accurately as they were ob-

6

tained, and to note down carefully the color of those parts likely to fade; my next was to hand the specimens to my friend, to be presented life-like by his quick and talented pencil. I will not deny, however, that we had our little hitches at the first outset; for Baines could hardly understand why I should lay so much stress upon details as I did. But my argument was this. I propose at some future day, if spared, to publish a work on the natural history of this and the neighboring countries, and which I intend to try to make really useful and reliable; besides, it will be an expensive work, and the public is entitled to fair value for their money. Now I cannot myself draw or paint a bird if my life depended on it, but I am always more or less able to tell at a glance whether the position, markings, etc., are correctly executed. However, by the time my friend has depicted half-a-dozen birds or so, we understand each other perfectly, and I am in duty bound to say that he never refused to make the necessary alterations when he found that my remarks were just and to the purpose.

But after having been thus successfully employed for a considerable period, it became evident that however much my friend was anxious to serve me by his pencil, and otherwise by his presence to be useful to me, he earnestly longed to return to Europe, chiefly, I believe, with a view of meeting with and getting redress from the famous Dr. Livingstone, then in England, who had so fearfully wronged the poor fellow by his hasty imputations on his honesty, as also to try to get some employment more congenial to his tastes than bird-painting. In fact, I understood that he was anxious to get the Royal Geographical Society of London to appoint him to some exploring expedition. Becoming gradually and fully aware of this, to him, all-engrossing feeling, and however much I thought it against both our interests—for my friend earned a certain though humble income by his present permanent employment—I considered it unkind to keep him any longer to his engagement, and accordingly bid him go. And thus we parted; and, may I hope, with mutual regret? I shall always gratefully remember his many acts of good-will and solicitude for my comfort and ease, during this truly distressing period of my life.

After Mr. Baines' departure I was fortunate enough to discover a very remarkable bird of the falcon tribe, not only quite new to science, but forming an altogether new and distinct genus. At a later period I had the very great pleasure of presenting it to my kind friend Mr. John Henry Gurney, one of the most distinguished and pains-taking ornithologists of the present day. I speak of "Andersson's Perm" (*Machærhampus Anderssoni*, Gurney), which English naturalists, considering I was its first discoverer, were pleased to name after me.

Of this very singular bird I obtained one specimen, a female, on the 10th of March, 1865; shot near to Otjimbingue by my servant, who observed another, probably the male; and, if I mistake not, I also saw it on more than one occasion in the same neighborhood.

When the specimen in question was brought to me, I instinctively suspected it was a feeder at dusk or at night, and exclaimed, "Why, that fellow is likely to feed on bats!" And truly enough it so turned out, for, on dissection, a bat was found in its stomach; and in that of another of these birds killed by my man some time afterward, several of those creatures were also met with. In this species the irides are bright lemon-yellow, extremities of mandible black, basil parts and gape bluish lead-color, and toes bluish-white.

Measurement of Male and Female.

	Male.		Female.	
	In.	Lines.	In.	Lines.
Entire length	17	8	18	2
Length of folded wing . . .	13	9	13	11
Length of tarsus . . .	2	2	2	5
Length of middle toe . . .	2	0	2	1
Length of tail	7	3	7	6
Length of bill	1	10	1	9

"The female specimen just spoken of," says Mr. Gurney, who so kindly and ably edited "Birds of Damaraland," "was presented to me by Mr. Andersson, and was added to the collection of Raptores in the Norwich Museum. Among the skins of birds left by Andersson at his decease, was the male specimen which he subsequently obtained; and this, on the sale of his collection, was secured for the British Museum, in the Ornithological Gallery of which it is now exhibited. These two specimens only differ from each other in the somewhat smaller dimensions of the male bird. The female example was described by me in the 'Proceedings of the Zoological Society' for 1865, under the belief that it was both generally and specifically new, and I suggested for it the name of *Stringonyx Anderssoni.*

"Mr. A. A. Bartlett very obligingly undertook to

mount this specimen for the Norwich Museum, and while the bird was thus passing through his hands it occurred to him that it certainly belonged to the same genus, and probably to the same species, as a bird in the Museum at Leyden, which had been figured and described by Mr. G. F. Westerman, under the name of *Machærhampus alcinus*, in the first volume of a scientific work published at Amsterdam under the title of *Bijdragen tat de Dierkunde*, etc.' This specimen had been purchased for the Leyden Museum from Mr. Frank, the well-known dealer in birds and animals, and was stated to have been brought from Malacca; but Mr. Bartlett was of opinion that this locality had been erroneously assigned to it, and that the bird was really a native of Damaraland, especially as many birds collected there by Mr. Andersson had passed through the hands of Mr. Frank about the same date as that at which the '*Machærhampus*' was acquired by the Leyden Museum; and it was therefore presumed that some accidental confusion of tickets might have caused a mistaken habitat to be assigned in error to this specimen. Mr. Bartlett's views on this subject were recorded in the ' Proceedings of the Zoological Society, for 1866, page 324; and as I concurred in his opinion, the female specimen from Damaraland, now in the Norwich Museum, was figured and described under the name of *Machærhampus alcinus* in the ' Transactions of the Zoological Society,' Vol. VI., Plate 29.

" This conclusion, however, has proved incorrect, two specimens of the true *Machærhampus alcinus*, agreeing with that at Leyden, having subsequently occurred, an examination of which has proved that the

Damaraland bird, though a nearly-allied, is yet a distinct species, and therefore entitled to retain the specific name of *Anderssoni* which I originally proposed for it.

"Of the two additional specimens of *M. alcinus* above referred to, one is in the possession of Count Turati, of Milan, as I am informed by my friend M. Jules Verreaux; but the locality where it was obtained has not been recorded. The second additional specimen, which is now in the collection of Viscount Walden, was obtained by the late Dr. Maringay at Malacca, thus confirming the correctness of the locality originally assigned to the Leyden specimen.

"Mr. R. B. Sharpe, in an able paper on this subject, published in the 'Proceedings of the Zoological Society' for 1871, thus sums up the distinctions between these two nearly allied species. 'The Malacca species coincides with the Damara bird in the form and style of plumage to having the white ring round the eye and the stripe down the throat, but differs in its larger bill, darker colors, brown abdomen, and long occipital crest; there seems, however, to be a difference in the white feathers round the eye. *M. Anderssoni* has a white superciliary line and a white spot below the eye; *M. alcinus* has the latter plainly mottled, but has no distinct supercilium, though the feathers round the iris of the eye are whitish.' "—*Editor.*

CHAPTER X.

Proceed to Cape Town—Surgical advice—Cape Town Museum and Library—Mr. Layard—Avi-fauna of Damaraland—Axel Ericson—Accumulation of misfortunes—Propose to return to Damaraland—Return to Otjimbingue—Wild and desolate aspect of the country—The Welwitchia.

TO proceed: on the 16th of May, 1865, by which time I felt myself strong enough to be moved with tolerable safety, I set out with my family for Walwich Bay, where I was fortunate enough to secure a vessel soon after our arrival. The voyage to Cape Town proved speedy and prosperous, having by a miracle escaped the terrible gale that swept Table Bay at this period, and which proved so disastrous to the shipping of that port. The unfortunate mail steamer, the Athens, the reader may perhaps recollect, was among the worst wrecks recorded, since neither ship nor human beings were ever heard of, having been lost within sight of the port, though such was the violence of the hurricane, that no one knew of the sad occurrence till the following day.

As may be supposed, I lost no time in obtaining the best surgical advice. Dr. R——, my regular medical attendant, after the most careful examinations of the wound, and after gathering all facts and particulars relating to it previous to my arrival in Cape Town, unhesitatingly came to the conclusion that I must submit to amputation—the more so as I had given him to understand that I was a ruined man, and had a family to provide for, and consequently required to be in a perfect state of health in the shortest possible time. Others, again, took a different view of the case, and declared that, though the leg looked deformed enough, and notwithstanding the small amount of union that had hitherto taken place in the bones, there was still hopes for me that I should walk one day. But on pressing these medicos for something more definite—for some substantial reason for their belief, and for the limitation of the time of my supposed recovery, they merely shrugged their shoulders and remarked, "We cannot give you any particular reasons, but nature works out strange cures at times, and we feel confident that she will do so in your case." Both parties meant well; the one thought only of how most readily and efficiently to restore me to health, while the other naturally imagined that I should be anxious to save the limb which had hitherto proved such a faithful servant to me.

But this hesitation and indecision could only prove injurious to my general health by keeping me in suspense as to the ultimate issue. And, therefore, to set the matter at once at rest, I determined to consult a friend in England, of considerable reputation as a surgeon of one of the first hospitals in London. Accordingly, I got my friend, Dr. R——, to draw up a report upon the disabled leg, accompanied by correct diagrams and measurements, and so well did he accomplish his task that it drew forth the most unqualified praise and admiration of my English medical friend, who consequently found no difficulty in forming and giving his opinion. And it amounted to this: "I would recommend amputation;" for though he laid before me another alternative, it was clear he himself put no faith in its efficacy. Armed with this weighty document—for my English adviser was well-known by report to most of the faculty in Cape Town—I presented myself before five of the most talented and experienced surgeons of the place, fully determined to abide by their verdict.

After a lengthy consultation, and notwithstanding Drs. R—— and B——'s opinions, four out of the five gentlemen decided to leave the leg alone, at least for another six weeks, when, if the union of the bones was not satisfactorily advanced, it would be time enough to think of amputation. "It was easy," they argued, "to take off the leg, but impossible to replace it." And at the end of the stated period the leg was found to be so much improved in strength, if not in appearance, that it was finally decided to "let well alone"; in fact, to permit nature to do the best she could for me.

I scarcely knew whether to be pleased or disappointed with the result, for, even should I ever be able to walk, it would be in such a crippled way as to preclude an active life in future. And I had heard so much of the excellence and superiority of artificial legs and arms over deformed natural limbs that I felt half inclined to have insisted upon amputation, with a view of verifying or falsifying such reports. But it was not to be. It is true I am now able to hobble about in a way, but it is only with pain and inconvenience that I can accomplish even a few hundred yards. And before

I arrived at this indifferent result, I had to suffer the most severe pain for many months. Indeed, nearly two years elapsed before I could dispense with crutches, and I have never been able to do without a stick. Three and a half inches of the large bone, and about half as much of the smaller, has been lost—removed, as already stated, in upward of seventy pieces and splinters. The deficiency in the length of the leg is tolerably compensated for by an artificial cork and leather boot, but no remedy has yet been found for its other deformities, which are the real causes of my not being able to walk.

During my stay in Cape Town I spent much time at the Museum, then superintended by my friend Mr. Layard, who not only paid me every attention in his power, but greatly aided me in comparing and identifying specimens of natural history, of which this institution possesses a large number. The collection of eggs, numbering upward of five hundred, and they are very good ones too, specially attracted my attention. The library attached to the museum possesses upward of 2,500 volumes.

These frequent visits to the museum, where I learned much, together with the numerous specimens of birds presented to me by friends and acquaintances, and shot in the vicinity of the Cape by a Swedish servant named Svante, who had accompanied me from Damaraland, enabled me to make considerable progress with my contemplated work, the "Avi-fauna of Damaraland," and the adjacent regions, for which, through the medium of a friend, I had now found a publisher, in the Messrs. Day and Son, the celebrated lithographers; and though the estimated cost of each copy would be five guineas, I was nevertheless enabled to procure upward of one hundred subscribers in the Cape Colony, which goes far to prove the wealth of the inhabitants.

While sojourning at the Cape I was joined, at his own particular desire, by a youth named Axel Ericson, from Sweden. His credentials were the best, and fully borne out by his subsequent conduct while in my service. He was a fair shot, and few surpassed him in preserving bird skins, which to me was of moment, as I was thereby relieved, in a degree at least, from the disagreeable task. Altogether he proved a very valuable addition to my little staff.

After such an accumulation of misfortunes and reverses as narrated in the preceding chapter, it may be well supposed that my means had not only diminished, but were altogether exhausted. Nay, after settling with my Cape agents, to whom I resigned all my worldly possessions—including my wife's property—I found myself a beggar in the truest sense of the word. Indeed, had it not been for my brother-in-law's * hospitality, I must have starved. Many a man might fairly have given way to despair at such prospects as were evidently in store for me. I loved independence dearly, and would be under obligations to no man as long as there was the slightest chance of earning a living by my own hands or brains. But with the best of wills to work for my bread, I was hardly fit for the lightest occupation. Owing to a money crisis, I believe, Cape Town at this time was in a state of something like temporary bankruptcy, and there were hundreds of men

* Now Postmaster-General at the Cape.—ED.

out of employment, far more capable than myself, and even had I found some friend to take pity on me, I could hardly have given satisfaction in my weak and enervated condition. I had already been too much confined, and it was clear that a sedentary occupation would no longer agree with my health.

In this dilemma it was not unnatural that I should turn my thoughts to the " old country," *i. e.*, Damaraland; for though I had lost my all there, it was equally true that there I had acquired everything, and why not try to make a second competence in the same land? Of course, there were now serious drawbacks which had not existed in the first instance, but I have been so accustomed to battle with troubles and difficulties of all kinds, that it requires a good deal to turn me from my purpose when once I have made up my mind to do a thing. My wife, however, was quite angry with me when first I broached the subject to her. " It was simply madness to think of it," she said; and my medical attendant was pretty much of the same opinion. In my weak state of health, and with a leg only partially healed, I should run too much risk. But I thought otherwise. The faculty had been able to do little or nothing to alleviate my sufferings, though they had done everything that kindness, close attention, and skill could apparently do. I had an idea that a return to old scenes and occupations, as well as to the air that had agreed with me so well for such a number of years, could not fail to prove beneficial. And when I argued this with another surgical friend, he quickly remarked, "You cannot do better; there are times when a man may be allowed to be his own physician, and your case is probably such a one." This settled the question.

But in my impoverished state, to will a thing of such moment was not quite to do it, as I should, of course, require a considerable outfit. And who would undertake such a risk? My name, it is true, I found stood as high as ever in the Cape mercantile community for honor and integrity. But the time for credit had passed away; for things were different now from what they were before. A man with £50 in his pocket might then have obtained supplies to the amount of several hundreds, while nothing but cash, or the very best securities, would now do. I had once begun my account with Messrs. V—— & Co., with upward of £2,000 to my credit, and I felt painfully the difference of my present position. Unfortunately, I have been gifted with a very sensitive mind, and a refusal would have caused me much pain and shame. Through very severe loses sustained in the business, I knew my late agents were incapable of assisting me at this juncture, nor did I apply to them. But the plunge must be made somewhere; and I am happy to say that, when at last I mustered up courage to take it, out of the half-a-dozen individuals to whom I applied for assistance, only one refused, and that for the smallest amount. Nay, the applications were not only readily granted, but were accompanied by sympathizing notes, and the expressions of most unbounded confidence in my integrity. I cannot express how pleased I felt at this proof of confidence. It showed that honesty and straightforward dealings will always bring their reward. And it affords me much pleasure to add that my supporters never found cause to regret their trust; for, under God, I have since been able to repay them, and thus save them from all risks, though I shall always remain their debtor for their kindness and liberality.

Having overcome this, my greatest difficulty, I lost no time in making the necessary preparations, and after some delay, caused by the want of a proper and cheap craft, I set sail for Walwich Bay, on the 2d of May, 1865, accompanied by the lad Axel, of whom mention was recently made, and another Swede, Captain Eeen, of the mercantile service, who had entered my employment. This place, after a short and prosperous voyage, we reached on the 9th of the same month, and, after a stay of a few days there, proceeded to my old quarters at Otjimbingue.

On the way there, the travellers' road, for a considerable distance, lies over as barren a country as can well be conjured up to the imagination. Here sand-hills, miles and miles in extent, rising several hundred feet in altitude, and changing their terror-inspiring aspect with every fresh and strong wind that blows; there a naked granite rock or bowlder, reflecting from its reddish looking surface a glaring and insupportable heat; or huge heaps of (black) "iron stone," neighboring perhaps a dazzlingly white limestone ridge, all destitute of vegetation. This is its appearance; and there are hundreds of miles along the west coast, northward and southward—even extending far inland—precisely like it. Indeed it might vie with the Great Sahara itself in sterility and dreariness; and the weary eye seems to range in vain over this howling wilderness, in search of some object worthy of attention. Nevertheless, there is to be found in this desert of sand and rock—more especially as one approaches the watershed of the periodical Swakop—an object of the highest interest to the naturalist, one that has of late years won for itself a world-wide reputation. I allude to the celebrated Welwitchia, a plant uniting within itself characters peculiar to many classes of vegetable productions, but of which, owing to some strange oversight, I omitted to make mention in my former works.

CHAPTER XI.

Defeat of Hottentots—Fall of a lawless marauder—Letter to the editor of the "Cape Town Mail and Advertiser"—Escape from shipwreck—Samuel, the Freebooter—Mr. Green's advance to the Cunene—Renewed disturbances—Great loss of produce—A new way to pay old debts—Letter to Jan Jonker—Jacobus Boyce.

DURING my absence from the country, the Hottentots had at last carried out their threats of attacking Otjimbingue, but the attempt had not only proved an utter failure, but led shortly after to the complete ruin of one of the parties concerned. I am informed that they appeared before my old place quite 2,000 strong; and had they been as brave as they were numerous, it would have fared badly with the Damaras that day, as they could only oppose to their enemies a comparatively small number of fighting men. But fortunately they proved the very reverse of courageous, for after having exchanged a few volleys at long range, they most disgracefully took to their heels, closely followed by the Damaras, who captured a considerable number of ride-oxen, which, in their hurried flight, they were unable either to find or to mount.

Not long after this signal and almost bloodless victory on the part of the Damaras, for I believe only one man was killed on their side, they mustered in very large force, and accompanied by a strong party of their old allies, the Rehobothians, followed up the enemy to his own place. Four or five distinct tribes of Hottentots had entered into an alliance, with a view of destroying the Damaras, but one of these under Henry Nanib, had made itself especially obnoxious to the latter and the Rehobothians, and it was therefore determined to try and punish this man first, as with his fall the others would certainly lose courage, and thus make them more inclined for peace.

They (the Damaras) found Nanib strongly intrenched, and assisted by numerous friends from adjoining parts. Such, however, of the Namaquas, who were with him under Jan Jonker, fled at the first onset, not, I believe, so much out of fear as out of sheer disgust with their friends, who had conspicuously shown the white feather in the late combined attack on Otjimbingue. In short, Jan Jonker was afraid to trust his life among them. Moreover, it was said that he and his people were really anxious for peace. But "a dog will always bark best on its own threshold," and so the Damaras and their allies found it now, for Nanib had been brought regularly to bay, and finding escape impossible, and being well protected by stone walls, natural and artificial, he and his people retrieved their reputation, offering the most resolute resistance. Indeed it is affirmed, and with perfect truth I believe, that had it not been for the presence of the Rehobothians, the Damaras would have been driven back with shame and slaughter. As it was they lost many men, but the day, somewhat inauspiciously begun, ended in the most complete victory, every one of the enemy, including the obnoxious chief, being slain. This was very satisfactory; and I verily believe there was not even a

Namaqua, except his own intermediate adherents, that did not rejoice in the fall of this lawless Hottentot commander. He had for years been the bugbear and bully of his neighbors, as well as of the white trader, whom he never failed to insult, rob, and even personally ill-treat whenever and wherever he found the opportunity. The country had truly been rid of a scourge and a pest!

This decisive victory had, as may well be supposed, thoroughly disheartened the enemy, and though no regular peace had been established, there seemed to be a tacit understanding between all parties that hostilities were to cease. The Rev. Mr. Volmer, indeed, a missionary among the "Red Nation" (the most numerous among the enemies of the Damaras), on his way through Otjimbingue, had been commissioned to offer peace to his flock. This was the state of affairs on my arrival in the country, which, however, will be better understood by the following letter that I, on the 6th of June, 1866, addressed to the Editor of the "Cape Town Mail and Advertiser":

"The kindly, nay, almost affectionate interest always evinced toward me and my 'adopted land,' by yourself and the Cape public in general, inclines me to the belief that any news from the 'old country' will not prove unacceptable to the columns of your valuable paper.

"As you are aware, I left the Cape lately with the following objects chiefly in view, viz.: to try and recover my health, and put a few pounds in my empty purse, and to add to and improve my stock of knowledge as regards my contemplated great work on the feathered tribes of these and neighboring regions—a work, the prospectus of which your and other important Cape papers noticed so favorably shortly before my departure.

"But before I say anything on the state of the country and my own future movements, etc., I cannot refrain from telling you of a wonderful escape from shipwreck that I have had; the circumstances are shortly these. There being a scarcity of suitable craft in Table Bay at the period I speak of, and a still greater dearth of cash in my pocket, my kind friend Spence (of the firm De Pass, Spence, & Co.), generously offered me a passage to Walwich Bay, via St. Helena, in their fine vessel, the Isabella Hartley. By a mere accident I was prevented from availing myself of this offer, but shortly afterward shipped in the Telegraph and arrived safely at my destination. Hardly had I landed my effects, however, when, to my astonishment, and sincere regret, I observed the Isabella Hartley on shore within sight, and so far as I am aware, she became in a short time a total wreck. This is the second time I have been thus marvellously preserved. Truly I have much to be thankful for when I remember the very many hair-breadth escapes that I have had, both by sea and land.

"But to proceed with my story. My return to Damaraland, with solitary exceptions perhaps, was hailed with universal satisfaction, and many a man less accessible to public applause than myself, might have felt flattered at the reception, for I find that though perhaps I have not been able to endear myself to the people, my absence had been felt as an evil—a no mean compliment. As it is, however, I feel more grieved than pleased, since it proves but too clearly how impossible it is for the natives to go on by themselves. In fact they are like children, who require an unimpassioned, judicious, and fearless parent to guide, judge, and even chastise where necessary. Were the country of greater intrinsic value than it is, and were it possible for the English Government to send a commissioner, I would strongly recommend such a step as the only means of finally restoring peace, order, justice, and confidence. The great curse of this country is the mutual distrust existing between every party. The only man, the Rev. C. H. Hahn, who from his well-known integrity, fearlessness, and knowledge of the country, its wants and population, could fairly challenge the necessary attention, confidence, and respect, is in a measure incapacitated from exerting these qualities in consequence of his position as a missionary. Politics and evangelization are difficult to reconcile in one and the same person. I truly grieve for this unhappy land.

"In their last engagement with the Hottentots, the Damaras had received effective and valuable aid from the Rehoboth-Namaquas, who had always proved themselves stanch friends and supporters of the Damara cause. But it would seem that the subsequent sharing of the spoil and other causes, by the time I arrived, threatened to lead to an open rupture. I am happy to be able to add, however, that I have for the present succeeded in arranging matters to their mutual satisfaction. Nevertheless I would not answer for the result when once my back is again fairly turned upon the parties concerned, the more so as the Rev. Mr. Hahn is just now absent on a long journey to the Ovampo, etc.

That cursed mutual distrust, above spoken of, makes a thorough reconciliation so difficult, if not impossible, between so many conflicting interests.

" In the very midst of these attempts at pacification reports spoke of an attack upon more than one party of Europeans now away to the northward, hunting and bartering. The leader of these marauders is one Samuel, once a subject of Jonker Afrikaner, but who, even before the Damara war of independence began, had separated himself from the tribe, and had ever since pursued a system of plundering and murdering. And, unfortunately, from the central and all but inaccessible position fixed upon by this freebooter, he was enabled seriously to annoy and injure inoffensive traders and hunters. The Damaras, it is true, had twice attacked and routed the villain, but in their usual careless way they had allowed him and most of the men to escape, and the consequence is that the rascal has again found means of reoccupying his former stronghold, and in greater force than ever, it is reported.

" A few days after these rumors had reached us, and after they had been duly discussed as to their probable correctness, letters reached me from several of my hunting acquaintances, confirming our worst fears, though not altogether without some cause for rejoicing in the midst of the ruin wrought by the scoundrels. Mr. Palgrave, who had been one of the parties attacked, but who by a most laudable determination and judicious defence had been enabled to turn the tables against the enemy, thus writes :

" 'On the morning of Saturday the 28th of April, I was at Namatoni, a large fountain near the edge of

Elosha, and about eight o'clock, just as I was sitting down to breakfast, we were surprised by about twenty Namaquas with some hundred bushmen, Berg-Damaras, etc., etc. One of my people instantly recognized among the Namaquas some of the same rascals who shot Messrs. Smuts, Todd, and Lewis in the Kaoko, in 1864. As soon as I could prepare my people, I attacked the party, routed them completely, killing several, six it is said, took two guns and six ride-oxen. My party, exclusive of one man who was with the cattle, and three others who ran away at first sight of the enemy, was only six in number, that is myself, Kenny, Svante, and three Damaras, and of these only four of us had guns. I regret that I must add that Svante and three Damaras were wounded. Poor Svante's wound is not very serious; he received the bullet on the outer side of the hip bone—the *ilium*—which it has very slightly splintered, and up to yesterday (Mr. P——'s letter is dated 12th of May) was progressing very favorably, when he was attacked by his old enemy rheumatism, which will, I am afraid, retard his recovery considerably. I reached Ondonga on the 7th inst., where I found your servant, Grendon, who at once placed your very nice house at my disposal, in which poor Svante is as comfortably housed as circumstances have permitted. I have said that I reached Ondonga on the 7th inst. Two days after, L—— came in on foot and reports that up to the 27th of April, he, T——, and K—— were outspanned at a fountain about forty-five miles north-east of Otjitno, where they had been very successful in obtaining ivory. On the morning of the 27th they were attacked by a party of Hottentots, who succeeded in taking from them three wagons, five horses, all their cattle, and 1000 lbs. of ivory. In short T—— and L—— lost everything except about 1000 lbs. of ivory, which they had a short time before buried, and another 1000 lbs. left in charge of Otjikongo; K—— saves five guns, but loses everything else. They were attacked very early in the morning, and were quite unprepared for action. I regret to say that not a single shot was fired by any of the party. T—— was wounded, one Damara woman killed, others captured, and two or three wounded. K——'s conduct in the affair seems to have been scandalous. L—— left again yesterday with your wagon and a party to fetch in the buried ivory and the wounded.' "

The reader may perhaps have guessed that the Svante of whom Mr. Palgrave in his letter makes mention as having been wounded, is my Swedish servant, whom I had sent with my friend to collect additional materials for my book on the natural history of the country. Notwithstanding some serious faults, Svante has always, from early youth, proved himself a devoted follower of my father and myself, accompanying us, when in his native land, not only on our shooting excursions, but when war was made on wild beasts; and latterly sharing with me in South Africa many a trying scene and situation by "flood and field." We are consequently much attached to each other. Poor fellow! though once possessed of gigantic strength and the most robust health, he is now but a shadow of his former self, and I am therefore not without some apprehensions for his final safety.*

* Andersson's apprehensions regarding the man in question were not groundless, for soon afterward lockjaw set in and he succumbed to his

"I have succeeded in inducing the Damaras to go in pursuit of Samuel and his murderous followers; but from the indifferent success that attended them on former occasions against the same men, I may perhaps be allowed to doubt their being able to effect anything that is likely to really benefit the cause of the whites in these parts. Still I must and will hope for the best.

"It was originally my intention to have started for the Ovampo country about this time, but I shall now be compelled to await the return of the Damaras from their present expedition, for though I might probably be strong enough to defend myself against the attacks of any marauders that may chance to cross my path, I should have gained but little, since the risk to individuals or very small parties must remain the same.

"Mr. Green informs me that he has at last, in company with young Smuts, and one John Pereira, succeeded in penetrating to the long heard of and long sought for river Cunené, and that the aspect of the country round about it greatly exceeds his most sanguine anticipations. He speaks in raptures of the scenery, which far surpasses that of the Okavango, as also does the river in general size and grandeur. On his way there, Mr. Green passed through numerous tribes, rich in cattle, cultivating the soil diligently, much given to barter, and all bearing a strong resemblance to the Ovampo, in their manners, habits, and general appearance. He met, moreover, with considerable civilization among one or two of the nations in question. One

wound, to the deep regret, as it would appear, not only of his master, to whom he was greatly attached, but of many others in Africa, who took a vast liking to him for his kind and obliging disposition.—ED.

chief was especially well advanced, being completely dressed like a European, whom he further imitated by living apart from his subjects, over whom he evidently exercised the most absolute sway.

"Mr. Green and party were everywhere kindly and hospitably received; only once did they experience anything like a rude reception, which, however, was soon turned into one of the most friendly nature. My friend attributes all this to the kind representations of the Ovampo chief, Otjkongo, who is not alone most friendly disposed toward Europeans, but possesses much influence with the neighboring tribes. The Rev. Mr. Hahn has just gone to Ondonga, with a view of trying to establish a mission there. I am sure we all wish him God speed!

"But though Mr. Green gives such a glowing account of the scenery, the country, and its capabilities, he speaks, on the other hand, in the most discouraging terms of any attempt at trying to establish a trade between the various tribes inhabiting the regions between the Ovampo and the Cunené, as well as those living on its banks. Not because of any unwillingness on the part of the natives to trade with other Europeans, nor from want of produce to exchange; but because the commerce, he says, is completely monopolized by the Portuguese, who, from the intimate knowledge they possess of the people and their wants, the exceeding small cost at which they travel—for they get food gratuitously from the natives, and their merchandise, as well as the produce obtained in exchange, are all carried by slaves—and the cheapness of their wares utterly forbids all competition. Thus, he assures me that the price paid for a single elephant tusk, say 50 lbs., weight, is eight to ten coins! Surely it is high time that the Cape Government remitted the exorbitant duty on guns and ammunition in favor of parties proceeding in the direction here indicated, so as to enable them to compete with some chance of success with the Portuguese. For, notwithstanding Mr. Green's dismal forebodings, I feel confident of success, could an outfit be obtained at the Cape on reasonable terms. I have yet to learn that a spirited and persevering Anglo-Saxon is to be distanced by a European of more favored climes, whether it be in the field of daring exploration or the more peaceable pursuit of commercial enterprise!

"But, my dear Mr. Editor, I am sadly trespassing upon your space, and for fear of exhausting your patience altogether, I will hasten to close this lengthy epistle. I have only to add, in conclusion, that the mission-work among the Damaras is progressing favorably. A few natives have been converted to Christianity, more are under preparation for baptism, a goodly number of children go to school, a nice church is in course of erection; and lastly, though not the least important, the natives are steadily acquiring habits of industry. The bed of the periodical Swakop, in front of the station, is for a considerable distance covered with newly sown corn-lands, and much of the ground on the banks is rapidly being converted into gardens. Altogether, the prospects are favorable, and all that is required to make the people and country happy and prosperous is permanent peace—and I am told there is some chance of this—and a better government. In short, we require an upright, well-to-do, fearless man, who would be prepared to deal out even-handed justice alike to the high and lowly, to the rich and the poor."

On the 22d of November, I again wrote to the Editor of the "Advertiser and Mail," to the following effect:

"When I last had the pleasure of addressing you from this country, I was led to speak rather hopefully of its present and future condition, but I am sorry to have to inform you that, instead of a peaceful settlement of the difficulties that have of late years caused so much strife and bloodshed, the country is once more thrown into a state of the utmost confusion, and the prospects of peace farther off than ever. The object of the present letter is to give you and the public the facts, so far as I am acquainted with them, that have led to this unhappy result.

"You will remember, I dare say, my allusion to a certain Hottentot marauder of the name of Samuel, who was levelling 'black-mail' on peaceful hunters and others, and that the Damaras had promised me to try to punish the villain, as well as to break up his stronghold. Month after month, however, elapsed without any signs of their intentions to redeem their solemn promises, till at last I fairly despaired of ever seeing them fulfilled. But all at once they (the Damaras) declared their readiness to proceed, and remembering the old saying, 'better late than never,' I saw them depart with joy and hope of a happy issue.

"But I had reckoned without mine host, for, not many days after the commando had left, rumors were rife that they had altered their intended course, which was to Samuel's stronghold on the confines of Damaraland; and this, in consequence of having learned by the way that the marauder, in anticipation of punishment for his many misdeeds, had already left his den with his people and ill-gotten booty and retraced his steps into Namaqualand, and instead of returning home they had followed him into that province. For should these rumors prove true, it was not difficult to see that they would attack any other Namaquas that might cross their path, and thus open a fresh old wound and grievance.

"And it turned out as I had anticipated, for a smaller party preceding the main body of the army, having encountered at an early period some Namaquas (altogether unconnected with Samuel), with whom was a white trader, who happened to be in their company, they at once fell upon and slaughtered the whole party, and then took possession of their effects. This was very sad; to say nothing of the attack on unoffending Namaquas, it was the first time, so far as I am aware, that the Damaras had been guilty of such an outrage on Europeans, for, unlike their more civilized neighbors, the Namaquas, who were in the frequent habit of abusing, robbing, and ill-treating the white traders they casually met, the latter had always been respected by them.

"And although on intelligence of the raid reaching Otjimbingue, the chief expressed regret for what had occurred, and, moreover, promised that on the return of the expedition the property of the traders should be restored to them—yet I could not learn that such restoration had been made.

"But to go back to the commando, which, after

vainly following the spoor of Samuel's wagon for a considerable distance into Namaqualand, were at length necessitated to retrace their steps, in which they appear to have suffered dreadfully from sickness (whereby very many died), and want of water and food. At this period, moreover, an advanced party of them, consisting of from three to four hundred stragglers, were surprised by a strong body of Namaquas, who were returning from a hunting expedition, and utterly routed, leaving forty-seven of their number dead on the spot. As a set-off, however, to this mishap, the main body of the Damaras soon afterward met the same party of Namaquas who, proud of their late victory, hesitated not to attack even them. But the Damaras not only showed a bold front, but steadily advanced on their foes, who, being all mounted, retreated to their wagons, which were 'trekking.' Here the Namaquas dismounted, and deliberately awaited the Damaras until so near that 'the white of the eye could be seen,' when they simultaneously fired a volley, and then remounting, they one and all fled for their lives, leaving their wagons, oxen, etc., a prey to the enemy. Notwithstanding the close proximity of the opposing forces on the occasion in question, it would not appear that any of the Damaras were killed, but six Namaquas were subsequently dispatched by them with the assegai.

"Previous to the occurrences mentioned, I had received tidings of another nature, that seriously affected me personally; namely, that a large party of Namaquas, headed by J. Boyce and J. Jonker, had made a sudden descent on Walwich Bay and the neighborhood, laying friend and foe alike under contribution, but more especially myself, who unfortunately had just forwarded a large quantity of valuable produce for shipment to Cape Town, nearly the whole of which was carried off. The worst feature in this case is that the outrage was principally committed by a Namaqua chief, with whom we had never been at enmity, but on whom, on the contrary, I, for one, had lavished much kindness and bestowed many handsome presents. He, moreover, owed me close on £100. I suppose the rascal thought it a very pleasant way of crying quits. This, as you may well imagine, has been a grievous blow to me, and one from which I shall not easily recover. Still, for the sake of the dear pledges of my affection, and those who so liberally and trustingly helped to equip me, I will not despair. Indeed, as far as my creditors are concerned, they are secure enough, for by dint of the most strenuous exertions and self-denial, I still hold property enough to make good all their claims. It is my poor family who will be the sufferers. But I feel that the Almighty, who has hitherto so mercifully and marvellously preserved me, will not abandon me in this my hour of need, and that my honest endeavors will finally be crowned with success. Away, then, with dark thoughts! cheerily once more on the boundless ocean of Hope!"

To proceed: Having by this time pretty well ascertained that the Damaras had no sincere wish for peace, and seeing that it would be hopeless for me to struggle successfully against so many contingencies of danger, without some guarantee from my enemies of being allowed to pursue my peaceable avocations unmolested, I addressed at this period a letter to Jan

Jonker, demanding whether he wanted peace or war; that for my own part, I was heartily tired of strife and bloodshed, and would be glad to come to a thorough understanding at once. On Jacobus Boyce, I did not deem it worth while to waste ink and paper, but would leave to the Damaras to deal with the ungrateful wretch as they saw fit.

CHAPTER XII.

Scarcity of wild beasts near Otjimbingue—The Leopard—Its resorts and food—Manner of surprising its prey—Wonderful bound—Accident to Axel—African Boer—Out of the frying-pan into the fire—Andersson's adventure—Temerity of the Leopard—The chasse—Dogs—The chetah—How it hunts—The wild-cat—Andersson's letter.

OTJIMBINGUE had once been a famous resort of wild beasts of various kinds, and though these had of late years been in a great measure driven or scared away by the largely increased population, a stray shot was occasionally obtainable at some of the smaller as well as the larger quadrupeds indigenous to the country. A visit from a lion was, on the whole, a rare event; but leopards, chetahs, lynxes (generally known as wild-cats), paid frequent visits to the sheep-folds, hen-roosts, etc. A favorite rendezvous of theirs were three small rocky, table-shaped eminences, largely strewn with bowlders—and consequently well suited for their hide-and-seek nature—within easy range of my house.

Before, however, I speak of these animals, a word or two regarding their natural history, etc., may not be out of place.

The leopard of Africa (*Felis Leopardus*), there very commonly called tiger or panther—the first in order, which Captain Harris tells us is very similar in appearance to that indigenous to India—is common throughout Damaraland, as also Southern Africa generally; but, from its cunning, active nature and nocturnal habits, is but rarely seen. It is about two feet seven inches high at the shoulder, and seven feet six inches in extreme length. The chin, neck, breast, belly, and inside of the extremities are white, the rest varying in different specimens between tawny, fulvous and reddish-brown, irregularly marked with spots of black which differ greatly in number, size, and appearance at different ages and seasons. It is monogamous, or solitary. In its wild state it is an exceedingly beautiful creature, its motions in the highest degree easy and graceful, and its agility in bounding among the rocks and woods quite amazing. Of its activity no person can have an idea by seeing it in the cages in which these animals are usually exhibited in Europe, humbled and tamed as they are by confinement and the cold and damp of the climate.

The chief resorts of the leopard are mountainous districts, where rock is piled on rock in frightful confusion, leaving between them fissures and caverns, more or less spacious. It is also met with in dense brakes and tangled coverts, where, if hard pressed by the hunter, it almost invariably takes refuge in a tree, should one be at hand; and if this be large and umbrageous, it is not without difficulty the animal is discovered, it having a marvellous faculty of concealing itself behind some knotty branch, or at the junction of the larger limbs with the trunk. Under such circumstances, moreover, it requires a practised eye and a steady hand to bring it down dead, as, if merely wounded, the chances are both man and dogs will fare badly. Nevertheless, this is the easiest and safest way of killing the leopard.

Its food is very various; indeed, hardly anything comes amiss to its voracious appetite and blood-thirsty nature; and, what is worse, it wantonly slays far more than it can consume, and thus becomes doubly destructive, so to say. It attacks indiscriminately birds, the rock-rabbit (*Hyrax Capensis*), monkeys, baboons, dogs (of the latter of which it is said to be specially fond), if they come in its way, antelopes, sheep, goats, and young cattle. It is said, indeed, that it causes the natives and colonists more damage than even the lion and other beasts of prey put together. It also preys on the ostrich, among whom, from that bird's want of hearing and smell, it commits great ravages. Indeed, I am inclined to believe that, of the large number annually destroyed in Damaraland and adjacent parts, whether by man or otherwise, two-thirds may be fairly charged to the leopard's account. I draw this inference, because out of the ostrich feathers brought to me by the natives for the purpose of barter, such of them as had been plucked from birds killed by the leopard were readily distinguished from those of birds shot by the hunter or captured in gins and pit-falls, by their jagged, mangled, and sawed look, occasioned by the teeth of the creature in question.

According to Methuen, even the "fretful" porcupine is not safe from the attacks of the leopard, for after describing the death of one of the last-named animals, he says, "It is a curious fact that on skinning it we found several bits of porcupine quills, upward of two inches in length, embedded in the flesh, with much attendant suppuration."

Elsewhere, the same author, after telling us that certain animals and birds have a propensity to lay in a supply of provisions for an emergency, goes on to say, "The Hottentots led us to the water near our camp, and showed us a singular phenomenon in the shape of a 'leopard's larder,' in which some savory morsels of flesh were stored away in the forks of a large olive tree, at about ten feet from the ground, and carefully concealed by some twigs, the leaves of which were just shrivelled."

As with the lion, the leopard always surprises its prey, either by stealing upon it cat-fashion, or from an ambush. As a rule, it fixes its fangs in the neck of the victim, and with such fatal accuracy that marks of one or both of them are usually found on or about the jugular vein, and, as a consequence, few animals thus seized escape with life. Nevertheless, although its strength is very considerable, it might be matched by a powerful dog were it not for its surprising agility. The extent of its bound when endeavoring to escape from an enemy, whether it be from a height or the ground, is at times almost beyond credence. Indeed, I myself was, on a certain occasion, an eye-witness to its wonderful powers in this way; it was under these circumstances: One evening, a little before sunset, while I was still suffering from the effects of fever, all my dogs suddenly began to give chase to some animal, which the distance did not enable us to distinguish. To judge, however, from the rapid alternating attacks and retreats of the pursuers, they evidently had a formidable antagonist before them. I was too weak to keep quite up with them, but my curiosity was so great that I almost did so. They were, I conjectured, from their steady, unbroken, deep bay, close upon the haunches of the enemy, yet I could not distinctly see either the dogs or the object of their pursuit; when all at once a magnificent leopard sprang right before me, from the topmost branches of a tall acacia, clearing, with a single bound, all his fierce assailants. I was so astounded at the magnitude of the leap—of which, without having seen it, a person can hardly form a notion—that, looking first at the tree and then at the place on which the beautiful animal alighted, I could hardly withdraw my eyes from the spot. Had the dogs been equally fascinated as myself with the fierce muscular action of the comely creature, they would certainly have lost their prey; but rage alone animated them, and before the panther had proceeded one hundred yards, they had overtaken and pulled him to the ground, when they fell on him with such ferocity that by the time I reached the scene of conflict, the poor brute gave no other signs of life than a quivering of the limbs.

Its disposition is fierce, cruel, and vindictive, and it has the reputation of being desperately courageous. Speaking generally, however, excepting in self-defence, or when wounded, the leopard will not attack people; though it does happen at times that when they approach too near to its hiding-place it will, without the slightest provocation, make an onset on the intruder.

Casualties from leopards in my vicinity were not of unfrequent occurrence. On one occasion, indeed, my Swedish lad, Axel, was beating some low bushes in search of game and specimens, when he suddenly found himself in presence of one of these beasts, who, apparently, was in the very act of springing upon him, its head being ensconced between its fore legs, as is its wont on such occasions. Being probably startled at the unexpected vision, the youth hurriedly raised his fowling-piece to his shoulder and fired. But the contents, unfortunately, only lodged in one of the animal's fore-paws, which it smashed, as was afterward ascertained, and before he could pull the second trigger he found himself in a deadly struggle with the exasperated brute. However, being a strong-limbed and courageous young man, he seized the leopard with both hands, and for some moments held it down to the ground by main force. Hearing cries of distress, some Damaras who were herding cattle hard by came up, but seeing the danger, they beat a precipitate retreat. My poor boy repeatedly pointed with his foot to the gun, but all in vain, and he began to despair of his life, as the beast had by this time dreadfully lacerated both his hands and arms, and consequently unfitted him for prolonged strife with such a fierce and powerful opponent. Providentially the dogs, though not the most courageous, came to the rescue, and by persistently worrying the beast in his hinder parts, finally compelled him to decamp, though not until he had killed one of the number. It is satisfactory, however, to add that he himself was shortly afterward destroyed by a party of natives, who, on hearing the poor fellow's cries, promptly ran to the spot, and afterward went in pursuit of the leopard, which died game, having slain a second dog;

two others, moreover, being accidentally shot by their owners in the general *mêlée*.

As I have said, the lad was fearfully knocked about and mauled. In some places, especially about the hands and wrists, the teeth of the animal had actually met in the flesh. I am, however, happy to be able to add that with care and quiet, he ultimately regained the use of his arms and hands, though not until after much and prolonged suffering.

On another occasion, a herd of mine espied a leopard among some rocks, and being armed he unhesitatingly discharged his musket, but either missed his mark, or very slightly wounded the brute. The next moment the poor fellow felt himself struck violently to the ground, with the teeth of the infuriated animal deep buried in his left shoulder. However, by the assistance of some dogs the leopard was made to retreat after awhile, but not until it had fearfully mauled the man, who, though he recovered temporarily, eventually died from the effects of the dreadful wounds inflicted.

Numerous other instances of the ferocity of the leopard have come under my own notice, and very many others are on record, of which I shall instance a few.

"Two African farmers returning from hunting, roused a leopard in a mountain ravine, and immediately gave chase to it. The beast at first endeavored to escape by clambering up a precipice; but being hotly pursued and wounded by a musket-ball, it turned upon its assailants with the frantic ferocity peculiar to this animal, and springing upon the man who had fired at it, pulled him to the ground, biting him at the same time on the shoulder, and tearing open his cheeks with its claws. The other hunter, seeing the danger of his comrade, sprang from his horse, and attempted to shoot the leopard through the head; but whether owing to trepidation, the fear of wounding his friend, or the quick motions of the animal, he unfortunately missed. The leopard, abandoning its prostrate foe, darted with redoubled fury upon its new antagonist, and so fierce and sudden was the onset that, before the Boer could stab it with his hunting-knife, the savage brute struck him on the head with its claws, and actually tore the scalp over his eyes. In this frightful condition the hunter grappled with the leopard, and, struggling for life, they rolled together down a steep declivity. All this passed far more rapidly than it can be described in words. During this dreadful scene the hunter first attacked had started to his feet and seized his gun, and after reloading it, he rushed forward to save the life of his friend. But it was too late. The leopard had seized the unfortunate man by the throat, and mangled him so dreadfully that death was inevitable; and his comrade (himself severely wounded) had only the melancholy satisfaction of completing the destruction of the savage beast, already exhausted with the loss of blood from several deep wounds from the knife of the expiring huntsman."

Again, another instance of the ferocity of the leopard occurred in the case of the Missionary Schmidt. "This worthy man had gone out with a party of Hottentots at another Moravian station to hunt some hyenas which had been very destructive to their flocks, and in company with one of the men entered a thicket in pursuit of a beast they had wounded. Instead of the hyena, however, the dogs started a leopard, which instantly sprang on the Hottentot and bore him to the ground. Mr. Schmidt ran forward to the aid of the man, with his gun cocked; but before he could find an opportunity of firing, the animal left the Hottentot and flew with fury at himself. In the scuffle he dropped the gun, but luckily fell above the leopard with his knee on its stomach. The animal seized him by the left arm with its jaws, and kept striking him with its paws and tearing his clothes in tatters from his breast. Schmidt, however, being a powerful man, succeeded, after receiving another severe bite or two, in seizing the leopard by the throat with his right hand, and held it down, in spite of its desperate struggles, for a few minutes, and until his strength was on the point of giving way, when a Hottentot on the outside of the jungle, who heard his cries, came to the rescue, and shot the ferocious beast through the heart, so that its death was instantaneous. Had any life been left, its dying struggles might still have proved fatal to Mr. Schmidt. As it was, he was so terribly lacerated that for several weeks his life was in the greatest danger. The Hottentot who was first attacked was less severely wounded, but his face was so much torn by the animal's talons that his eyes were filled with blood, and he was unable to render any aid to the missionary who had so generously come to his aid."

"While in this helpless state" (rheumatic fever), writes Gordon Cumming, "Mr. Orpen and Present (a native follower) had gone up the river to shoot sea-cows, when they fell in with an immense leopard, which Present wounded very badly. They then sent natives to camp to ask for dogs, of which I sent them a couple. In about an hour the natives came running back and said that Orpen was killed by the leopard. On further inquiry, however, I found that he was not really killed, but fearfully torn and bitten about the arms and head. They had rashly taken up the spoor on foot, the dogs following behind, instead of going in advance. The consequence of this was that they came right upon the beast before they were aware of him, when Orpen fired and missed him. The leopard then sprang on his shoulders, and dashing him to the ground, lay upon him, growling and lacerating his hands, arms, and head most fearfully. Presently the creature permitted Orpen to rise, and come away."

Where were Present and all the natives, that not a man of them moved to assist the unfortunate Orpen? He goes on to say: "According to an established custom among all colonial servants, the instant the leopard sprang on him, Present discharged his piece in the air, and then, dashing it to the ground, he rushed down the bank and jumped into the river, along which he swam some hundred yards before he would again venture on *terra firma*. The natives, though numerous and armed, had likewise fled in another direction."

The teeth of the leopard, or rather its saliva, I presume, are reputed to be of a very poisonous nature. Certain it is that men bitten by the animal seldom recover from their hurts until after a length of time and much suffering.

I should remark that when a man has been bitten by a tiger, and the beast has afterward been killed, the

Damaras melt some of the fat, which is poured into the wound along with a powder produced by pounding a portion of its teeth. They also, I am informed, take the moist soil out of the river-bed, which, after being cooked, or prepared in some way or other, is applied as a poultice to the wounds. A tiger's bite, the natives moreover assert, is less dangerous if inflicted at noon than at an earlier or later period of the day. It is a curious fact that the custom of applying a portion of the fat, entrails, or even the flesh of the creature (whether quadruped or reptile) held to be poisonous to the wounds of a man that has been bitten by it, or of taking the same internally, should be prevalent among nearly all the tribes of Southern Africa.

Numerous instances of hairbreadth escapes from the leopard are also on record, among which that of Moffat the missionary is, perhaps, not the least remarkable, the rather as, in the avoidance of the threatened danger, he incurred another of even a more perilous nature, thus verifying the old saying, "Out of the frying-pan into the fire.

"In one of my early journeys," he writes, "I had an escape from an African tiger and a serpent, no less providential. I had left the wagons, and wandered to a distance among the coppice and grassy openings in quest of game. I had a double-barrelled gun on my shoulder, which was loaded with a ball and small shot. An antelope passed, at which I fired, and slowly followed the course it took. After advancing a short distance, I saw a tiger staring at me between the forked branches of a tree, behind which its long, spotted body was concealed, twisting and turning its tail like a cat just going to spring on its prey. This, I knew, was a critical moment. I moved about as if in search of something on the grass, taking care to retreat at the same time. After getting, as I thought, a suitable distance to turn my back, I moved somewhat more quickly; but in my anxiety to escape what was behind, I did not see what was before me, until startled by treading on a large cobra-da-capello serpent asleep on the grass. It instantly twisted its body round my leg, on which I had nothing but a pair of thin trousers, when I leaped from the spot, dragging the enraged and venomous reptile after me, and while in the act of throwing itself into a position to bite, I, without turning round, threw my piece over my shoulder and shot it.. Taking it by the tail, I brought it to my people in the wagons, who, on examining the bag of poison, asserted that, had the creature bitten me, I could never have reached the wagon. The serpent was six feet long."

Happily, I myself never came within the clutches of a leopard, though on one occasion, had not prudence got the better part of valor at a critical moment, I might have found myself in a very awkward scrape.

Cantering one genial afternoon past one of the wooded knolls recently spoken of, near to Otjimbingue, with a splendid eagle (*Aquila bellicosa*) slung to my saddle, I was treated to an exquisite view of one of the creatures perched most picturesquely on a projecting rock. With body expanded to its utmost size, nerves strained apparently almost to bursting, leaning well forward from the bowlder, one of its hind legs being firmly planted on an adjoining stone, tail swaying meaningly to and fro, and with eyes dilated and glittering, fixed steadily on some object immediately below, it hung, as it were, on the clear-cut horizon, the very beau-ideal of a feline picture.

I was within a couple of hundred yards of the brute, but so intensely was his gaze riveted on some other passing object that it either was not aware of my presence, though in full view of me from its elevated position, or it lost sight of its own danger in trying to compass its natural impulses. Reining in my steed cautiously, I contemplated admiringly for a few moments the striking scene, varied by the contrast of a large herd of many-colored sheep and goats just emerging from some low brushwood at the foot of the rock—evidently the object of the leopard's fascination—frisking and gambolling in their satiety and fulness, totally unconscious of the close proximity of their dreaded and deadly foe.

Only one barrel of my fowling-piece chanced to be loaded, and that with the very smallest shot, having shortly before discharged the other at the eagle spoken of; but the temptation to have a shy at the fierce marauder was too great to be withstood, and being always much of a creature of impulse, I quickly made up my mind to the risk. I felt confident that if I could but bring a huge stone that rose close to the animal between me and him unperceived, a sudden leap or two would bring me face to face with him, and give me a chance of despatching him with even such an indifferent missile as I had then at command. Accordingly I rode on quickly until out of sight, when I immediately faced round, and having reached the foot of the rock alluded to, I dashed boldly on the panther. He heard me coming, and I was only just in time to catch sight of his hind-quarters as he disappeared round the very stone that had hitherto concealed me from view. Being a tolerably good snap-shot I might perhaps have given a good account of his seat of honor, but fortunately my eagerness did not outrun my discretion at this critical moment, and I forbore to fire. And right glad was I, after reflection, at having refrained; for though a well-directed shot at his head might have killed or blinded him, a charge of dust shot in his breech could only have served to exasperate the brute, and would have made the issue at least doubtful.

There were several native villages close to the knolls in question, and as I passed them on my way home I warned the inhabitants of the danger; but either they cared not or they had not the means to avert it, for the next morning, having occasion to go by some of the werfts, I found that the leopard spoken of had played sad havoc in one of their sheep-folds, having remorselessly killed several of its inmates, besides wounding many others.

The temerity of the leopard is sometimes almost incredible. I remember an instance in point which occurred during my stay at Otjimbingue. A Damara who was herding my cattle came one morning to tell me that a leopard had entered one of the huts on his werft, occupied by a young woman, during the night, and there remained till daylight. On finding herself thus unexpectedly visited—the man went on to say—she gave the alarm, and on hearing the voices and steps of her friends approaching, the girl made a rush for the door and gained the open air unmolested. The people, however, would not believe it possible that there had been such an animal as she described in the hut, and much less that it could still be there: it was merely her fancy, they laughingly remarked—a dream in short. But the woman stuck to her tale, and insisted upon the leopard still occupying the hut; and though they refused to credit her, not one would enter the hovel to disprove or verify the assertion by ocular demonstration. It had the effect, however, of keeping the natives awake for the remainder of the night, and just as day was breaking they observed, to their surprise, a full-grown leopard quietly emerge from the hut in question, and make for the adjoining rocks!

The secret was now soon explained, for it appears that the object of the brute's visit to the hut had been a dog which had taken refuge there, and which he had at once killed, remaining unconcernedly to feast upon the carcass until gorged or scared away by the return of day.

A somewhat similar story is told by Delegorgue, the African traveller:

"Seeing a crowd of people of both sexes in earnest conversation, and gesticulating violently," he writes, "I went up to them to inquire the cause of their ex citement; but before they had time to reply I noticed, extended on the ground and attached by the four legs to a stout pole, a long and slender panther, over the head of which was thrown a *our-gobo.* She was quite dead; the blood still flowed from numerous wounds. This is what I learned:

"The preceding night, between eleven and twelve,

when every one slept, three living beings reposed in a cabin, wherein was a half-extinguished fire. A woman and her child occupied the inner end of the left side of the building; a dog the outer end to the right. The panther, who incessantly prowls about during the night, had from a distance scented the dog, and, creeping forward on her belly, placed her nose to the aperture; up to this time there had been no noise. For an instant the beast hesitated; but the victim is so near. The door gives way—the dog barks, and is immediately torn to pieces.

"At the cries of the woman, who could not escape by the door, except by passing the dog and the panther, whose claws and fangs constantly opposed her, a number of armed men ran to the spot—and see the singular expedient they had recourse to. The door is closed and securely fastened. Four men pass their *ourkondas* through interstices in the door, the points of their weapons crossing in like manner as bayonets, and thus preventing the savage animal from either lifting up or opening it. These men remain without, each holding a second assegai in his right hand in readiness for any emergency. At the same time a hole, ten to twelve inches in diameter, is made on a level with the ground, at the upper end of the cabin, to facilitate which operation fires were lighted round and about the latter. Presently the woman and her child—both half dead with fear—were drawn through the aperture in question, which was afterward effectually closed with sticks, mats, etc. The dog and the panther now alone remained in the hut, where the beast was heard to bound repeatedly against the walls, which it essayed to tear down with its teeth.

"The Amazoulous turned to advantage this rage of despair; a hundred, two hundred *our-kondas* were passed through the sides of the slightly constructed hovel, and presently their sharp and cutting points converged about the furious beast. Sometimes she tore away the spears with her claws, at others seized them with her teeth; but a number of the weapons wounded her, and when, frantic and roaring, she rushed upon the door, to which she was naturally attracted by the light of the fires, the four warriors posted there riddled the fore-part of her body with their assegais. She had already received more than a hundred wounds, without counting the loss of her eyes, when with a desperate bound she pierced herself to the heart.

"This is not a fabulous relation; I myself saw the woman, the child, the panther, and the weapons used to destroy it. I have inspected the bloody arena; and I have moreover brought away the skin and the head of the animal in remembrance of the event, and of the presence of mind of the Maputa."

Again: "The leopard, when famished with hunger," writes Gordon Cumming, "is exceedingly audacious. The night was pitch dark, so that nothing could be seen; but Molleyon told me that a lion and a leopard were prowling round us, endeavoring to obtain the venison of the zebras, which hung in festoons in the trees beside us, and next moment I heard the voices of both, the lion roaring and the leopard shrieking wildly as they sprang after the dogs. At length their boldness increased; the lion chased the dogs with angry growls within twenty yards of where we stood, and the leopard actually sprang into the centre of my larder beside the fire, and was making off with a large fragment of ribs, when the dogs went gallantly at him. He turned upon them, and so terribly lacerated two that they soon afterward died of their wounds. We now snatched up large flaming brands from the fire, and, meeting the lion as he advanced, sent them flying in his face, when I fancy he made off. I feared to use my rifle lest I should shoot the dogs. The horses and oxen, though much alarmed, did not endeavor to break loose, being still very much fatigued from the hardships they had undergone."

On another occasion, Gordon Cumming tells us, "A panther at night came within ten yards of my fire, and killed Craddock, and disabled Wolf, my two best elephant dogs."

The chasse of the leopard, by both colonists and natives, is commonly conducted on foot, the hunters being accompanied by dogs, of which the more there are the better, as they are the greatest of safeguards from this fierce and agile beast; and, though the native fox-like breed are awful-looking creatures, I have never found any others equal to them for daring or pertinacity.

In the vicinity of Otjimbingue, should the leopard be very destructive to the herds and sheepfolds, the Damaras at times turned out *en masse* to hunt him, in which case he seldom escaped with life, though too frequently at the cost of several of their most courageous and best dogs, and severe wounds and bruises to one or more of the men themselves. A leopard on such occasions has been known to cast himself, in rapid succession, on five or six different assailants, severely wounding each and all, and not unfrequently maiming some for life. When at these times, I would here remark, an individual is attacked by the creature and cast to the ground, it not unfrequently happens, should the opportunity offer, that he seizes it by the ears; and, if he be strong and agile, holds it fast until his companions come to the rescue and despatch it, which they are then enabled to do with tolerable ease and safety. If a gun be not at hand, a blow with a *knob-kiêri* on the nose or chest will prove sufficient to put it *hors de combat* for a moment, or, it may be, kill it outright. Though the leopard, as said, is commonly hunted on foot, yet once on a time, as what follows will show, the creature is pursued on horseback.

"After partaking of some refreshment, having just returned from an elephant hunt," says Gordon Cumming, "I saddled up two steeds and rode down the bank of Ngatwani with the Bushmen, to seek for any game I might find. After riding about a mile along the river's green bank, I suddenly came upon an old male leopard lying under the shade of a thorn grove, and panting from the great heat. Although I was within sixty yards of him, he had not heard the horses' tread. I thought he was a lioness, and, dismounting, took a rest in my saddle on the old gray, and sent a bullet into him. He sprang to his feet and ran halfway down the river's bank, and stood to look about him, when I sent a second bullet into his person, and he disappeared over the bank. The ground being very dangerous I did not disturb him by following then, but

I at once sent Ruyter to camp for the dogs. Presently he returned with Wolf and Boxer, very much done up with the sun. I rode forward, and on looking over the bank the leopard started up and sneaked off alongside of the tall reeds, and was instantly out of sight. I fired a random shot from the saddle to encourage the dogs, and shouted to them. They, however, stood looking stupidly round, and would not take up his scent at all. I led them over his spoor again and again, but to no purpose; the dogs seemed quite stupid, and yet they were Wolf and Boxer, my two best. At length I gave it up as a lost affair, and was riding down the river's bank when I heard Wolf give tongue behind, and galloping back, I found him at bay with the leopard, immediately beneath where I had fired at him. He was very severely wounded, and had slipped down into the river bed and doubled back, whereby he had thrown out both the dogs and myself. As I approached, he flew out upon Wolf and knocked him over, and then, running up the bed of the river, he took shelter in a thick bush. Wolf, however, followed him, and at this moment my other dogs having heard the shots, came up from camp, and bayed at him fiercely. He sprang out upon them, and then crossed the river bed, taking shelter beneath some large tangled roots on the opposite bank. As he crossed the river I put a third bullet into him, firing from the saddle, and as soon as he came to bay I gave him a fourth, which finished him. In the conflict, however, the unfortunate Alert, who was still going on three legs, with his breast laid bare by the first waterbuch, was wounded as usual, getting his face torn open.

The leopard is not unfrequently taken in traps of various kinds. Most commonly, however, these are constructed of large stones and timber, on much the same principle as the common rat-trap. On the beast being thus captured by the Cape Colonists, notice is usually given to the neighbors, who assemble at the spot, when the creature is baited by all the curs in the vicinity, in order to train them to meet it in the field; but it seldom dies without first killing or severely maiming one or more of its assailants.

At other times, we are told by Lichtenstein: "The leopard is taken by hanging a piece of raw flesh upon a bush, in the midst of which an assegai is so ingeniously fastened, the sharp point being upward, that when the panther springs at the meat he falls upon the iron, and is struck by it to the heart."

Notwithstanding the naturally savage disposition of the leopard, he is capable of being domesticated and tamed when captured young and judiciously managed, as I myself can testify, having reared one of these animals. It is true that, like the chetah, or hunting-leopard, of which presently, he was fond of a fowl, pig, or puppy, and managed to snap up numbers that came feeding or gambolling unsuspiciously in the neighborhood of his kennel, when, with an unerring blow of his paw, he would knock his unhappy victim down, and the next moment fasten his teeth in its neck with the force of a vice. I have myself stood by his side when an unlucky cur came within his reach, and nothing but forcibly separating his jaws would make him relinquish his hold, and that long after life was extinct in his prize. Yet he was very tame, allowing any one almost to approach, caress, and stroke his sleek and glossy sides, and enjoyed very much a romp with me or the full-grown dogs, some of which seemed to relish the fun nearly as much as he himself. This animal found its way to England, and, for aught I know, may now be an inmate of that interesting collection of wild beasts to be found so well and humanely cared for in the Zoological Gardens, Regent's Park, London.

The chetah, or hunting-leopard, of the Cape Colony (*Felis jubata*), which Harris tells us is similar in appearance to that of India, is about the size of a greyhound. The belly and inside of the extremities white, the rest pale yellow studded with small black spots, larger over the back and on the outside of the thighs. As with its congener, the leopard, it confines itself chiefly to mountainous districts, where it preys on the rock-rabbit and such of the antelopes as it can contrive to circumvent; and when it takes up its abode in the vicinity of the colonists or natives, it is very destructive both to the sheep-fold and the hen-roost. Though of a savage and intractable nature, the chetah in India and other Eastern countries is regularly trained to the chase, and proves a valuable ally to the sportsman. Though somewhat out of place in these pages, perhaps what follows, showing the manner in which the creature acts, may not be altogether without interest to the reader.

"On one occasion," says Harris, "I saw three chetahs in the field. Coming on a herd of antelopes, one of them was quickly unhooded and loosed from his bonds. As soon as he perceived the deer, he dropped quietly off the cart on the opposite side to that on which they stood, and approached them at a slow crouching canter, masking himself at every bush and irregularity that lay in his way. As soon, however, as they began to show alarm he quickened his pace, and was in the midst of them at a few bounds. He singled out a doe and ran it close for about two hundred yards; when he reached it he, with a single blow of his paw rolled it over, and in an instant was sucking the life-blood from its throat. One of the other chetahs was slipped at the same time, but after four or five desperate bounds, by which he nearly reached his prey, he suddenly gave up the pursuit and came growling sulkily back to the wagon. On these occasions, and when the deer is pulled down, a keeper runs us, hoods the chetah, cuts the victim's throat, and securing some of the blood in a wooden ladle, thrusts it under the leopard's nose. The antelope is then dragged away, while the chetah is rewarded with a leg for his pains."

My own experiences, however, as to the teachable qualities of the chetah, are altogether at variance with those generally ascribed to it; and I had a good opportunity of judging of the nature and habits of the animal, as an acquaintance of mine brought up one in my immediate vicinity, than which a fiercer or more intractable brute never came under my notice. Its disposition, in fact, was the very opposite to that of the leopard spoken of a page or two back. But, then, it is not of course fair to judge of a whole species by a single individual. Moreover, the animal in question was much teased and annoyed, more especially by the natives, whom he learned to hate with the most deadly hatred; and, unfortunately, several children were bitten by him in a fearful manner, one, if not more of them, dying from the wounds it inflicted. But, indeed, with the exception of myself and one or two others, not a European dared to approach within his reach. Kindness and gentleness had no effect upon this fierce brute, and it was only by completely cowing his nature that we ventured to interfere with him. Now and then he would manage to break, or otherwise free himself, from his bonds, when, with fearful yells and imprecations, the terror-stricken natives would be seen running wildly to and fro in search of shelter; but I never remember him doing any mischief to the people on such occasions. Woe, however, betide any smaller animal, such as a puppy, a pig, or a fowl, that then crossed his path. The chetah in question unfortunately succeeded one day in escaping, never to be recovered; and from its fearlessness of man and local knowledge it became more destructive to the hen-roost and the sheep-fold than one in its wild state would have been.

The wild-cat (*Felis catus*) was common in the neighborhood of Otjimbingue, and is generally distributed over Damara and Great Namaqua Land, and, indeed, throughout most parts of Southern Africa. As soon as evening sets in, or even before darkness has enveloped nature in her nightly shroud, a harsh, wild, and disagreeable cry often greets the ear of the wanderer, and adds greatly to the dreariness of an African solitude; it is that of the wild-cat calling to her mate, or others of her congeners.

There is probably not a more destructive animal to the poultry-yard, pigeon-house, and even to the sheep-pen (which it not unfrequently enters for the purpose of killing the young lambs and kids), than the wild-cat. It is said to have an especial relish for the heads of birds, often leaving the rest of the body untouched. It sometimes takes up its quarters in the immediate neighborhood of man, and unless quickly dislodged or killed, will prove a serious evil to a homestead. I remember a case in point. One of my servants always kept a number of fowls, which were generally housed in a small shed abutting on his cottage. For a long time great depredations were committed among the birds, and knowing the thievish propensities of the natives, the Damaras were generally thought to be the culprits, though never detected. One night, however, hearing a terrible clucking and fluttering of wings in the hen-house, the man hastily dressed himself, and, with candle and gun in hand, rushed into the shed. The first sight that met him was the headless trunk of his favorite cock, quickly followed by those of others, and, on looking upward, he espied to his surprise a huge wild-cat perched between two hens, who were apparently paralyzed with fear. Delighted at having at last discovered the real depredator, and having an opportunity of punishing the wily, persevering, and daring marauder, it may be well supposed that he lost no time in giving him his *quietus*. The skin now graces my collection.

The wild-cat is an exceedingly fierce and spiteful animal, and will not unfrequently turn upon his pursuers, be they men or dogs, when hard pressed. St. John, in his "Highland Sports," mentions a remarkable instance of the beast's courage, ferocity, and tenacity of life. "I have heard many stories," writes this author, "of their attacking and severely wounding a man when their escape has been cut off. Indeed, a wild-cat once flew at me in the most determined manner. I was fishing at a river in Sutherlandshire, and, in passing from one pool to another, had to climb over some rock and broken kind of ground. In doing so I sank through some rotten heather and moss up to my knees, almost upon a wild-cat, who was concealed under it. I was quite as much startled as the animal herself could be, when I saw the wild-looking beast rush out from between my feet, with every hair on her body standing on end, making her look twice as large as she really was. I had three small Skye terriers with me, who immediately gave chase and pursued her till she took refuge in a corner of the rocks, where, perched in a kind of recess out of reach of her enemies, she stood with her hair bristled, and spitting and growling like a common cat. Having no weapon with me, I laid down my rod, cut a good sized stick, and proceeded to dislodge her. As soon as I was within six or seven feet of the place, she sprang straight at my face, over the dogs' heads. Had I not struck her in mid-air as she leaped at me, I should probably have got some severe wound. As it was, she fell with her back half broken among the dogs, who, with my assistance, despatched her. I never saw an animal fight so desperately, or one which was so difficult to kill. If a tame cat has nine lives, a wild-cat must have a dozen."

The skin of the African wild-cat is probably not equal in value to that obtained from the same animal in colder parts of the world. Nevertheless, the fur is soft and warm, and accordingly the skin is much prized by the natives, who convert it into carosses. Very large numbers of wild-cats are annually destroyed in Damaraland, but being a prolific animal, the population scanty, and food abundant, it does not appear to decrease, as the case is in more civilized and populous countries. Like the domestic cat, it produces at a litter an uncertain number of kittens, sometimes only two or three, at others double the nnmber.

[The Editor would here remark that though Andersson makes no mention in his "Notes of Travel" of having killed large game at this period, either in the vicinity of Otjimbingue or elsewhere, it would appear from a letter to a friend, now lying before me, that, when on short excursions from home, he met with considerable success with antelopes, for he says: "I have lately returned from a short shooting excursion, during which I saw much game, but shot wretchedly. The number of koodoos (you will remember the noble creature from Wood's beautiful picture in 'Lake N'gami') that I met with almost exceeds belief. Some of the scenes that I witnessed, strongly reminded me of a well-stocked deer-park in England. Thus I have counted upward of fifty koodoos in a two hours' ride, out of which perhaps there no were less than twenty stags. The koodoo, when seen in its native wilds, is truly a magnificent beast. But notwithstanding my vile shooting, I carried away some fine heads, which I am about to present to my wife, who is clamorous for losses sustained; for, you must know, I was compelled to part with my former very handsome collection of heads and skulls *for bread*. I think I have already told you I can ride on horseback pretty well; the only drawback is the shape of my artificial boot, which has a deep hollow between heel and the toe, into which the stirrup is continually slipping, thus causing me to lose command of one leg. But, notwithstanding, I fairly rode down a gemsbok, one of the fastest of African antelopes, the other day."]

CHAPTER XIII.

Departure of elephant-hunters for Ondonga—Accident to Andersson—Departure for Ovampo Land—Arrival at Jacongava—Omapjee—Wild dogs and koodoo—Remarkable flowers—Huge snake killed—A gemsbok shot—Wagon stuck fast in the mud—Bushmen come to bivouac—Arrival in Ovampo Land—Escape of Andersson's people from Samuel.

BUT it is high time, after this long digression, to return to my little narrative. Latterly, the elephant-hunters, my best customers, had made Ondonga, as the residence of the chief of Ovampo Land was called, their head-quarters, it being a convenient centre from whence to make excursions in quest of the beasts in question. As a further inducement, the chief was known to be exceedingly well disposed toward Europeans, and corn and vegetables could always be obtained there, which was not the case in Damaraland, where, indeed, little besides cattle was procurable from the natives.

Knowing all this, and that the overland route to the Cape was unsafe, and that there was now no longer a field for the adventurous trader at Otjimbingue, I determined on following my friends to Ondonga, for which market I, when at Cape Town, had laid in a good stock of suitable goods. But just as I was on the point of starting, news of the attack of the Hottentots upon the Europeans, as mentioned in a preceding chapter, reached me, and of course put an end, for the time at least, to my projected journey. It is true I was perhaps strong enough to defend myself against any attack these scoundrels might make on me; but I should have gained little, even if successful in beating them off. This unexpected delay, coupled with the trivial amount of barter to be done at Otjimbingue, left much time on my hands, in which I occasionally absented myself for a few days from home, the better to enjoy the pleasure of the chase. During the last of these trips, however, I had the misfortune to fall from my horse, or, rather, he fell on me, bruising in a frightful manner my still very indifferently cured leg. It was a mercy, indeed, that the leg was not altogether smashed; as it was, the accident entirely crippled me for upward of a month, and caused me great pain for a long time afterward.

This very long and compulsory stay at Otjimbingue would, as may be supposed, have been monotonous and tedious enough had it not been for my literary labors—the securing of specimens of Natural History, and in improving my knowledge of the habits of the birds and beasts found in the vicinity—which occupation enabled me, pleasantly enough, to while away many an idle hour. On the 22d of September, 1866, however, I despatched my people with the wagons to Ondonga, and on the 29th of December of the same year I myself set off for the same destination.

[With the exception of three chapters on special subjects, inserted hereafter, Andersson's "Notes of Travel" end here, and the only account we have of his after proceedings is to be gathered from his journals, which I have copied all but *verbatim;* but these (his journals) seem never to have been *corrected*, even in the slightest degree, by him, since they were written, which will account for any little discrepancy or ambiguity that may be found therein. And though, owing to ill health and his disabled state, which prevented Andersson from exerting himself or enjoying the pleasures of the chase, as he was wont to do in former times, these journals may not contain much matter to interest the general reader, still it is to be hoped their contents will prove acceptable not only to the naturalist and the sportsman, but also to the future traveller in Ovampo and Damara Land, as showing the manifold difficulties he will probably have to encounter, and the risks he will run from the insalubrity of the climate, etc.—*Editor*.]

JOURNAL.—*Journey from Otjimbingue to Ondonga.*

"*Saturday, 29th December.*—Effected with great difficulty a start from Otjimbingue a little before noon, and reached Omarun all right after about four hours' steady travelling. Mr. K—— and the 'trek oxen,' though poor, answered well enough; however, the only real good front ox that we have the herd managed to lose last night. The Damara sent in search of the animal returned without it; must start him off again to-morrow. The country begins to look most cheerful; everything is green. How different from my last visit to these parts! I do love it during the rainy season; one feels, and really gets new life. The weather is pleasantly cool, even slightly chilly during the night.

"*Sunday, 30th December.*—Left bivouac at an early hour; reached Jacongava after about three and a half hours' travel. Shot a fine specimen of *Agthoracicies*, but did not get a sight of nest. January, Hans, Abraham, and Kamapge joined us in the afternoon, but went away again, intending to be with us in earnest to-morrow, except the first-named, who will go ahead with a view of collecting the people, and slaughter things.

"*Monday*, 31*st December*. — Left Jacongava at 3.15 P. M.; bivouacked at 5.55, under 'Sugar Loaf Peak,' which I took it into my head to ascend, a height (and many parts quite perpendicular) of not less than from 1,200 to 1,500 feet above the plain. Prodigious exertion, considering my crippled condition. But the sight one gets from the top of this lofty hill is worthy of some trouble and pains. In fact, Damaraland, at least this portion of it, here lies like a map spread out at one's feet. It affords unquestionably the best view of the country of all the numerous hills that I have ascended. Unfortunately I had not time enough to contemplate the fine prospect at my leisure, as I had numerous bearings to take. The afternoon, however, was lovely, and though the descent was troublesome and painful, I enjoyed, on the whole, my trip very much. I trust only I shall not feel the effects to-morrow.

"*Tuesday*, 1*st January*.—In a few months I shall have passed my fortieth year. Forty years! an ordinary lifetime; and what have I done? A bankrupt in purse and health; and as to what I have performed, it is *apparently* very little; and yet I have worked desperately hard, setting danger, fatigue, pain, and troubles at nought. God help me, poor fellow! But regrets are vain, and I ought not to indulge in them. Let me try and make the most of the few years left to me here on earth, should it please God to spare me. Could but peace and quiet be obtained for this unhappy land I might yet do well, and leave my wife and children provided for. I long to be settled in this land, in order that I may ascertain what can be made of *Omappi* and *Oronge*.* I don't half like to leave for the Cape until I get some one to occupy both places. I ought to have a garden as well as corn land ready ere many months are passed. I, moreover, want to leave the trees at Omappi. A kraal ought to be constructed for strangers, that they may not pitch their 'tents' at random, and thus wantonly cut down the bush. Left bivouac at 8.40; reached Katondeka at 9.50. Road very stony; abundance of water in limestone pits. Omatake can be seen from here (Troch., 17, 10½). Off again at 3.25; came to a vley at 5.20 (Troch., 79 92). This place must hold water for many months after the rains have ceased. Off a third time at 6.40. Bivouacked at 7.40; but this must be an error, as we have been at least an hour and a half on the road. Travelled well. Feel very poorly.

"*Wednesday, 2d January.*—Left bivouac at 6.5. Came to a pit in a small river at 7.40, called Otjovargande. Delayed here about twenty minutes, after which we journeyed on till 9.15. Travelled well; country bushy and stony, and road consequently circuitous. Off again at 10.30. Did not reach Katjongo (Otjakatjongo) till 1.10 P. M. Off again at 4.5. Bivouacked at 6.35. 'Veldt' very dry hereabouts: the rain has as yet been very partial. Some men came up

* Two small properties lately presented to Andersson by the Damara chief, of which we shall have more to say presently.—ED.

with ostrich feathers; obtained about a pound in barter, which is an unexpected windfall.

"*Thursday, 3d January.* — Left bivouac 6.22; reached Omappi at 9.22. Travelled rather slowly; country somewhat dry hereabouts, but the small rivers in the neighborhood have rain. Set about making a 'stranger's kraal' without delay; have selected a spot a little below the fountain, and near a pit of water which is never dry.

"*Friday, 4th January.*—Desperately hot; it is evident we shall have a change with the new moon, perhaps to-night. Broke ground near the fountain with a view of testing how far one can grow corn without irrigation. I don't see why the experiment should not succeed during the rainy season. Kamoja and Jacob returned late in the afternoon; the former had killed a koodoo and wounded a giraffe.

"*Saturday, 5th January.*—A slight rain fell last evening, as I had fully anticipated, and this afternoon it came down in torrents for about three hours. I am so glad we had comfortably finished the sowing and planting; and if corn can really be grown without irrigation, it will now have a fair chance. We have let a stream of water into the enclosure from the fountain; but after the rain had ceased I caused it to be diverted to its original source. I feel half inclined to leave a man or two behind, and yet have no one to be trusted that I could possibly spare.

"*Sunday, 6th January.*—Little or no rain fell during the night, though it looked threatening. To-day also the sky looks lowering. Kamoja brought in a portion of the koodoo he had shot on the 4th ; but I fear it will spoil in this unpropitious weather.

"While reading the Bible, I was suddenly startled by loud shouts of 'Gun! gun!' coming evidently from Jacob, who was washing clothes at the fountain. The Damaras at once set off, and while looking around trying to account for so extraordinary an alarm, I espied, to my utter astonishment, within less than a hundred paces of me, a koodoo chased by two wild dogs, who were in such close pursuit as to jeopardize momentarily the poor creature's life. John endeavored to cut off the animal, but the dog 'Snook' had just caught sight of and was ranging alongside of it, which prevented the man from firing. Thus chased, the koodoo described a perfect circle round the wagons, followed not only by my own dog, but the '*wilde hunde*,' which fearlessly pushed on right through the people. Shouting at the top of my voice, I drew the attention of the gunners to the whereabouts of the quarry, which was at last successfully turned and shot within one hundred yards of us. It was a fine full-grown cow, and we were now, therefore, well off for meat. I had the carcass conveyed to the wagon for inspection and measurement.

"*Monday, 7th January.*—Set all my people to work in clearing out the 'vley' above the fountain, and, as the colonial men arrived, they severally and jointly, of their own accord, assisted in the operation, and by sundown, therefore, a great deal had been effected. But I fear it will take a month to clear out the place thoroughly, it being filled up with such a mass of dung, clay, and stones. The most remarkable feature is the quality of the latter, thrown in apparently purposely. I have lately discovered two deep water holes in the very top of the rock, and as they seem to me higher than the general level of the 'vley,' I doubt not but that they may be made subservient to the filling the same. I foresee the usefulness of this piece of water, if it were thoroughly cleared and filled. In the course of time I hope to see it, or rather the sides, covered with vegetation, and perhaps may live to see the children scull a boat on it. Cloudy atmosphere. A tremendous flight of locusts passed like a searching fire within view of the place. It sickens the heart, such devastating and harassing sights.

"*Tuesday, 8th January.*—Sent Hans and Kamoja out in search of game. The former brought in a stembok only; Kamoja ditto. Have done another good day's work at the 'vley.' Rather hot. In the evening talked to the colonial men about their wishes as regards my place on the Omarim river. Set before them my conditions, to which they did not seem to object. The corn is appearing above ground. Have strengthened the fence. Did a little more to the 'vley,' which begins to show the effect of our efforts; still it will take another month to get it quite clear.

"*Wednesday, 9th January.*—Left Omappi at 1.25; bivouacked at 6.20, perhaps fifteen to twenty minutes delay. 'Veldt' beautiful, and much superior to anything we have yet seen. It has evidently rained heavily in these parts.

"*Thursday, 10th January.*—Started from our bivouac at 11.35; reached Omavuram exactly after an hour's travel. Held on till 3 P. M., when we halted a short time. Observed in our progress a most singular flower, resembling a *Neileca*. The flower itself was very plain, but surrounded by a very pretty *curled* fringe of a yellow color. I wish I were as much a botanist as a zoologist, and I doubt not my present journey would yield me a rich harvest. This valley looks rich. Off again at 4.10. Reached Epako at 5 (here Troch. stands at 95, 23½). Sky rainy-looking. All the hunters unsuccessful; Hans wounded a gemsbok. Saw some giraffes.

"*Friday, 11th January.*—Showery during the night and the day looks lowering. Hans killed a gemsbok as we travelled along. Left Epako at 8; stopped at 9.15 to cut up gemsbok. Reached Otjim at 12 (Troch., 69, 22½). Delay about forty minutes. Damara werfts here. Heavy rains all round. Fancy I have found a new species of lark, which has a very pleasant call-note, and secured a few.

"*Saturday, 12th January.*—Left Otjim at 4.10 P. M. Reached Otuiova (made memorable to me years ago by the loss of a horse) at 8.5. Nearly half an hour's delay (Troch., 40, 49½). Plenty of water, in fact, the river is running slightly. Observed a most magnificent creeper, with a leaf to match, being many inches in diameter each way, and of a whitish hue beneath. The flower is lilac and puce, approaching to crimson in the corolla. Collected a number of bulbs as we came along; I wish I had a garden to plant them in at once. Pity I don't know anything of botany, as I might enjoy myself very much with the flora of the country, which seems rather rich. Of birds and birds'-nests I can see none, which is singular, as the country appears most favorable. I never saw a prettier place than that we have just left. Off again at 9. Came to a sudden halt at 10.40 in consequence of a heavy shower of rain. I am disappointed, wishing to have slept and spent the Sunday at the next regular watering-place. Ascended a small granite '*Kopy*,' or rocky eminence, in the neighborhood, where I observed a new bird.

"*Sunday, 13th January.*—It being Sunday, and the sky threatening more rain, we stay here for to-day. Obtained several birds'-nests; but it is getting late, most birds having young, or the eggs are hard sat on. Heavy rains in the afternoon. The country is pretty hereabouts, being diversified by round granite 'kopies,' and bowlders.

"*Monday, 14th January.*—Left bivouac at 6.5. Reached Kothongonika at 10.35; quite forty minutes delay. Road pretty fair (Troch., 90, 19½). Pits here deep, but they are nearly all in disuse. The small river that passes this place is said to find its way to Ongoo-ona; it may probably take its rise a little east of the range of hills seen to the eastward. As the cattle did not return till late, we bivouacked here. People out in search of game, but found nothing.

"*Tuesday, 15th January.*—Left Kothongonika at 5.40. Came to a halt at 9.35 (Troch., 55, 99½), at a small water course, the first we met with this morning. Country fine, but monotonous. The usual vegetation, acacia, much mingled with thornless, large-leaved trees. Omara and some other conspicuous hills are seen very clearly from this spot. Even Okonyenja was visible a short time before we halted. Killed a huge snake, seven feet ten inches long, said to be poisonous. Off again at 11 A. M. Reached Otjikongo at 3.30; perhaps ten minutes' delay. Part of road heavy

(Troch., 14, 83½). Found a large number of Berg-Damaras, and spoke to them of the passing of the wagons of white men, and also as to their camping near to Samuel, which they deny, but say they have heard the Bushmen ahead were in the habit of doing so. I am determined to put a stop to this; kindness has evidently no effect on these ungrateful creatures. A slight shower of rain, and more evidently to be expected.

"*Wednesday*, 16*th January.*—Went to the top of a neighboring 'kopy,' where I had a fine view of most of the surrounding country; can even make out the west extremity of Omuvereredo and Omatako. Men out hunting; but just now there is no game in this neighborhood. Left Otjukango at 2.20 P. M. Bivouacked at 7.40. Travelled steadily: no water, but met with several places that after good rains would hold the precious liquid. The sky looks threatening, and rain has fallen this afternoon some distance ahead.

"*Thursday*, 17*th January.*—Left bivouac at 6.35. Reached Kotjorongonde at 10.45 (Troch. 25, 42½). Travelled steadily. Mounted my horse in hopes of getting a shot—was not disappointed; but fairly missed a stag hartebeest with both barrels. My people, with one exception, were equally unfortunate; Kamapge, however, knocked over a gemsbok and badly wounded a quagga. Saw much game, hartebeests, gemsboks, zebras, etc. Very unwell. Fear this ride has done me harm.

"Heavy rains during the night; I am sorry for my poor people, and would give them my last coat and shirt were there fewer that stood in need of covering, and if I was certain of being able to replace the articles in this country. The rain, nevertheless, comes most opportunely, as I hope it will supply us with water during the next ordinarily waterless stage of twenty miles. Many Berg-Damaras here. January tells me he has heard that these men killed more than one of Mr. Green's trek-oxen, and that he passed over the offence unpunished. Can hardly believe it, as it would be the height of bad policy to do so for fear of a repetition of the same.

" Picked up a good many shells * this morning, but they seem to me only one or two kinds. How difficult they are to find! It is of no use to follow the ordinary rule for their detection. The only time, apparently, that they can be searched for with any likelihood of success is after a shower of rain, when they sometimes crawl about. Spent a very wretched night, and this morning I am very ill—no dieting avails. Stormy throughout the past day, and the night looks threatening.

"*Friday, 18th January.*—The night, somewhat contrary to expectation, turned out fine, and I was in hopes we should have had a fine morning, but we were doomed to disappointment; for just as we had inspanned the rain came down in torrents and continued unabated for about an hour-and-a-half. Left Kotjorongondi at 6.5—Came to a halt at 10.5 at a valley, river running parallel between the low range on our right, and the larger to our left. It must have its source

* What sort of *shells* does Andersson speak of both here and elsewhsre? Can they be the *cowrie-shells* which serve as *coin* in parts of Africa?—ED.

some distance off. No delay, but road heavy in consequence of the rains ; also winding. Saw hartebeestes and ostriches, and tracks of at least half-a-dozen lions. Off again at 12 ; halted for the night at 2.10 at a small water on a branch of the aforesaid Omurambe—the first water we have seen. Ascended a small 'kopy,' with a view of getting bearings—saw numerous tracks of koodoos ; one of the men observed the new buck, but, as usual, he got away unharmed.

"*Saturday, 19th January.*—Left bivouac at 6.50 ; came to a halt at 10.55 (Troch., 103, 62½). No delay—travelled steadily, but slowly—not quite sure of the time to half-an-hour, as my watch once stopped. Road heavy in consequence of rains during the past night. Course nearly parallel to the small, low ridge we crossed yesterday afternoon. Off again at 1 ; came to a halt at 3.50, the weather looks very threatening,

"*Sunday, 20th January.*—Heavy rains before midnight last night ; I had bivouacked in a nasty place, the grass and other vegetation being so luxuriant as to render moving about inconvenient. It must have rained early in these parts. The soil on the Omuramba we have been following is black as pitch, and evidently very rich—what would I not give for an acre or two of it at Omappi ! Left bivouac at 5.45. Travelling difficult in consequence of the '*doorslagt*' (inundation) ; and as we approach the fountain Naidaus, the wheels of the vehicle not unfrequently sunk to the naves, and if we had had a load we most assuredly should have stuck fast. Road open till within less than an hour of the fountain, which we reached at 9.45 (Troch., 241, 93½)—could not find a dry spot on which to outspan. It has rained fearfully here lately; I wish we were safely away, but the weather continues very threatening—bagged the first couple of ducks I have seen this season, *and dined on one* with great relish. It is the first *meat* meal I have tasted for many days; but I fear the consequences of such an indulgence.

"*Monday, 21st January.*—Left Naidaus at 6 A. M., but we had hardly gone twenty minutes before we stuck irretrievably in the '*doorslagt;*' and, while trying hard to get out, the rain came down and made matters still worse. Two hundred or three hundred yards off it seemed to be a little drier, and there I sent the people and the cattle, I myself remaining with the wagon, a prisoner almost, for, excepting getting into the mud over my knees, I could not move. Our position was very awkward, to say the least of it, for should it rain during the night, of which there seemed every probability, we might not be able to extricate the wagon for days to come; however, it is not the first time my patience has been tried. The herd reported having seen and called to two Bushmen, but they bolted. I am not anxious for myself or my people, but seriously so for our cattle; these once lost, our situation would indeed be desperate. It is seldom that one can recover them from such expert marauders, as they have a way of scattering with their ill-gotten booty in so many directions that pursuit becomes almost hopeless.

"*Tuesday, 22d January.*—A terrible thunderstorm passed to the northward of us at dusk last evening. I watched it with the utmost anxiety, but fortunately only a slight shower overtook us; and, thank God, after a few hours' exertion we got the wagon out safely, though not until we had unloaded everything, but even now the situation of our camp is anything but satisfactory. It is true we are on hardish ground, but within a few paces of us it is so saturated with wet as to be all but impassable. Two Bushmen made their appearance; spoke to them about their relative position to the white men and Samuel. In reply they said the latter was no friend of theirs, but in this matter I won't altogether take their word.

"Thousands of shells about—how difficult to find, but when once discovered, what quantities may not be secured! I cannot satisfy myself that there are more than one or two kinds — five say. At one time it threatened to rain, but it passed away, leaving a pretty serene sky. I wonder how long we shall be stuck here; the Bushmen declare that the country ahead is one continuous '*doorslagt!*' What's to be done? If we cannot get on, it will be necessary to send messengers to Ondonga.

"*Wednesday, 23d January.*—Left our sticking place at 12.55—road for the first hour or two very bad, as we were frequently on the point of coming to anchor in the mud; but afterward it became tolerable. Unfortunately, we followed Trompo's direction, and, as a matter of course, went all wrong. I insisted on turning right in toward the mountains, and had sent Abraham a-head to examine the road, but he did not return till the mischief was done. Bivouacked at 7.5—found a guinea-fowl's nest, containing no fewer than fifteen eggs; Abraham and Ryker killed a gemsbok.

"*Thursday, 24th January.*—Left bivouac at 5.30; got to Nondas at 8.35. This is the place Mr. Hahn intends to make a missionary station for the Bushmen; and it certainly is one of the most picturesque spots in Damaraland. It is situated on a splendid grass flat, surrounded on two sides by distant mountains, and the pasturage in the vicinity is illimitable; but as a take off, the water lies deep, and I see neither garden ground nor wood. Thousands of shells in the neighborhood; one seems different from those I have already met with. Off again at 1.45; reached a water at 6.30. Road excessively stony—my inside quite shaken to pieces. We bivouacked near the spot, and will probably pass the mountain to-morrow.

"*Friday, 25th January.*—Left bivouac at 6.5; came to a halt at 10.43 in the bed of what appeared an 'Omurambe' No water here—perhaps half-an-hour's delay, having lost the road. Off again at 12.25. Reached some pits at 3.30; about fifteen minutes' delay. At this place Mr. Green once killed several elephants—a strong shooting 'screen' in ruins may still be seen. Passed to-day a spot where a number of Totties (Hottentots) had evidently encamped; it was probably the party who followed up my wagons. Very poorly—once so faint as hardly to be able to hold up my head.

"*Saturday, 26th January.*—Left bivouac (Korovicar) at 6—came to a 'vley' at 9.15. Fully half-an-hour's delay in cutting a road, which, moreover, was very circuitous. Travelled unusually slow—we are leaving the hills fast behind us; even Otzikoto, they say, is past; if so, I and Mr. Galton differ widely as to its position; he lays it down much farther west than I do.

"*Sunday, 27th January*.—I find I have lost a day; it should be Sunday, not Saturday—am sorry for the blunder, as I wished to have passed it quietly. As it is, we must get to a regular water; off again, therefore, at 12.5. Reached Evambo at 3. P. M.—quite forty minutes' delay—road very stony and ziz-zag; distance to-day (exclusive of delays), five hours—find my dead reckoning comes out wonderfully accurate. I have recognized the most conspicuous peaks in the Omanbonde range, which was carefully fixed, and it has proved of immense service to me; ascended a tree, whence I obtained a splendid view of the mountains we have just left behind us—can perceive, also, some low ranges to the westward in the direction of Sarskab. Water boils at 206 degrees Therm. in the shade; shortly after our arrival, 85, height above sea, 3,085 feet. This Evambo resmbles Otjkoto on a large scale, in fact it must be a little lake after heavy rains; but it has only the *roundness of its form* in common with Otjkoto, for the water is quite shallow and the ground muddy; still these circular spots are very singular. How are they formed? I can only conceive by the ground falling away beneath; in other words, strong springs, or even bodies of water, undermine the localities, but the former still remain to be accounted for.

"*Monday, 28th January*.—Left Evambo at 1.18—reached Kajothononutyi at 10.10. Travelled famously, and the road was very good and not so circuitous as usual. Part of country very fine; but almost devoid of animal life—a *bird* is truly a *rara avis*. Off again at 1.15; after three hours' travel came to a pit, with about a northern course; hence, very westerly, quite north-west, I fancy—road execrable at the beginning, stony, bushy, and 'doorslagt.' It had rained heavily in one locality. Large park-like tracts of *omutali* trees—bivouacked at 6.25. By climbing a tree I could just catch a last glimpse of post range, the last landmark hence to Ondonga—raining to the westward and southward.

"*Tuesday, 29th January.*—Left bivouac at 5.20 A. M.—reached Little Onamotoni at 9.45, quite twenty minutes' delay—road winding; but though it passes through a very woody part, pretty well cleared of bushes, we clear away the last remnants of obstructions. By climbing a tree I can just make out Onondova flat, and the east extremity of Etoska. Another short half-hour's travel brought us to Great Onamotoni, the fountain passed by myself and Galton on our journey to Ondonga, now some sixteen years ago.

"What a noble place it is—fine open view toward Onondova. After very heavy rains the whole flat must, I fancy, be one immense sheet of water. I think I can detect large patches of it now; herds of wildebeest in view; the men missed the fine bull. I understand that the road here takes a great sweep to the eastward. We had not been long outspanned before a terrific rain-and-hail storm came on—I am so glad we have got thus far, as such torrents could not help converting many of the flats that we have passed into one immense 'doorslagt.' At dusk Kamapge killed a bull wildebeest; a most opportune reinforcement to our exhausted larder.

"*Wednesday, 30th January.*—The water had much increased this morning on the flat; in fact, it appeared to me to be steadily advancing. Found some new shells after a very diligent search. In the afternoon it came on to rain heavily, and the night threatens to be dirty.

"*Thursday*, 31*st January*.—Raining nearly throughout the night, and continued this morning till near noon, when it cleared a little. Some Bushmen were here yesterday who informed us that Chykongo (the chief of the Ovampos) has sent a number of his men to attack Samuel, five of whose men have been to Ondonga at the command of Chykonga, who called them there with a view of instituting inquiry regarding their villainous dealings with white men. The Bushmen further told us that the Ovampo have orders to try and kill Samuel if they don't find his 'werft' too strong. I do hope Chykongo will earnestly exert himself to get the fellow out of the way. It would be foolish to try to make peace with such a faithless set; nothing short of an utter extermination will ever give us peace and quiet in that quarter. Cattle and men driven half frantic with mosquitoes and a species of gad-fly which literally swarm about these parts.

"Left Amaloixe at 1.30. Scarcely had we entered on the flat before we got among rills of water, and about half-way we crossed a small river flowing waist-deep toward Etoska, which we found one immense sheet of water, though, of course, quite shallow. It was a pretty sight, and but once in a time to be met with in these parts of Africa. It has been, and continues to be, a puzzle to me from whence proceeds this body of water. The relative height of these parts and of the river Okovango seems utterly to exclude the possibility of its coming from the latter. This flat lies some four thousand feet above the sea, whereas the Okovango, even when struck by myself, cannot be the fourth of that height. Observed large numbers of water-fowl and waders. Came to a halt for the night at 7.45. This long stage will enable us to reach Otjhako doa Mosenga at an early hour to-morrow morning.

"*Friday, 1st February.*—Left bivouac 5.45; reached the last-named place at 8.45. Overtaken by a small Ovampo caravan on the way to procure copper. They informed us that some of my friends the elephant-hunters, as also one of my own wagons and people, are away to the Ovaguamli, hunting and bartering with the natives, I suppose. Much water on this flat likewise, and lots of water fowl. Journey on again at 11.40—came to a halt for the night at 5.10, having fairly left the great flat behind us, and entered the last bush before coming into glorious Ondonga. On the way we saw many wildebeestes; also found a new shell, a fine, large, and handsome species.

"Having now entered Ovampoland, I despatched a messenger to the chief, Chykongo, informing him of our arrival; and, while awaiting a message from him, had the satisfaction to receive a letter from my people, informing me they had reached Ondonga in safety. It would appear, however, they had had an almost miraculous escape from the clutches of Samuel, who had followed their tracks for many days, and only desisted from the pursuit on finding himself unable to overtake them; and as for some time past I had entertained the most serious apprehensions that they had fallen into his hands, I now made a solemn vow never again to expose them to risks not shared by myself.

"*Saturday, 2d February.*—Wanted to have gone ahead on horseback, but finding myself unequal to a long ride must postpone it till to-morrow. Left bivouac at 6.5. Came to a halt at 12; quite half-an-hour's delay. Road very sandy and bushy. Had several narrow escapes with the wagon; indeed, we damaged one of the steps. Off again at 1.45. Came to a halt at 6.25; also about half-an-hour's delay. Road worse, if possible, than in the forenoon. It was quite touch-and-go in many places, and unfortunately the shaft oxen are bad. Disappointed at not reaching Ondonga; but if we had gone on till dusk we should not have been so far off. Still very uneasy. It is now more than a month since I touched meat; bread, or rather 'cokies,' and now and then a little arrowroot, constitute my sole diet.

"*Sunday, 3d February.*—With the first return of daylight I was in the saddle, eager not only to meet my people once more, but to gaze upon that country which, some sixteen years before, I had visited in company with my esteemed friend Galton, to whom the public is so much indebted for his valuable contributions to science.

"Ovampoland, or rather Ondonga, as that portion of the country is commonly called, has since then undergone many changes. Bloody civil wars had swept like a hurricane over its quiet rural beauties, immolating or dispersing one-half of its industrial, gay-hearted, and inoffensive population, and leaving but the fame of the vast herds of cattle that once gave additional charms and importance to the country. The exactions and contributions of foreign auxiliaries called in by one or other of the contending parties, and the insidious and destructive 'lung sickness,' left but a small remnant of these, their chief wealth. Old Nangoro, the obese king spoken of by Mr. Galton, who was chieftain on my former sojourn here, had died under very suspicious circumstances, and more than one other ruler of the country had subsequently met with a tragical death. But there had now been peace for some years, and the country itself presented the same beautiful appearance as had enchanted me on our first becoming acquainted with it. The like magnificent trees, both forest and fruit, were observable everywhere, and the landscape, as heretofore, was dotted in all directions with patriarchal-looking hamlets, and further enlivened by groups of men, women, and children, occupied in their several vocations. The cheerful twitterings and warblings of numerous birds, moreover, added an additional charm to the scene. I have seen many lands and places, some perhaps, strictly speaking, more beautiful; but among the extensive savannahs, or the interminable forests of South Africa, which so long has been my home, there was but one Ondonga.

"To proceed. A few hours sharp riding brought me to my people, who were encamped near to the chief's 'werft,' and whom, with the exception of one or two down with slight fever, I was happy to find in good health and spirits. Axel had, I ascertained, collected few eggs or shells, but a good many specimens of birds—among the rest three or four new species, and another example of the *Stringonis Anderssonyx*, the nondescript named after myself. An additional pleasure was afforded me on this occasion by meeting many of the elephant hunters, who had of late years made Ondonga their head-quarters; and who, on hearing of my arrival in the country, had come to greet me. Some of them I had not met for years. Poor fellows! they had labored hard to retrieve their broken fortunes, though with little success, as elephants had become scarce, and so excessively wild as to bid defiance to the most experienced and persevering sportsmen. My friends were, moreover, excluded from the best 'veldt,' situated in the near vicinity to their inveterate enemies the Hottentots, and which, in consequence, they ventured not singly, or in small parties, to visit. As a set-off, however, to the pleasure of thus meeting with my people and old acquaintances, I was sorry to hear that the late excessive rains were likely to produce a great deal of sickness in the country this year. As I afterward learned, indeed, not a few individuals had already fallen victims to fever, or were then suffering from its effects. Thus was a journey of very considerable extent, attended by some real danger and many inconveniences, speedily and safely accomplished; and as by taking a route different from that pursued by Mr. Galton and myself, I was enabled to rectify much of the map that I had constructed of Damaraland, besides adding largely to its details, which map I have since sent to the Royal Geographical Society in London. As regards my researches in natural history, moreover, I was enabled to corroborate much that was previously somewhat doubtful, as also to add no inconsiderable quantity of new matter to my previous store. On the evening of this day, therefore, though still very ill in body, I retired to rest with great satisfaction, and truly grateful to Providence for the many mercies and blessings vouchsafed to me during my recent wanderings."

[Here Andersson's journal ceases for awhile, and in this and the two succeeding chapters, we have a continuation of his "Notes of Travel."—*Editor.*]

CHAPTER XIV.

Chykongo—Appearance of the country—Description of the homestead—The chief's werft—The soil—Agriculture—Times of scarcity—Fruit trees—Minerals—The flora and fauna—Ichthyology—Domestic animals—The inhabitants—Their amusements—Religion and superstition—Attack on Mr. Hahn's party.

ON the evening of my arrival at Ondonga I received a visit from Chykongo, the paramount chief of Ovampoland. He is perhaps fifty years of age, but appears younger. His figure is commanding, though slightly inclined to corpulency, and his face intelligent; but if the eyes are closely examined they will be found somewhat sinister in expression, especially if he is at all unpleasantly excited. But, taken altogether, the Ovampo ruler is certainly by far the most chief-like in aspect and bearing of all the native sovereigns between the Orange River and the Cunené, with whom I am acquainted.

But Chykongo did not succeed to his present elevated position quietly. Immediately on Nangoro's death, which, as recently observed, I have reason to believe was sudden and unnatural, the sovereign sway was assumed by Chypanza, his elder brother, though I imagine this was quite in accordance with the law of succession in the country. There was at the time a strong party who inclined for another chief, at the head of which was Nakonjona (a remarkably intelligent and fine-looking man), but Chypanza, dreading his influence, caused him to be put out of the way. On this, the younger brother of the murdered man, the present chief Chykongo, sent for assistance to Jonker Afrikaner, the famous Namaqua freebooter, who shortly afterward appeared in Ovampoland with a considerable force. For awhile he amused himself by laying heavy contributions of cattle, etc., on the natives, besides slaying very many of them.

After varying fortunes and manœuvrings, it would seem that at last an open fight between the people of Chypanza and those of Chykongo took place, in which the latter were victorious, entirely dispersing their adversaries, many of whom fled for protection to neighboring rulers. Since then Chykongo has governed the country, and with the same tyrannical power and freedom as his predecessor, Nangoro, but he seems less reserved with his subjects, who address him much more familiarly.

Having now given some account of the chieftain of Ovampoland, it may be proper to say a few words regarding the country and people he rules over. True it is that in Lake N'gami these subjects are slightly touched upon; but as the Ovampos are a fair type of the nations and tribes dwelling between Ovampoland and the river Cunené, of whom I shall hereafter have occasion to speak, I deem an apology unnecessary for making a short *résumé* of what is said respecting them in that work, adding thereto such information as I have since acquired. It will save repetition hereafter, when, in due course, I shall have occasion to introduce to the reader the people in question, whereby he will be saved the tedium of twice going over the same ground, as it were.

Ondonga, that is the grain-growing portion of Ovampoland, which is situated some three thousand feet above the level of the sea, and runs from south-south-east, to north-north-west, is of very limited extent, not being more than about forty miles in length, with an average breadth of ten or twelve. It is very level, with frequent extensive though shallow depressions, which are filled with water during several months of the year, and that portion of it, therefore, is rendered useless for agricultural purposes, otherwise nearly all of it would be available land. About one-fourth of the whole is cultivated. It is a beautiful, open, and for Africa highly cultivated country, environed on all sides with interminable and dense forests—in short, a perfect oasis in the desert. In the fall of the year, indeed, the landscape presents a boundless expanse of yellow waving corn, studded with primitive-looking homesteads, while here and there, whether alone or in clusters, arise gigantic, wide-spreading, and dark-foliaged trees. In short, after the traveller has perhaps for weeks and weeks together toiled through pathless forests and the thorny brakes, which have not only torn his garments and other belongings to tatters, he finds himself in Ondonga, it seems to him a perfect elysium. Such, at least, on my first acquaintance with the country it appeared to me.

The population of Ondonga is considerable. When in company of Mr. Galton, we were anxious to form some idea of its density, and by counting the houses in a given extent of country, and taking the average number of individuals to each, we came to the conclusion that there were about a hundred people to every square mile. There is but little pauperism ; the crippled and aged, moreover, seem to be carefully tended and nursed. What a contrast to their near neighbors, the Damaras! who, when a man becomes old, and no longer able to shift for himself, leave him to perish on his own hearth, or carry him into the desert or the forest, there to die of hunger or to be devoured by beasts of prey.

There are neither towns nor villages in Ondonga, if we except perhaps the chief's werft, which, from its great extent, might almost come under one or other of these categories. Each family, often consisting of father, grandfather, children and servants, resides by itself in a very patriarchal sort of way. Their houses, or rather huts, are circular in form ; the lower part consisting of slender poles, about two feet six inches high, firmly driven into the ground, and further secured by withes, or other bands, the whole being plastered over with clay. The roof, composed of rushes, is in shape not unlike a beehive. The height of the hut, from the ground to the apex of the roof, does not much exceed four feet, and its circumference outwardly is about sixteen. The reason for their thus entombing themselves, as it were, is probably partly as a protection against the cold, and partly on account of the great distance the wood has to be conveyed from the forest.

Besides the hut in which they themselves dwell, the homestead consists of various other erections ; viz., the "palaver-house," or that wherein councils are held ; several beehive-topped baskets in which the grain is stored away ; pens for the cattle and goats, etc., the whole being surrounded by a high and strong palisade, and it may be a thorn fence in addition. The pathways, or walks, leading to the several buildings enumerated, which are also lined on both sides by rows of poles, are exceedingly tortuous, and to a stranger perfectly bewildering.

The residences of the great differ but little in design from the homesteads of the commonalty; but they are on a much more extensive scale—that of Chykongo, the paramount chief, for instance, being something like half a mile in circuit. The defences, moreover, are very much stronger, the outer palisading, as well as that on either side of the pathways leading to the several buildings, consisting of two or more rows of poles or planks, instead of single ones, and these so closely placed together as almost to exclude the light, and consequently impervious to ordinary fire-arms. Indeed, it would require cannon to knock them down; and I have no doubt it is intended they should prove impregnable, if not to ordnance, at least to such weapons as are at the command of the natives. Without fear of being thought to exaggerate, I will venture to affirm that at least one or two hundred thousand stout poles, together with a great many planks, or rather slabs, for saw-mills have not as yet found their way into Ondonga, were made use of in the construction of the werft in question; and as all the homesteads in the surrounding country, though on a very much smaller scale, are similarly constructed, it may readily be conceived what millions upon millions of young trees must annually be felled for their construction and needful repair.

In the erection of the residence of the paramount

chief of Ondonga, be he who he may, I should add the whole population is compelled to assist ; each man contributing his quota of materials and labor, and that without remuneration of any kind ; but on these occasions a great quantity of beer is consumed, and, as I imagine at the chief's expense.

The soil of Okovango, which chiefly consists of a fine loose sand on a clay bottom, is very fertile, as may be inferred from the fact that little or no manure is ever applied to the land. Two species of cereals are indigenous to the country, viz., the so-styled Caffir corn (*Holcus Suluceni*), a flattened, roundish seed of a reddish-yellow color, and a much smaller kind, not unlike canary-seed. This, which is called *omahange*, is the most prized, and is chiefly used for food, whereas the former is, for the most part, converted into beer. Both yield an enormous return ; two thousand grains and upward being commonly obtained from a single ear of the last-named.

Besides grain, they cultivate small quantities of beans, of which there are also two sorts—one brown and the other white ; both are very palatable, the last quite a delicacy. But, strange to say, neither kind is much prized by the natives themselves, who prefer corn. Tobacco is likewise extensively planted, but their way of preparing it quite destroys any flavor it may possess. It is mashed together in a hollow piece of wood, by means of a heavy pole, into little round balls of the size of an orange, which when dry are broken into smaller pieces. Calabashes are besides largely produced, but only to be converted into vessels for holding food, beer, etc. Pumpkins are rarely seen.

The cultivation of corn is associated with much toil and labor. Indeed, from the first preparation of the soil until the grain is cut, housed, and cleaned, it is one continuous course of hard work. When the first heavy showers have fallen they begin their operations. The seed, however, is not sown broadcast as with us, but little holes are made at regular intervals, into which a few grains are deposited. As soon as the plants are sufficiently grown, these, with the exception of one or two that are left, are pulled up and transplanted elsewhere. This is going on almost incessantly, and it is amusing to observe how the area on which the corn was first sown grows under the process. Thus a field of grain that in the first instance was only half an acre in extent is eventually converted into one of many acres. As a matter of course, a large field of corn rarely ripens at one and the same time; but this is of no consequence, as only the ears are severed from the stalk. The ground, I should add, is carefully weeded by a small one-handed hoe, the only farming implement in use among these people. From the first dawn of day to dusk, the women, and at times the men also, are employed about the cornfields.

Notwithstanding the care and labor thus bestowed on the cultivation of the soil, and the uncommonly large yield, still times of great scarcity occasionally occur. The soil consists, as I have said, of fine loose sand on a clay bottom; consequently, as the evaporation is always great, and there is little or no shade, the ground is rapidly exhausted of its moisture, and unless replenished at regular intervals by copious tropical rains, it becomes incapable of yielding the usual produce. In former times, when the Ovâmpo possessed many cattle, an occasional failure of the crop, though always more or less calamitous, was of less consequence, since they could then fall back on a meat and milk diet until the return of more favorable seasons; but such is not the case at present, their enemies having of late years despoiled them of a large portion of their herds. However, as all the tribes bordering on Ovampoland are more or less corn-producers, and as the rains are not everywhere equally uncertain, it follows that a supply may in general be obtained from one or other of their neighbors, sufficient at least "to keep the wolf from the door."

Magnificent trees, both fruit and forest, whether alone or in groups, dot, as said, the Ondonga landscape. Preëminent for beauty among the former stands the palm, the glory of the tropics, the stem of which, before branching out, often rises to a height of fifty or sixty feet. But this tree is even more useful than ornamental; for, independently of its rich brown clusters of well-tasted fruit, its wood, broad leaves, and fibres are applied to a hundred beneficial purposes.

Next in rank comes, perhaps, a huge-stemmed, wide-spreading tree,* with small elongated leaves, yielding in ordinary years tons and tons of a small, apple-looking fruit; but it is only in appearance, for it contains a strong kernel, surrounded by a fleshy pulp, which defies your utmost efforts to detach it.

* This tree at times attains to an astonishing size. Indeed, the branches of one that we measured spread over a space of ground one hundred and forty feet in diameter, or four hundred and thirty-two in circumference.

By removing the skin, however, an agreeable, sweet, acidulous flavor is obtained. As the fruit begins to ripen it falls to the ground, where it is carefully gathered by the natives, who convert it into a kind of beer. This is done by simply removing the peel, and then throwing it into some vessel partially filled with water. In a day or two it is fit for use, and is said to be very intoxicating. I cannot say that I like it, but when mingled with the ordinary beer obtained from malted corn, it becomes a cool and pleasant beverage.

Then there is a rich, dark-foliaged, and dark-stemmed tree, producing a small yellow acorn-looking (minus the cup) fruit, which is apparently highly prized by the native population. To my taste, however, it is too sweet and insipid. Single fig-trees are met with everywhere, and grow frequently to enormous dimensions. The fruit is plentiful, but not very well flavored. Besides those mentioned, there are some other kinds of fruit-trees, but let the aforesaid suffice.

There are no rivers in Ondonga, only an "omuramba," or periodical water-course, containing grass as well as water, which intersects nearly its whole length, and never dries up entirely even in the hottest summer. From the level nature of the country, however, it hardly drains an area of half-a-mile on either side; and in extraordinary wet seasons, therefore, the country is half under water, from which cause, as will naturally be inferred, it becomes extremely unhealthy. But more of this hereafter.

Neither are there minerals in Ondonga, or, in fact, in any part of the extensive country surrounding it that is claimed by the Ovampo. Iron these people obtain by barter from neighboring tribes; and copper is brought to them, in the shape of ore, by the Bushmen who inhabit the border country between Ovampo and Damaraland. With gold and silver they are unacquainted, as also with all other known metals except the two just named.

The climate of Ondonga cannot be looked on as healthy, the natives at all times suffering more or less from ophthalmia, dysentery, and fever: for none of which diseases have they any specific. In very wet seasons, moreover, when the rains, generally lasting from January to May, have been unusually heavy, and the country, as a consequence, laid half under water, a kind of intermittent fever (to which foreigners and strangers are equally as liable as the natives) extensively prevails, causing the mortality to be frightful. This disease arises, no doubt, from the excessive amount of evaporation that takes place after the downpourings have ceased. Nevertheless, the country generally cannot with propriety be called either swampy or marshy; for, as said, the soil is sandy, and neither reeds nor rushes will thrive in it. With the exception of the "omuramba" spoken of, none of the "vleys" hold water throughout the year, and consequently there is no encouragement for the formation of decomposed matter.

Independently of the risk the stranger who visits Ondonga runs from one or other of the diseases spoken of, he will surely be plagued almost out of his life by certain insects. Among these may be enumerated the white ants, which, in an incredibly short time, deface and destroy everything they come across. A room left deserted for a short while will be found to have large heaps of earth on the floor, which if not speedily removed will shortly grow into hills. The posts of the veranda of my house in Ondonga became so incrusted, even to the rafters, with their mud-work, as to give me the idea of a torrent of lava having run down their sides. The thorn-fences, moreover, look in a short time as if a herd of mud-bespattered elephants had been rubbing their bodies against them.

The evil just mentioned, however, is but trivial compared with that inflicted by a kind of bug of a shining brown color. During certain months of the year these insects literally swarm everywhere, invading and destroying all they meet with. You open your clothes-box, and myriads are seen scampering off, though only to hide themselves in the linen. Examine any one piece, and scores are found secreted in its folds; and, to cap the evil, they get into one's food. Every crack and fissure in a loaf of bread, if left exposed for only half an hour, harbors its dozens. Ugh! If you chance to kill one of them, which a slight pressure of the finger will effect, the squashed parts adhere to the digit, and make the eating of the bread anything but pleasant. Such a sight would, I am sure, act on many persons like a dose of ipecacuanha. Others of the pests to which one is subjected at Ondonga are the common house-fly,* the mosquito, and mice.

* We, in Europe, who are annoyed enough at times by the common house-fly, can hardly form an idea as to the number of these insects in Southern Africa. Methuen, in his interesting work, when speaking of a visit paid by him to a Boer, says, for instance: "A hot wind was blowing at the time, and the Dutchman's house was perfectly full of flies, and garnished with the usual appendages. A number of green boughs were

The flora of Ondonga is comparatively poor; the paucity, or rather the want of variety, is probably to be accounted for by the uniform character of the soil.

Nor is its fauna richer, at least the animal portion. The cause here is even more apparent, viz., the open and cultivated nature of the country. Now and then a steinbok, a ducker, a hartebeest, and so forth, may be seen, and during the dry season an occasional herd of migratory springboks. But in the dense bush that surrounds Ondonga on every side we find an occasional elephant, as also the eland, the gemsbok, the giraffe, the koodoo, etc.; to say nothing of beasts of prey that usually follow in their wake, such as the lion, the leopard, and the hyena. The last-named beast is, however, not only a constant resident in the country, but literally swarms everywhere.

But what Ondonga wants in animals is amply made up for by the quantity and variety of the feathered creation. Indeed, I know no other country in the world, of an equal extent (the reader will recollect that Ondonga is only about forty miles long, and one-fourth of that in breadth), that can boast of such a number of different kinds of birds. It is true, many are only temporary residents, arriving with the return of the rainy season, and taking their departure on the gradual drying-up of the "vleys" and other waters. During my last visit, I ascertained the existence of many species, but want of space prevents me from giving even a list of them.

suspended overhead to attract the flies, which the good vrow from time to time enveloped in a wet sack, and then shaking the sack's mouth, deposited it in a corner. The contents did not appear to be far short of half a bushel."

Fish are also abundant in the "omuramba," or periodical water-course spoken of, which, as I have said, never dries up entirely. Of these the natives are fond, and catch them during the hot time of the year by means of bee-hive shaped hand-baskets, which are dropped suddenly over the fish when appearing in view. But this rude process is only successful with the smaller species, and where the water is shallow; the larger ones are speared. There are several kinds; but I cannot remember having identified more than the barbel (*Glanis Siluris*), and the mullet (*Mugil Africanus*), though *Claria Capensis* is probably found, too. The barbel attains to an enormous size and fatness, being not unfrequently captured six, seven, eight, and even nine feet in length.

The domestic animals of the Ovampo are the ox, the goat, the pig, the dog, the cat (which I myself lately introduced), and the barn-door fowl. Horses, of which of late years a few have been brought into the country, don't thrive; for the most part, indeed, they die at the end of the rainy season of the so-called "lung-sickness," the disease that annually carries off so many animals, both wild and tame, in Southern Africa; those that survive, however, are said to be exempt thereafter from the epidemic. Neither have sheep succeeded; those that have been imported from Damaraland, or elsewhere, have for the most part succumbed to a disease designated the "blood-sickness."

The cattle, which are of a fair size, differ in nothing from other native breeds, but the cows give little milk. The goats—nearly the whole of which are black, or of a darkish color—are very diminutive; but people who have had opportunity of comparing them with breeds elsewhere, say they yield more milk than others of double the size. The pigs are also black, or nearly so, and very uncouth looking, being bony and lanky. The head is particularly ugly. The flesh is, however, palatable. The dogs, which are larger than those found with the Bushmen, are of a lightish color, with dark gray muzzles. The fowls, a species of bantam, are very small, but capital egg-layers. I hope shortly, however, to supply them with a more useful breed.

A word now as to the inhabitants of Ovampoland, who, as a race, are fine-looking people, and have nothing of the real negro type in their features. The men are tall and well-formed, and their upright, manly figures are set off to great advantage by a broad, stiff leather girdle. This, with a slip of dressed skin (more frequently the inside of an ox's stomach) in front, and the apology of a piece of hide behind, is the only covering they indulge in. Though they have now been for nearly twenty years in communication with Europeans, and eagerly buy our guns, ammunition, etc., they strictly eschew everything approaching to clothing. They do not even make use of the skins of wild or domestic animals as coverings during the night. One can only account for this apparent perverseness of their taste by the fact that they look on their own lubricous and next to naked persons as a far prettier and more respectable sight than the most dandified Brummel costume; but let the cause be what it may, their going thus denuded of dress must ill agree with their constitutions, for during the rainy seasons they evidently suffer much from the cold. With the exception of ear-rings, composed of beads or shells, the men display but few ornaments.

Their arms consist of the bow and arrow, a dagger-shaped knife, and the "knob-keerie," a short, straight stick, or rather club, with a heavy knob at the end; a most formidable weapon in experienced hands, as a single well-directed blow is sufficient to fell the strongest man to the ground. The natives of Africa, moreover, throw it with very great dexterity, seldom failing to hit the object aimed at. Harris, indeed, when speaking of the Matibili, goes so far as to say, "They rarely miss a partridge or a guinea-fowl when on the wing."

The features of the women, though coarse, are not unpleasing, and in early life many of them are very good-looking. As a rule they are exceedingly plump and well fed; and, curiously enough, I have never seen among them any of those thin and scraggy females, who are so common in Europe. And though they retain their roundness even in old age, it is seldom they become corpulent. As with the men, they lubricate their persons with grease and red ochre, and are as innocent of clothing as their lords and masters, wearing only, like them, a belt about the waist, and a slip of skin before and behind. Their persons, however, are profusely ornamented, or rather loaded, with various colored beads, and strings of round pieces of ostrich eggs, the latter resting gracefully in front.

But the Ovampo ladies have their fashions, as well as those of more civilized countries. On my first visit to Ondonga, they, for instance, wore the hair (the artificial portion of it at least) straight down the back, each elf-like lock being fastened to a sort of comb, as depicted in "Lake N'gami." Now all this is changed, and the hair is worn *en négligé*. Thus a few locks descend behind, while others are thrown coquettishly over the head and part of the face. Then again, at the period I speak of, it was customary for the fair sex to wear, as ornaments, heavy copper rings about the ankles. Now this fashion is altogether dispensed with, and the rings in question are used for a very different purpose, viz., to prevent servants and slaves, if suspected of the intention of running away, from carrying out their purpose; for when several of the rings are attached to the legs, which renders even the process of walking somewhat difficult, it is next to impossible for them to effect their escape. Both the men and women, when grown up, I should add, chip the middle tooth of the under-jaw.

The Ovampo are a light-hearted people, and, among other amusements, delight in music and the dance. Almost every evening, indeed, when the labors of the day are over, there are balls, which, in their way, are remarkable performances, and in which both sexes take part. The women stand in a ring, singing, clapping their hands, and keeping time with their feet, while the men join in a kind of chorus. Individuals of the male sex now and then spring into the open space, and challenge their companions "to kick me here if you dare and can," presenting at the same time their caudals as a mark, but with a threatening "beware of your own." He who succeeds in making the highest leap, and planing the most vigorous kick on the inviting spot, is warmly applauded by the women. But who shall blame the Ovampo if they think that kicking each other in the way described is rare sport, and a graceful and interesting amusement? Every country for itself. Their musical instruments are of a very simple kind, consisting of the well-known African "tom-tom" and a sort of guitar.

The staple food of the Ovampo may be said to consist of a kind of stir-about and milk, and though partial to meat, it is seldom they slaughter their own cattle; chiefly for the reason, I believe, that as a man's wealth and influence are judged of by the number of his herd, he is loth to make inroads on the latter, but on very special occasions. With the exception of the hyena, and for a reason hereafter mentioned, they eschew not the flesh of any other animal, whether tame or wild. That of the dog would appear to be especially welcome to them. What is more than strange, however, is that both flesh and fish, even when in a high state of putrefaction, are eaten by them with great gusto, and singularly enough, no evil consequences would appear to follow the banquet. What would doctors and inspectors of meat say if assured that not only putrid but diseased meat was perfectly healthy; but it must not be forgotten that those who partake of such dainties with impunity, live and breathe in the purest of atmospheres during the greater part of the year. Beer is the favorite beverage of the Ovampo, and if they can afford it, they drink it in large quantities.

These people, so far as I am aware, worship nothing, either in heaven above or on earth beneath; whence one is led to conclude their religion, should they really possess one, must go in a very small compass. Still they would appear to have a dim idea of a future state, as may be inferred from the awe and reverence evinced by them when the subject of death is mentioned. But, after all, may we not entertain incorrect notions in this matter as regards the Ovampo, attributable, not improbably, to our insufficient knowledge of their language and habits, and to shyness on their part to reveal such subjects as those in question to strangers. Certain it is, however, they are very superstitious, and the "Rainmaker," as well as other diviners of coming events, are, as a consequence, held by them in high honor and repute.

As with some other South African tribes, the Ovampo never bury their dead, their chiefs excepted; but so soon as life is extinct, the corpse is borne to some out-of-the-way place, and there left to be devoured by birds and beasts of prey. The hyena, more especially, indulges in this revolting kind of food (hence the antipathy of the natives to partake of his flesh, as mentioned a page or two back), and becomes at length so emboldened as, in failure of dead, to seek out living subjects. It is, therefore, not uncommon to hear of these beasts attacking and killing, not only full-grown women, but men, of which several instances came under my own notice during my stay at Ondonga. Previously I had always despised the hyena as a sneaking, cowardly brute, whom a child was sufficient to scarce away; but during my present travels in Ovampo and adjacent countries, I honestly acknowledge that I never felt myself quite safe when sleeping in the open air, unless protected by powerful and watchful dogs.

The Ovampo are an industrious race, and the men, contrary to the custom of most other African tribes and nations,, work fully as hard as the women. Besides taking part with the latter in the cultivation of the soil, they tend the cattle when pastured in the distant forest, furnish wood for the huts and enclosures, dig the wells, and perform various other laborious occupations. When, moreover, they have time to spare from their several duties, it is often employed in trading with their neighbors, for which purpose they not unfrequently make journeys of several hundreds miles in extent; on these occasions, they exchange iron and copper rings and beads, hoes, spear-heads (assegais), and a few other simple articles of their own rough manufacture (there being artisans, so to say, among them) for iron, copper, etc., etc. The women are never idle, as the men are. Independently of household duties, nursing their children, milking the cows and goats, they assist their husbands and brothers in field labors, reaping the grain, storing it away, etc.; but let them be engaged in what manner they may, they always seem a merry, happy set, laughing and chatting together, and making sport, as it were, of labor.

The morality of the Ovampo is much on a par with that of the Damaras and other South African tribes, which is not saying much in their favor. Polygamy is practised to a great extent, and a man may have as many wives as he can afford to maintain. Our guide, on the occasion of my first journey to Ondonga in company with Mr. Galton, was said to have no fewer than twenty, two of whom, I found to my astonishment, were mother and daughter; and Nangoro, the then paramount chief, boasted of no fewer than one hundred and three help-mates. Women in that country, it is to be observed, are looked on as a mere mercantile commodity, an article of commerce; in short, should the man be poor, the price he pays for a wife is two oxen and one cow; but if his circumstances be good, three oxen and two cows are expected. The chief, however, is an exception to the rule, as in his case the honor of an alliance with him is supposed to be sufficient compensation to the parents of the girl.

A stranger passing through the country would be inclined to look on the Ovampo as honest, and they are probably as much so as most of the African tribes. Such was the first impression of Mr. Galton and myself when we visited Ondonga. A more intimate acquaintance will probably dispel the illusion. It seems to me, indeed, that their apparent honesty arises rather from fear of the consequences that might ensue, than from a desire of "doing as they would be done by." And no wonder, for the chief rules them with a rod of iron, and should any of his subjects be suspected on good grounds of theft, conspiracy, or other serious crime, he takes not the trouble legally to investigate the case, but invites the unfortunate individual to an entertainment at his own "werft," where he is plied with intoxicating drinks until all sense of consciousness is lost, when "Jack Ketch"—there really being such a functionary attached to the chief's establishment—steps behind the victim, and either stabs him with an assegai or cuts his throat, and that with as little compunction as he would slay an ox or a sheep. Should, however, this course of proceeding be thought too open and dangerous, the doomed man is waylaid and put to death at a distance.

The Ovampo are a peaceably inclined people, and

seldom, I believe, resort to arms, except in self-defence, or when a question arises as to the succession of a chief. Apparently they are obliging, hospitable, and kind-hearted; but their disposition at bottom, it is to be feared, is treacherous and cruel, as indeed was shown by their dastardly attack on the Rev. Mr. Hahn, who, in company with my friend Frederick Green, visited their country in 1857, for though ostensibly well received by the then paramount chief, Nangoro, the seeming kindness shown by him to the travellers was, as it turned, a mere *ruse de guerre;* for just as they were about to depart they were suddenly and furiously attacked, and that by the monarch's orders. Fortunately, however, they were not altogether unprepared, hints having been previously given them as to what was about to happen, and, by the determined resistance made by them, they not only succeeded in securing their own safety, but completely defeated the enemy. The loss on Mr. Hahn's side was only a single native attendant, who was killed near to the missionary's wagon previous to the commencement of the fight, whereas that of the Ovampo was very considerable, many being either killed or wounded; and among the former one of the sons of Nangoro. Nangoro himself, moreover, is reported to have met his death on this occasion (a statement at variance with the general impression, as elsewhere stated, that he came to his end by foul means), for although not present at the fight, yet on hearing the repeated discharges of firearms he became so excited and terrified that he dropped down dead. It was supposed that the assailants of the European party numbered at least six hundred fighting men, all armed with bows and arrows, assegais, and "knob-keerie," while the travellers could only muster thirteen capable of opposing the enemy. The victory gained by them was, therefore, truly wonderful, and deserving of being chronicled among other heroic deeds.

CHAPTER XV.

Lung-sickness—Symptoms of the disease—Inoculation said to be a preventive—The virus—Inoculation not always effective—Cure of the disease—Periods at which horses are liable to be attacked—Flesh of infected cattle—Refutation of Dr. Livingstone—Origin of the disease unknown.

A WORD now regarding the so-called "lung-sickness" (pleuromonia), to which occasional allusion has been made in these pages, as also in "Lake N'gami," that is so terribly fatal to both tame and wild animals in Southern Africa, and which, unless an effectual remedy be applied on the first symptoms appearing, almost invariably ends in death. It seems to me that this insidious disease bears some affinity to the dreaded "rinderpest" which of late years has so ravaged England and other European countries, in which case some useful hints may be gained by learning the treatment resorted to in Damaraland and the adjacent regions for the cure of the "lung-sickness." I have therefore thought it right to subjoin the result of my own experiences, which have not been few, regarding this disease. And I speak with some authority, as during my long sojourn at Otjimbingue, I myself have possessed very large herds of horned cattle, and unfortunately lost upward of two thousand by "lung-sickness."

The outward symptoms of pleuromonia are: The infected beast loses his appetite, his breathing becomes hard and labored, he is seized with a short, dry cough, the hair becomes partially raised, and has a rough and ruffled appearance, just like that of cattle on a cold morning. As the disease increases in violence, the beast, no longer able to support himself, lies down, too often to rise no more; the breathing becomes more difficult, the cough more frequent, a frothy matter exudes from his mouth and nostrils, and the eyes close as if in sleep. When the disease has arrived at this stage, no known remedy can possibly restore the poor creature; he is then abandoned to his fate or the butcher's knife. When not quite so far gone, however, it occasionally happens that he recovers from his desperate condition, in which case he may be considered safe for life, only he is much weakened, and will never be himself again. This is especially observable in "draught oxen." If such be slaughtered, it is not uncommon to find the whole of one lung, and perhaps half of the other, destroyed. I have known an ox on one occasion to remain without eating and drinking for twenty-one days, and afterward recover; but, generally speaking, a week, or at the outside, a fortnight, will decide his fate. If the attack be severe, he never eats during the while, but occasionally sips a mouthful of water, which is always placed within his reach.

To the best of my belief this insidious disease may be present in the blood for weeks, nay, months, before there is the slightest outward appearance of sickness; and I am led to this conclusion from the fact that when, after perhaps only a few days' illness, the infected beast dies, it will be found on dissection that more than half of the lung is gone, which never could have occurred in so short a time. Then, again, it is confidently asserted that, on the first breaking out of "lung-sickness" in a hitherto untainted district, it will not unfrequently be found, on carefully tracing it to its origin, that many weeks have elapsed since the cattle—the presumed cause of the epidemic—passed through it.

As a preventive for the disease in question, or, as many believe, a cure for it when had recourse to in its early stages, inoculation, on the same principle as with human beings, is very largely practised in Southern Africa; the success of the operation, however, much depending on the manner in which it is performed, and the quality of the virus employed. Of the latter, I have seen people use such as had been obtained from cattle that had died of the disorder in question; but this, I consider, was highly injudicious, and even dangerous. In my own case, it was always procured from the lung of an ox in the first stage of the malady, that was killed for the special purpose, care being taken that no blood or other extraneous matter was mingled with the lung itself, which is found partly imbedded in, and imbued with, a certain liquid—in short, the virus. Such portion of this and of the lung as may be required is removed and placed in a large-mouthed bottle, or other vessel, carefully excluding the air. In a hot climate such as Damaraland, virus should never be used more than a week old; I, for my part, indeed, never ventured to employ any that exceeded half that age. The best virus has a clear, transparent, yellow look.

Various plans for applying the virus are adopted. Thus some people, after cutting a portion of the lung of an ox that has died of pleuromonia into small bits, will insert one of these into some part of the body of the animal under treatment for that disease, while others will only dip a piece of twine or thread in the liquid, and afterward apply it in a similar way. There are those, again, who prefer administering a wine-glassful of the liquor internally. My own plan, which certainly was as successful as that adopted by my neighbors, was to pour a small quantity of lung-liquid into a small, flat dish, in which I further put a number of single-stranded cotton wicks, two or three inches in length. One or two places are chiefly selected for operating upon in an infected beast—viz., the tail and the dewlap. For my part I preferred the former, as being more distant from the vital parts, for it not unfrequently happens that the virus, if too strong, or too plentifully administered under certain circumstances, say, for instance, in hot and sultry weather, will kill instead of cure. This is especially the case when the animal is already tainted with the disorder.

All things being in readiness for the operation, the ox is secured (with native cattle not unfrequently both a difficult and dangerous operation), one of the cotton strings just spoken of, after being knotted at the end, is then reeved through the eye of a moderately large sailmaker's needle, which is afterward passed through the tail within three or four inches of the extremity, care being taken not to touch the bone. The needle is now withdrawn, the thread being left, having first been run forward and backward several times through the small orifice made by the needle, so as to make sure that the virus has come in full contact with the blood. The time required for it to take effect varies according to circumstances and climate, but usually from four to fifteen days elapse. There are those who insist on a fixed period; but this is absurd, and shows that the men who advocate so senseless a theory know very little of what they are talking about. The only safe way of ascertaining the point is to examine the tail a few days after it has been operated upon. The signs of its proper ripeness are a swelling and a slight exudation of yellow matter, resembling the virus. When such is the case, this is supposed to have done its work, *i. e.*, spread over the system and returned whence it came. Most people deem it necessary to cut off the tail a few inches above the spot where the needle was passed through it; but others merely scarify it. It is, I believe, safest to adopt the former course, though you thereby deprive the poor beast of his only means of defence against tormenting flies. It not unfrequently happens that the tail has to be cut once, twice, and even a third time, so that nothing but the merest stump remains, giving the brute a curious foreshortened appearance.

Contemporary with the thickness of the cauda there frequently appears on one or both sides of the basis or root of the tail a swelling, or lump, as if caused by a musket ball that had passed through the body of the animal, and lodged on the opposite side, just within the skin. The instant this protuberance is observed, a knife must be drawn across it, and a finger or two inserted within the aperture, when, by a little humoring, a small round or oval kernel, of a hard, compact substance, is extracted. The utmost vigilance should be exerted in discovering these "balls," or they will cause infinite trouble, and perhaps the death of the beast;

for, after a very short time they identify themselves, so to say, with the surrounding flesh, which in a few days grows hard and cancer-like. The "balls" in question must be removed at all hazards; in short, the knife should be freely used daily, for the swelling not unfrequently spreads over one or both of the hind quarters, passing downward into the legs, and in a few days lameness ensues, and with it the fate of the beast is sealed. A merciful master will no longer hope against hope, but shorten the poor animal's sufferings by instant death. The wounds are cleansed at least once a day. Pails of fresh water and a solution of common salt should always be held in readiness for the purpose. Sulphate of potash is also used, but is more expensive, and certainly not more efficacious than common nitrate caustic of some kind—none is cheaper or more to the purpose than bluestone or blue vitrol—which should likewise be freely employed.

Though vaccination is generally successful, still it often happens that the beast dies after the operation has been performed, and after the virus has apparently taken proper effect. And yet this could not well have been the case; in short, the disease must already have made such progress when the preventive was applied as to frustrate its intended purpose, or it may be that the two—the disease and the virus—were for a time contending, as it were, for mastery, and that finally the disease got the upper hand. Only in this way can I explain the matter. Doctors may say, "You have perhaps used bad virus, and if so it was quite sufficient to annul the intended effect." I will not gainsay that this, in some instances, may have been the case with others, but, from the terrible losses suffered by me within the past two years, hardly as regards myself, as I have been most cautious in the selection of the matter employed.

From what has been said, it will be seen that the inoculation of cattle and its attendant cares are most trying and laborious. It is, indeed, impossible to realize this severe and harassing duty unless one has personally witnessed it. It taxes a person's utmost patience, strength, and health. I have had as many as two hundred head of wild cattle to attend to daily for many consecutive months, besides a host of other equally important duties.

This disorder also occurs among horses, when it is called "Peripneumonia;" but whether it is of a precisely similar nature as that to which horned cattle are subject, I am not prepared to say. Many of the symptoms are certainly similar; but with horses the disease is far more rapid and terrible in its effects, the animal seldom surviving more than twenty-four hours after the first attack. If it does it will probably recover; but if only mildly attacked it will be liable to the disease again and again, and may finally die of it. It is further to be remarked that, unlike "lung-sickness" with cattle, who are liable to the disease under all circumstances and in all places, there are certain localities in certain countries where horses are altogether free from the scourge. These are generally high plateaus in mountainous regions situated at a considerable elevation above the level of the sea. Moreover, it is only at certain seasons of the year that horses are liable to it. Thus in Damaraland they are quite safe from June to

October, and even as late as November and December. Sheep and goats, as well as horned cattle, die of "lung-sickness," though only occasionally, as it would appear. With these animals, however, the disease would seem to be of a less infectious nature. In short, one or two may perish out of a flock, leaving the rest untouched.

The epidemic in question also occurs among certain wild animals, and mostly during dry and arid years, but it seldom, so far as I myself have observed, proves fatal to any very serious extent. Dr. Livingstone, however, tells a very different story. "During our stay at Chonuane," he writes, "a number of tolos, or koodoos, were attracted to the gardens of the Bakwains, abandoned at the usual period of harvest, because there was no prospect of the corn (*Holcus Sorghum*) bearing that year. The koodoo is remarkably fond of the green stalks of this kind of millet. The feeding produces that state of fatness favorable for the development of the disease, and no fewer than twenty-five died on the hill opposite our house. Great numbers of gnus and zebras perished from the same cause."

The flesh of cattle that have been slaughtered for the "lung-sickness," I should remark in parenthesis, may be eaten with perfect impunity, at least in Southern Africa. For more than two years hardly anything else appeared on my table, and in no one instance has any disagreeable consequence followed. Probably the strength of the poison is destroyed by cooking. The only parts we avoided were the ribs, to which the diseased lungs were more or less attached. And even these parts, as well as the lung itself, were consumed by my native servants and the dogs without any injurious effects. The experience of my neighbors was the same, and remains so to this day. "Lung-sick" meat, I should add, is easily detected by a yellowish fluid and little pimples of the same color disseminated throughout it. To a practised eye these become apparent even in the flesh of cattle slaughtered before the disease has had time seriously to affect their health.

I had written thus far when I recollected having read something on the same subject in Livingstone's first work, and, on referring to it, found to my utter astonishment the following paragraph, a direct contradiction, as will be seen, to what I have just stated.

"When the flesh of animals," writes the famous explorer, "that have died of this disease is eaten, it causes a malignant carbuncle, which when it appears over any important organ proves rapidly fatal. It is more especially dangerous over the pit of the stomach. The effects of the poison have been experienced by missionaries who had eaten properly cooked food, the flesh of sheep really, but not visibly, affected by the disease. The virus in the flesh of the animal is destroyed neither by boiling nor roasting. The fact, of which we had innumerable examples, shows the superiority of experiments on a large scale to those of acute and able physiologists and chemists in the laboratory; for a well-known physician in Paris, after careful investigation, considered that the virus in such cases was completely neutralized by boiling."

However much the practical Doctor may sneer at results obtained in the laboratory, it will be seen by what he says that the physiologists and chemists are on my side; the reader must therefore judge for himself whether mine or the great traveller's statement as to the wholesomeness of the meat of animals that have suffered from "lung-sickness" is the correct one.

In conclusion, I would remark that the true cause of this epidemic, as well as that of the "rinderpest," is unknown, and although innumerable speculations have been hazarded on the subject, it would seem we are as far from the truth at the present day as when these terrible scourges first appeared. I would further observe that so powerful is the poison of the "lung-sickness," that when the animal's body has been fully imbued with it, its hide suffers seriously, its strength and durability being in a great measure gone.

CHAPTER XVI.

Ovampoland—Missionary labor—Rev. Mr. Hahn's reception—Prospects of success—Difficulties to contend with—Civilization and Evangelization—Deceitfulness of the native character—Labors of the missionary—Enthusiasm in Germany.

IT was stated in a recent chapter as probable that Ovampoland would shortly have the benefit of missionary labor. Not very long before my visit to Ondonga, indeed, the Rev. Mr. Hahn, whose station is Otjimbingue, had been there for the express object of ascertaining the suitability of that country for the purpose, and returned home quite charmed with what he had seen and experienced, and full of enthusiasm for these benighted lands. Chykongo, the paramount chief of the Ovampo, as well as the chiefs of neighboring regions, had not only received him well, but had expressed a desire for teachers of the new religion, and presented him with ground for building and agricultural purposes; so that my friend at once put himself in communication with a missionary society in Finland, which would appear to conduct their labors on much the same principle as the Rhenish Society, or that to which Mr. Hahn himself is attached.

My own first impressions were favorable to the establishment of a mission in Ondonga, but on more mature reflection I must say I consider the prospect of success is, at the best, very doubtful. First, there is the fever to contend with, and though that difficulty may possibly be overcome, as it has been in other parts of the world, by a great sacrifice of life, still it must always remain a very serious drawback; then the very ease, good-nature, and good-humor of the inhabitants are likely to prove stumbling-blocks, devoid as they are of all interest and enthusiasm for anything but beer-drinking, barter, and cattle-lifting. At first, from the novelty of the thing, there may, and probably will be, a slight show of success; but gradually, it is to be feared, the work will languish for want of proper support, and ultimately, perhaps, die a natural death, as many similar enterprises have done before it.

Now that I am on the subject of religious missions, a few words from an impartial pen in regard to those in Southern Africa may not be without interest to the reader. That the missionaries do much good it is impossible to deny, though the good they effect is, in reality, quite different from that which a large portion of those worthy men imagine. Thus, instead of evangelizing the natives (only a very small portion at least), they are civilizing them, which, although not the ulterior object, I consider a grand achievement. They are far too fond of making the two—evangelization and civilization—go hand in hand, and use their best endeavors to let the former precede the latter, which, to my mind, is the greatest possible mistake. Of late years, however, it must be admitted, they have somewhat changed their tactics, and the effects for the better are quite apparent. I have often put the question to missionaries, as I do now to every intelligent reader, how is it possible to make a degraded savage—a being too frequently very little elevated above the brute creation—one who has no other thought or desire but how he shall fill his belly, ease his neighbor of his cattle, and so forth—how is it possible, I would ask, to succeed in making such an ignorant being understand and realize the mysterious doctrines of Faith, Justification, and Salvation? Surely it will be necessary first to raise such a wretch from his beastly degradation; to show him the way, and gradually provide him with the means of earning an honest living by his own exertions and ingenuity; to teach him that the good things of this world were given for our use, and not abuse; to show him that filth and filthy habits are an abomination, and that cleanliness and comforts are really things worthy of being acquired; to teach his children to read and write; in short, to inculcate habits of cleanliness and industry, to give him correct notions of "meum" and "tuum," to prove to him that instruction and education are superior to wealth. I say, first do all these things, and there is some chance of ultimately evangelizing these benighted nations.

If the missionary persists in pursuing a different course; if, in his anxiety to be able to report favorably of his congregation—and what pastor has not that ambition?—if, in short, he insists upon making Christians of his rude listeners before they are civilized, what will be the consequence? I would tell him, they will be Christians in appearance, while in heart they are hypocrites. And I regret to say that this is my experience of more than one mission in South Africa. The native is by nature oily and cunning; he soon finds that in order to keep in the good graces of his teacher it will be necessary for him to accommodate himself to his wishes; he learns quickly and glibly to quote Scripture; to have Christ's name mixed up with every second sentence he utters; to say, "If it pleases God," "If I am spared to live," no matter how trivial the occasion. And thus the worthy missionary, ay, even the most practical, is, without a direct fault of his own, too often wofully imposed upon. The very honesty of the man proves the rock on which his best hopes and aspirations suffer shipwreck. Why do we so often hear of missionaries dying prematurely? The cause is not always disease, suffering, or hardship, but they die of a broken heart, having at the eleventh hour discovered the hollowness and insincerity of those members of their little congregations in whom they perhaps most confided. I have known such men.*

If you ask one of these worthy men, "Well, I hear you have got another convert; what of him, do you really think he is a Christian?" "Oh yes, he is." "But how can you tell?" Of course he will say, "His practices are a test of his character." "But how are you to know what he says and does, you cannot always be present?" "No, true; but what I cannot see and hear, others do for me. Besides, his own countrymen, from a kind of jealousy of his new privileges and exalted

* Dr. Livingstone, ever candid and practical, writes as follows:—"On asking an intelligent chief what he thought of them (alluding to some native Christians), he replied, 'You white men have no idea how wicked we are; we know each other better than you do; some feign belief to ingratiate themselves with the missionaries; some profess Christianity because they like the new system, which gives so much more importance to the poor, and desire that the old system may pass away; and the rest—a pretty large number—profess because they are really true believers.'"

rank, keep a close eye on his movements." What short-sighted mortals we are! A hypocrite will always find means of deceiving both friend and foe. The more you watch him, the more he watches you. In my own humble opinion, a far surer test of the sincerity and reality of the Christian converts' faith would be their conduct when, after a few probationary years, they were distributed over the neighboring country, instead of being always kept together in one spot, as is now the invariable custom with missionaries. For, as it has been truly said, "unless habits of self-reliance are cultivated, and opportunities given for the exercise of that virtue, the most promising converts are apt to become like spoiled children."

I shall probably draw down on myself very severe censure for this unreserved statement; and there may be those who will negative its truth altogether, but it is the fact. And I speak with some authority, from having had considerable dealings with the *soi-disant* converts in question; and I should have no difficulty, were it needful, to find numbers of people to bear me out in what I have said. It must not, however, be supposed for a moment that I bear ill-will toward the missionaries; on the contrary, these worthy men have my best wishes; and it is because I mean them well that I now run the risk of being misunderstood, and perhaps abused. Were I not interested in their success, I should probably not care to expose their weak points. Those who know me will acknowledge, I hope, that I have always been a friend to missionary institutions, in deeds as well as words, and that consequently I make this disclosure from no ill-will to them.

A stranger on arriving at a station that has been established for some time in the distant interior, I would remark in parenthesis, can form no idea of the tremendous efforts and the immense amount of manual labor that it has probably cost the founder in its erection and construction. Every stone, every piece of timber in those substantial buildings, has been fashioned and placed in its proper place by him solely; that fine piece of garden ground has all been dug and planted by the same hand; that stout cattle pen, that magnificent well has been raised and dug by his own good right arm; nay more, the materials had frequently to be brought from a considerable distance. All this, and much more of the same kind, this toilsome man has accomplished, besides acquiring the language, teaching the children, attending to the sick and needy, composing sermons, being present at frequent prayer-meetings, giving advice, and holding consultations with the chief and strangers, and so forth. And it must not be supposed that his helpmate is idle meanwhile. Her duties are hardly less trying and laborious. She prepares the corn, makes the bread, churns, washes and irons the linen, attends to her own children, if there be any, visits and nurses the needy, helpless, and sick, instructs the infants, teaches the girls to sew, and a hundred other offices requiring time, patience, strength, and health. And the result of all this is too frequently premature old age. I have seen more than one blooming missionary bride in the course of a few years lose the roses from her cheeks entirely, her once elastic step had become measured and languid, the eye has lacked lustre, and the whole form bowed and altered wofully. And yet you will never hear a word of complaint from these patient and self-sacrificing women, who in their greatest troubles have always a kind word for the stranger, smilingly inviting him to a seat at the hospitable board. One sees that it is not the possession of either silver or gold which supports them so nobly; they feel that if there is a reward for their patience and self-immolation, it is in a hereafter. Truly I envy them their contentedness and cheerfulness.

With missionaries within the boundaries of the Cape Colony, or on stations that have been long established, and have easy access to civilized life, the thing is widely different, as they may be said to lead a life of comparative ease and comfort.

The children of missionaries, at least of the Rhenish Society, are educated in Germany at the expense of the society, and at the death of the head of the house the widow is pensioned off with a small allowance, very insufficient, as I believe, for her necessities; the rather as from thenceforward she has to shift for herself in every way. It must be very hard in old age, not only to lose a husband, but to be ousted from under the very roof raised, perhaps, by the beloved one, and made comfortable by her own thrifty housewifery. Under the present system, stations are called "missionary property," a misnomer certainly!

The missionaries, when settled beyond the pale of civilization, are almost entirely dependent on the natives for their supply of animal food; and as money is generally unknown in such places, they have recourse to barter for obtaining the needful supplies. I believe it was originally forbidden the members of the Rhenish

Society to obtain by barter more cattle than was absolutely necessary for their own support. Of late years, however, this regulation has been less strictly adhered to, and many missionaries at the present day increase their too often insufficient incomes, not only by trading with the natives, but by following certain trades, such as those of wagon-makers, blacksmiths, and the like, whereby, they say, the societies to which they belong are enabled to extend their influence, besides teaching the people useful handicrafts, which statement, on the face of it, seems fair enough.

But, as regards trading, the opinion of people in Southern Africa differs greatly. One often, indeed, hears the question asked, "What have missionaries to do with trade? They have enough to live upon without depriving other men of their bread;" or, "What becomes of the enormous sums subscribed for their use?" Missionaries being allowed to trade, in short, causes much bad blood among many of the European settlers at least. I myself do not agree with those who would prevent these men from trading. Indeed, I don't see how they could well exist without it; but this I would say, do not allow them to conduct the business in person, but leave it to their wives, or other responsible persons.

Trade and barter, in the course of time, are apt to taint the least selfish and honorable mind with a feeling of avarice, or a desire to accumulate money. At first, moderate profit may suffice, but eventually, perhaps, the trader is induced to overstep the bounds of moderation, which the wily native soon discovers. He is always suspicious, and steadily refuses to understand the reason why the missionary comes from distant lands to settle among strangers. It seems to him perfectly absurd that a man should make so long a voyage merely for the purpose, as the missionary tells him, of doing good to their fellow-men. In a native's eyes everything has its marketable value. A missionary may flatter himself that his own good conduct and precepts will be a test of the sincerity of his profession ; but once turned trader, and four-fifths, perhaps more, of his little congregation, will judge him in that character, and should they, perchance, find he has been overreaching them in any way, they will thereafter value their spiritual teaching accordingly.

The missionary appears, under diffierent circumstances, in a two-fold character, as it were. Thus, in Europe, he is the representative of self-abnegation, self-sacrifice, devotedness, moral courage, and so forth, all which he really is. Who has not seen immense crowds, such as not even royalty could attract, rush to a church when it is rumored that a missionary will preach ; a very large proportion are led there by mere curiosity and a desire to hear wonderful tales of hunger, thirst, sickness, or of miraculous escapes from savage beasts and still more savage men. Abroad—in South Africa at least—where European settlers are numerous, the missionary, instead of being looked on as a wonderful being, is by many of them viewed rather as an interloper—one in short, who has the monstrous audacity to set right the degraded natives, and to secure valuable lands that the latter ought to have possessed, and so forth. Thus in Europe enormous sums are cheerfully subscribed for the propagation of the Gospel among savages, while abroad, in South Africa at least, the poor missionary, the distributor of the money, is too often subjected to odium and suspicion.

Nothing is more common, moreover, than to hear missionaries stigmatized as "meddling politicians." If the accusation be true, then nothing is more easy than to account satisfactorily for such an assumption of the rights which they exercise. Their very social position and education compel them, as it were, to such a course. What is more natural than that the poor, degraded beings under their patriarchal rule should look up to them in every emergency for advice and comfort? Even when, after years of severe labor on the part of their teachers, their intellects have been cleared of Cimmerian darkness, and raised perhaps to an equality even with that of their missionary, the old habit of looking to him for a decision in every important matter clings to them. I have known missionaries who have made the most strenuous exertions to rid themselves of such a duty, at least in all that relates to politics, and for a short time they may have succeeded; they have even gone so far as temporarily to estrange themselves from their congregation by their obsinate adherence to refuse advice. But what father can resist the pleadings of his child, when, with infantine confidence and reverence, he throws himself on his more mature age and experience for help in difficulties? And so it is really with the missionary and his congregation, who stand in the relation to each other almost of parent and children. But the fact is the neighbors are jealous and suspicious of his motives. Were he the pastor of some European settlement, no such outcry or complaint would probably be heard.

The South African missions are very numerous; more so, some think, than the country requires. Certain it is that from the somewhat different teaching at the various stations (several societies and sects being represented), they prove a sad puzzle to such of the converts as, from circumstances, are necessitated to remove from one mission to the other, as not unfrequently happens in the more civilized districts.

They—the missions—which are chiefly German, are very liberally supplied, not only with funds, but with ready-made clothes; none of your slops, but good useful stuff that the best of us might wear. Most of the missions, indeed, annually receive chest upon chest of these valuable contributions, worth, probably, in the aggregate, many thousand pounds sterling.

The Germans, and probably other continental people also, would appear to be very enthusiastic about missions, as also very liberal contributors thereto. Even the lower classes freely take part in the good work. The Rev. Mr. Hahn told me that he himself knew a poor girl to deposit in the begging box a sum which constituted the whole of her savings during sixteen years of severe labor. I remarked to him: "Had you no compunction in accepting of the noble gift?" "None whatever," my friend replied. He might be right, but I was too blind to see it. Surely, the widow offering her last mite, as recorded in Scripture, was not meant as an example to be followed. If so, what becomes of the maxim, "Charity begins at home.' God forbid that I should sit in judgment on such weighty matters; but when Christ commanded His disciples to go into the world and preach the Gospel to the Gentiles, he forbade them to carry either scrip or bag, assuring them that their Heavenly Father would provide for their wants. It therefore seems to me that a portion, at least, of the stupendous contributions now raised in Europe for the support of missions would be equally well spent at home.

The reverend gentleman just named mentioned another circumstance, showing how enthusiastic the Germans are in regard to missionary enterprise. We were talking of the large debts that the African societies ventured at times to incur on the strength of such enthusiasm. "Suppose," said I, "your mission owed ten thousand pounds"—a very large sum in his country—"in what manner would you clear yourselves of the debt, and still continue your labors with unabated vigor?" "Oh!" he replied, "nothing would be easier; we should write to some influential friend of the mission, stating our urgent wants, and the money would be forthcoming in due time." Astonishing!

In concluding these few observations on the South African missions, I would remark that, taken as a whole, there are probably not more respectable and worthy men than the missionaries individually. I sincerely admire their courage, their devotedness, their enthusiasm, their total disregard of personal interests. What other men would abandon home, friends, comforts, in short all that renders existence valuable and pleasant, to bury themselves for life in desert and pestilential places, among barbarous tribes and nations, who, moreover, are utterly incapable of appreciating the sacrifice they have made, and for which sacrifice they, in return, too often receive only ignominy, treachery, and persecution, or it may be even death itself? Truly, it requires something like superhuman enthusiasm, and a true Christian spirit, to enable them to struggle successfully and submissively against such a condition. God speed and bless the labors of the lonely missionary in his arduous path!

CHAPTER XVII.

Prevalence of sickness—Despatch of ivory to Otjimbingue—Departure of elephant hunters—Study of Portuguese—Attack of fever—Birds shot by natives with arrows—Goat carried off by a hyena—Ophthalmia—Samuel attacked by the Damaras—New species of storks—Visit to Chykongo—Dr. Livingstone—A thief caught in the act.

HERE Andersson's "Notes of Travel" cease altogether, and henceforth it is only from his Journal, which he kept regularly posted up until within a few days of his death, that we have an account of further proceedings.—*Editor.*

JOURNAL.

"*Monday, 4th February,* 1867.—Palgrave came down during the night; looks very well; does seem to think that getting Samuel out of the way would be of much use; but surely some beginning ought to be made, or we have no earthly chance of ultimately bettering our condition.

"*Tuesday, 5th February.*—Chykongo (the chief) has assured me he will abide by his promise to the Europeans some time ago in regard to Samuel and his party. It is now understood that we withdraw to some healthier locality, while waiting the result of this affair. To go away altogether without knowing the fate of Samuel (as far as it can be known) would be folly. Chykongo might prove treacherous were we gone.

Many people are sick; a Damara died yesterday, and others are expected to follow. Raining; the country literally steeped in water, though here and there dry; all the intervening parts are submerged. I don't wonder it is unhealthy.

"*Wednesday, 6th February.*—Went out with Axel to hunt water-hens and procure eggs; succeeded in both objects. Rainy in the afternoon.

"*Thursday, 7th February.*—Poor Axel down with fever, and I myself feel very queer. God grant that I may escape! Even Green had an attack. Chykongo does not at all like the idea of withdrawing all my people; he has taken a fancy to Een,* and is very loth to part with him, assuring me that there shall be no danger to him or my property from Samuel. I don't think it will be of any great advantage to me to let Een remain; but I should wish to show my appreciation of Chykongo's kindness to white men by acceding to his wishes. Have sold the long rifle to Pereira for three hundred pounds of ivory; but I shall make nothing by the bargain, as sooner or later I must order a similar one from England. I have now more than three thousand pounds weight of ivory, which my people have collected in Ovampoland, and hope that quantity will be increased by several hundredweight before reaching Otjimbingue. Heavy, soaking rain all round.

"*Friday, 8th February.*—Took another emetic, which has caused me much pain. Could Green have given me too great a dose? Have made up my mind to remain here, and send Een home with the wagons;

* The sea-captain that Andersson took into his service when in Gothenburg.—ED.

I cannot say I like the arrangement, but there is hardly an alternative.

"*Saturday, 9th February.*—Continue very ill; am quite sure I am suffering from some other disease beside dysentery. My head aches dreadfully; have got much writing to do, but am utterly unfit for it, or, indeed, for work of any kind.

"*Monday, 10th February.*—I am just a little better; my wagons and people are off. The atmosphere has cleared up lately and I think we are likely to have fine weather for awhile. Axel continues poorly. Palgrave arrived; his people are getting better.

"*Tuesday, 12th February.*—Exceedingly unwell; Palgrave left. Chykongo paid me a visit yesterday; to-day he sent me some corn, of which I told him I stood in need, and also a young ox.

"*Wednesday, 13th February.*—T—— arrived; says Een has gone to Ovaquambo. The hunters talk of finally breaking up their camp in a day or two. It is high time; they are a vacillating, dilatory set. H—— returned; he has had an attack of fever since he left, and is still weak.

"*Thursday, 14th February.*—Signs of the rain returning; much thunder and lightning in the distance; even a little rain fell.

"*Friday, 15th February.*—T——, H——, H—— and Pereira, started for the hunting veldt, and consequently I am now alone, and fear I shall have a long and tedious time of it.

"*Saturday, 16th February.*—Tormented to death at night by the mosquitoes, and by flies in the daytime. Spent a most horrid and restless night; in fact, sleep was out of the question, and I therefore sat up to read and write. Have taken up a Portuguese Grammar, together with a Dictionary obtained from Palgrave. It does not seem so difficult a language, only I have no one to help me with the accents and pronunciation. I am determined, however, to know something of it, as in the event of reaching the Portuguese settlement, it will serve me in good stead. It has struck me as a good plan to get as far as Hombe, and there leave Axel while I proceed to Massamedas. Chykongo called on me, and took a fancy to my pea-rifle, which he insisted on buying, but I should not like to part with it. Moreover, I could never obtain from him a fair price. He sent me two large bull-elephant tusks, weighing together about one hundred and thirty pounds. He is also desirous of possessing two of my double detonating rifles; for flint guns he seems not to care. My head continues to ache; still, on the whole, I feel better. Axel, thank God, is so far recovered as to be able to resume his shooting. Goliath continues weak. H—— returned for a boy who had run away. Quantities of eggs continue to be brought us of the *Gall pumila* and *Eupl taka.* Raining all round, but far away.

"*Sunday*, 17*th February.*—Paid a state visit to Chykongo, dressed in my best. Tasted his beer for the first time. He insists on having my pea-rifle; offers a rather nice-looking double-barrelled rifle in exchange. This is a nuisance, the greater, as the pea-rifle can never be of any manner of use to him.

"*Monday*, 18*th February.*—Chykongo returned my visit, and brought me an ox as a present. He came for the pea-rifle, and I have let him have it. I find the rifle he offers in exchange shoots perfectly true, only the sight is too clumsy. It is of a very small bore. I know the gun, it was once Jones's; the locks are defective. Axel out shooting. Brought home ten ducks and geese, which are a valuable contribution to the larder. He obtained also some eggs, though of ordinary kind. A heavy shower of rain late in the afternoon. Letters from Pereira and H——. T—— is ill, and no improvement with the Damaras. They only got to the outskirts of the bush. Deluged with rain. I pity H——; may the poor fellow keep his health.

"*Tuesday*, 19*th February*.—Tremendous showers in the afternoon. Much improved in health; able to eat any thing I like; a state of things not experienced for several months.

"*Wednesday*, 20*th February*.—Hard at work mapping out the last of my route, and preparing a new sheet for my contemplated journey to the Portuguese settlements. Of Mr. Hahn's information I can make nothing. Some Ovaka here yesterday, with whom I sent word to their chief that I was desirous of visiting him as soon as the rains, as well as the sickness, abated. The sextant that I obtained from Palgrave is a powerful instrument, but in bad condition. Have put it a little to rights, as also the box containing it, which was in a ruinous condition. Both my watches are out of order; at times they go, while at others they stop. This is a very serious drawback. Axel away to the Omuramba, but got nothing; says the place is impassable from mud, etc.; brought home a nest of *Nictarina Callaris*.

"*Thursday*, 21*st February*.—Axel out the whole day in search of specimens, but was unsuccessful in that respect; he bagged, however, seven couple of ducks. The natives brought in some new eggs. At last I am in for what I long dreaded, viz., the fever, which, as usual, threatens to be very severe.

"*Friday, 22d February.*—Continue very ill; can hardly hold up my head for five minutes together. The tongue, however, does not look so bad as might be expected. Received at last the long expected note from Een, dated Ovaquambo. He had succeeded in getting about twenty cows, three of which were for an old debt. The chief, Navremas, is desirous of seeing me; he is annoyed at my not sending him a double-barrelled rifle. One of his head-men has run away from him with a number of cattle, and he begs me to get Chykongo (with whom, he says, the man has taken refuge) to send him and the cattle back.

"*Saturday, 23d February.*—Axel laboring assiduously in the vleys, but to little purpose. He complains of the difficulty of getting the birds to take wing, owing, no doubt, to their being so much hunted. The only two that he secured were shot with arrows by native lads beneath the surface of the water, one of them actually holding itself fast to a grass stalk by the bill.* A trifle better; able to sit up, but great pain in my right leg; sores are forming all over and around the large wound in front, and much redness in most parts. The heel is excessively tender.

"*Sunday, 24th February.*—Somewhat stronger this morning, but feel giddy and head sore. Cannot get a night's rest, owing to slight delirium and the mosquitoes.

* This is corroborative of what many assert to be of frequent occurrence, but which many, on the contrary, stoutly deny.—Ed.

Sent for and spoke to Chykongo about Navremas. Told me he would do his best, but said the chief in question was a bad man, and that his people were always running away from him. Told Chykongo that, if he would send a man with me, I would remonstrate with the half-mad chief upon his conduct. Should Chykongo really restore the cattle it would be a great triumph for me, and might be of value in my dealings hereafter with the native chiefs. Chykongo is suffering slightly from fever. My leg continues very queer; it can be nothing but an old ailment that has returned in the shape of erysipelas.

"*Monday, 25th February.*—Not quite so well today; able, nevertheless, to do some little work. Axel busy in collecting and cleaning shells; succeeded in getting a goodly number.

"*Tuesday, 26th February.*—Axel's success in the vleys is now apparently at an end. The water-hens refuse altogether to show themselves, and few or no eggs are obtainable. Jacob down with the fever. This is a great misfortune; the greater as Goliath is not gaining strength. Thus both my servants are incapacitated. Looked over and scarified some of Pereira's sick cattle.* He never asked me to do so, but don't

* This poor man, who was exceedingly well-educated, speaking several languages, and who for a length of time was in the employ of Mr. Andersson, recently met his death in a very sad way. Several articles had been stolen from him by some Bushmen, whom he succeeded in capturing at the werft of their chief, and who, by the aid of some Damaras, were conveyed to his wagon. Night, however, overtook the party halfway, and Pereira, therefore, resolved to wait until morning before continuing his journey. He was followed, unobserved, by three Bushmen, friends of the captives, who shortly before daybreak crept stealthily upon

like the poor fellow to lose them for want of a little attention.

"*Wednesday, 27th February.*—Cannot obtain sleep at night for mosquitoes. With the exception of headache, a slight weakness and pain in the left leg, I feel pretty well, and, if not worse again, shall have hopes of being in a fair way of recovery. Chykongo sent me the skin of the lion killed by his Bushmen. Axel shot a fine bustard, but of what species I know not.

"*Thursday, 28th February.*—The hyena took a goat of mine last night. He was followed by Axel a considerable distance. The poor goat was actually devoured by the beast while still living. The dogs, though they followed the hyena, dared not attack him. Suffer from a severe headache, chiefly above the right temple, but do not think it arises from the fever; it must be a cold. Goliath, since I gave him the quinine,

his place of bivouac, and by the light of the fire, alongside which he was sleeping, discharged three poisoned arrows at him. The first entered the left breast; he started up and seized his rifle, and while in the act of firing, another entered his arm below the shoulder, causing him to drop his gun, and the next moment the third struck him in the stomach; but the latter did not penetrate. With the deadly shafts still embedded in the flesh, poor Pereira discharged his rifle at the murderers, who fled, and made their escape in the obscurity of the early morn. He then summoned the Damaras to his assistance. The arrow which entered the flesh of the arm was cut out, but the other, which entered the breast, and appeared to have passed round the blade-bone, could not be extracted. He was carried on a rude stretcher, hurriedly made for the purpose, to his veldt home, where he lingered in great agony for five days. "The Bushmen's poison," the narrator of poor Pereira's death goes on to say, "is usually very fatal in its effects; but in this instance it had evidently become weak either from exposure or age. Otherwise he would not have survived the fatal shafts for more than a few hours."—Ed.

is evidently getting stronger. Jacob continues ill; he complains chiefly of his head.

"*Friday*, 1*st March*.—Notwithstanding a bad headache, went with Axel in search of ducks; but we were very unsuccessful, bagging only two couples between us; we, however, saw very few, and hardly any other kind of birds. Picked up a good many eggs of the *P. Minor;* but it is the second lay, and not one nest had half its proper complement of eggs. Showery a little before sunset; Jacob somewhat better.

Saturday, 2*d March*.—Literally eaten up by the mosquitoes at night; can get no rest for them, and dread the return of darkness. Letters from Palgrave and Green, with a sketch of map of their late route; I am very glad of this, as I can make nothing of Mr. Hahn's information. They have encountered great difficulties in their progress, what with fever and "doorslagt." The messenger says he is to return to the wagons, but not to remain. I hope thus once more to hear from my people.

"*Sunday*, 3*d March*.—My eyes very bad; I begin now to think it is the real ophthalmia. Chykongo paid me a visit, and informed me he had heard that the Damaras who conveyed my letters to Otjimbingue have just returned, less two of their number, who were killed in a skirmish with some Bushmen. Chykongo's two sons accompanied the Damaras. Mr. Hahn has gone to the Cape. Chykongo says also that the Damaras have at last attacked Samuel and taken everything from him; but we shall know better when the people arrive. The sky looks threatening; I suppose we shall have some rain with the new moon. A poor

Damara woman died; got her buried with difficulty, as we were short-handed. Poor creature! she had been in a sinking state ever since my arrival; don't suppose I could have done anything for her.

"*Friday, 15th March.*—Nearly a fortnight since I opened my Journal, and now it is with difficulty I can make the needful entries. I don't know what demon of perverseness possessed me to go out shooting when I was blind with ophthalmia, but eagerness for knowledge overruled common prudence.

"During my illness, Chikaongombe (one of the two sons of Chykongo just spoken of) returned with three or four Hottentots, and fully corroborated the statement of the Damaras as to their attack on Samuel, and the success attending it. It appears that the Totties (Hottentots) had just left the mountain with their 'treck,' with a view of coming here, when the Damaras arrived; still the marauders loitered three days, and when attacked were in a state of intoxication, and unable to oppose their assailants. The plunder obtained by the Damaras consisted of two wagons (besides one which was burned), all the oxen, some guns, and one or two horses, leaving the Totties with one wagon, seven horses, and a few milk cows.

"Samuel is now on this side of the mountain, and apparently it is his intention to come here; still I am told there are those in his camp who strenuously oppose his taking this step, urging that it can only lead to the destruction of the whole of them. Chikaongombe, who came here with three or four Hottentots, left again yesterday, is sanguine of success, and hopes to bring back with him both Samuel and his followers.

Have had a conversation with one of the Damaras, who returned lately from Otjimbingue, and who repeated the story of the Bushmen having treacherously killed two of their party because they would not give them meat. I have come to the conclusion that Bushmen, as a race, deserve no pity. The Berg Damaras are not, I fear, one whit better. It now turns out that the very men who occupy Otijkongo, and who professed friendship for us, proved themselves arrant traitors; they have, in fact, carried the news to Samuel of my having passed their werft. One of the Hottentots told Jacob that such was the case. Well, if I ever pass that way again I will make such an example as will probably scare them for the future. The Damaras bring another piece of news from Otjimbingue, which is almost too good to be true—viz., that Jonker has returned the cattle and wagons taken from Egger and Trinbo, together with a small portion of the feathers. The thing is not impossible as the result of Stewardson's mission to him on my account. Kamahero* has sent me a letter to demand the rest of the things, and a large commando has passed on to T. Boyce's. I may thus really have a chance of having some value for my stolen property. Did not get much rain at change of moon, but there has evidently been a heavy downfall in many other directions. Employed yesterday and to-day in writing letters to the hunters, Chykongo having promised to give me a man as far as Ovagandjera, whence they are to be forwarded. I hope the messenger will not fail me after all my trouble and the real pain I have undergone in writing, having had, in

* The Chief of the Damaras.—ED

a measure, to feel my way across the paper. Have also written to my wife and V. D. Byle and Co.

"Poor Axel, who fell ill of fever two days after myself, and was compelled to take to his bed, is very unwell; so extremely weak. I forgot to notice that the Damaras told me it had rained very heavily in Damaraland before they left—both the Omaruni and Swakup were running—and on passing Omappi * they found it full of water; and as they only saw the fence surrounding the grain, and nothing green, I suppose it was washed away. Still I fancy some little corner will escape, and thus enable me to prove whether grain will grow without irrigation in Damaraland.

"*Monday*, 18*th March*.—Again several days have elapsed since I was able to post up my Journal; in fact, I have tried my eyes too severely by writing and other occupations; but shut up in darkness as I am, I cannot lie on my back idle day after day. Axel is now convalescent, though, of course, very weak; but plenty of strong food will soon put him on his legs again. The woman continues very ill, and last night, unfortunately, Karatoe, her husband, also fell sick; Goliath, moreover, is constantly ailing. Yesterday it drizzled nearly the whole day. Kombonde, the heir-apparent, visited me hurriedly on Saturday night; he is said to be very kind and civil to white men. I could not judge of his appearance, except that he seemed tall; but Axel tells me he is good-looking and very manly. Letters from H—— and Palgrave; the former is only a few days' journey from hence, having come to a dead lock in consequence of sickness and death among his

* Andersson's newly-acquired little property.—ED.

people; he has lost his *soi-disant* wife and brother-in-law. He himself and his father are just recovering. Poor people! he asks my advice what to do, whether to return here or proceed; to adopt the latter course while alone he is afraid, on account of Samuel. Shall advise him to push on to Damaraland as fast as he can, as he can do no good here. Palgrave dates his letter fifty miles south of Ovagdjena, where he has been trying to sell his horse; but after a delay of ten days failed in getting the cattle promised him in return for it. The chief (Typaska) did not even send him a basket of corn. Speaks of great drought at the place where he writes from, and of having 'trecked' the whole day without finding water; but it is so in this 'changeland;' either you are knee-deep in water, or suffering the pangs of Tantalus. I don't think I shall trouble myself to visit the chief just named, now that I am acquainted with his stingy nature; it will, moreover, save me a gun, which is something gained.

"*Tuesday*, 19*th March*.—Sent off Kerger's boys. Feel feeble in my legs to-day; hope fever is not the cause of my debility; eyes excessively weak.

"*Wednesday*, 20*th March*.—Thunder and lightning all around. Chykongo sent me a pig, a welcome present. Lost a calf in a singular and sudden manner. Karatoe and wife continue very poorly; Goliath down every second day with some sort of complaint; this morning a cow has kicked him. Axel has had a serious relapse, and fell to the ground suddenly as if subject to falling sickness.

"*Thursday*, 21*st March*.—Axel very feverish nearly the whole night; moaned and raved dreadfully. This morning he can hardly move or speak; he looks very ill, and I much dread the result of the present attack. Chykongo here.

"*Friday, 22d March.*—Thank God! Axel something like himself again; at least, he is only weak, but otherwise able to eat, sit up, and even walk a little. This is a great relief to me, and if he has no return of the fever to-day I shall have hopes the poor fellow will speedily recover. Took a ride for the first time for nearly a fortnight, but fear it rather hurt me, as my eyes cannot bear the light. I must, however, take exercise of some kind in order to obtain sleep, which, of late, has quite deserted my pillow. Thunder and lightning, and even a few drops of rain, but nothing in earnest. Goliath, Karatoe, and wife continue *in statu quo*, and poor Jacob is suffering from boils under the arms.

"*Saturday, 23d March.*—Karatoe is dead; poor fellow, how soon all was over with him! The wife is rather better. My little family is in a sad state, not one being well. We shall have some difficulty in burying the man, being so short of hands. Eyes bad, but fancy it is more of a cold than ophthalmia.

"*Sunday, 24th March.*—Buried Karatoé, but obliged to carry him to the grave myself. At last we have got some rain; it began about five, and is still pouring down as I write (eight o'clock) Axel is getting a little stronger.

"*Monday, 25th March.*—Went out 'egging,' and observed a couple of storks that were new to me; got a double shot, but too far off. They were black beneath, with white breast and neck (all round), black on the shoulder, otherwise of a grayish hue, bill red. Overtaken by heavy rains; these have evidently now set in in good earnest. Jacob's ailment is clearly dysentery; cannot cure the disease with the medicines hitherto administered; must try the regular treatment. I am very helpless now, having to do all sorts of work myself. To-day I have been doctor (of both man and beast), cobbler, tailor, sempstress, etc., etc., besides having to stable horses and donkeys, look after cattle, etc. Chykongo sent me some mats, but they are not so well made as the one I so much admired.

"*Tuesday, 26th March.*—The morning set in rainy, but the rain soon ceased and the day became fine, though the sky remained densely clouded. During the morning my time was occupied in much the same manner as yesterday; but in the afternoon I took a long walk, rather longer, in fact, than was comfortable; suffer very much in my toes and heels when walking far. Found a couple of valuable nests. It is rather more than three weeks since I fell sick, and yet my eyes trouble me much; at a little distance everything looks dim and obscure.

"*Wednesday, 27th March.*—Eight hours in the saddle to-day, scouring the country in search of specimens and eggs; had long shots on three several occasions at the huge red-billed storks, but although I heard the shots rattle on their plumage like the pattering of raindrops on a house-top, they took not the slightest notice. No improvement with Jacob, must give him a second emetic to-morrow.

"*Thursday, 28th March.*—Too tired for the ride I had proposed to myself. The hyena killed one of my goat-kids last night; will, if possible, destroy it by poison, which I shall place near to the grave of poor Karatoe, the scent of whose corpse will probably attract it to the spot. I half killed the beast two days ago, he having for the second time murdered some chickens. Warm day, thunder and lightning all around; shifted the sheep kraal.

"*Friday, 29th March.*—Several hours in the saddle; took with me the rifle in hopes of again falling in with the large storks that I have lately endeavored to knock over with small shot, but could find none. Sun very hot; felt exceedingly poorly on returning home; head and neck ache. Jacob very sick; don't know what to do with him.

"*Saturday, 30th March.*—Took a short ride in a new direction. No water in the vleys; met with five Eforemas, and certainly killed one of them, but could not find it in the long grass; shot a quail of a species new to me. Omitted to notice that the hyena devoured the poisoned carcase I had laid out the other night, and has probably received his quietus; I am thoroughly glad of this. Seems inclined to rain.

"*Sunday, 31st March.*—Paid Chykongo a visit, the first I have made him for a very long time. He was with me yesterday; took me into his Sanctum through the most serpentine walks, lined on both sides with treble, and even quadruple, rows of poles or planks. Why, the place would stand cannonading; no native enemy could possibly take it, provided it was well supplied with water and provisions. Inquired of the chief as to the breed of dogs I had seen about, which I thought might be a cross between the native and some mongrels belonging to the Europeans; but it seems they are purely natives. They differ a good deal from those of the Bushmen, and the face is generally blacker. They are of all colors.

"*Monday, 1st April.*—Eight hours in the saddle, and riding hard a great part of the time. Saw comparatively few water-fowl, and those excessively shy. Very unlucky in my shooting; lost three ducks and two small herons, and returned home very unwell. Jacob again down with his old complaint. The old woman and Ouairi very poorly; were it not for Axel and Kaniko, I don't know what I should do. The weather hot; fancy we shall soon have rain again. Saw three or four Okafema; they wear 'hats' on their posteriors as the Ovaguamyama.

"*Tuesday, 2d April.*—Stayed at home, not being very well, and sent Axel out shooting in my stead.

"*Wednesday, 3d April.*—On horseback for some hours in search of specimens, and obtained a few. Feel very poorly; head-ache, pain in breast and stomach; finished roughly chapter on the Ovampo.

"*Thursday, 4th April.*—Axel away to the Omuramba, but not very successful. Myself very poorly; my legs won't carry me for five minutes together; have all the symptoms of fever about me; —— also ill. Not one of us now in health, Chykongo told me that this is a very unhealthy time, and truly he is right.

"*Friday, 5th April.*—Confined to bed nearly the whole day; such curious pains in the bowels. Toward evening, Axel started for the Omuramba, intending to sleep there, with the object of getting out early tomorrow morning. Weather very hot.

"*Saturday, 6th April.*—Oh, misery! Axel returned from the Omuramba at an early hour, deadly ill of fever. This is terrible! I would fain hope, however, that the attack will pass away quickly. I suspect he has of late taxed his strength too much. I myself continue poorly; but able to sit up and do a little writing, etc. I even skinned and prepared one of the pair of beautiful little geese killed by Axel. Fine breezy day; nevertheless, the heat is great.

"*Sunday, 7th April.*—Worse and worse. Jacob apparently seriously down with fever, and, with the exception of a solution of quinine in a small bottle, which I reserve for my own use, the whole of mine is gone. Fortunately Axel is a little better to-day, and able to attend to his ordinary duties. I tried to do something myself, but from excessive weakness could not accomplish much. Chikaongambe returned, but without the Hottentots who accompanied him from hence. I was much afraid such would be the case; the fellows were no doubt spies, and heard enough while here to arouse their suspicions. Samuel talked of retracing his steps to Otjeronjupa; thus we are in the same position as before, as regards this wretch. Chikaongambe says that some Damaras have followed the Totties and captured five of their horses. What fools, not to have endeavored to kill the marauders! How am I to get my wagon here in safety? *

"*Monday, 8th April.*—Very hot day; after sunset thunder and lightning, and the night promises to be dirty. Axel and Jacob very poorly. Have at last succeeded in getting a herd from Chykongo, or we should

* On its *return* from Otjimbingue, Andersson means.—Ed.

have been quite helpless. Poorly myself, but able to knock about a little, and do some work.

"*Tuesday*, *9th April.*—Spoke to Joseph about accompanying me; told him my intention of starting on my journey to the Cunené very soon; but fancy he seemed rather unwilling; at present he is ill with fever. Axel and myself a trifle better, but Jacob and the rest remain very poorly.

"*Wednesday*, *10th April.*—Chykongo with me; informed him of my purpose of setting off next month, and asked for Chik and a few people, which he readily promised. But though I talk of departing from hence, shall I be able? Not one of us is well; all are so indisposed to-day that, had not I myself been able to crawl about a little, we should have been in a very awkward position. None of those who have been long ill gather strength, notwithstanding that I feed them well; but I want quinine. Chykongo promised to sent word to Pereira as to what has taken place with Samuel; this will relieve my mind in that quarter. Presented the chief with a handsome pair of ear-drops of steel, and a cow. Weather frightfully hot. Tried my sextant for the first time, but it was as much as I could do to hold it against the fiery orb. Somehow my observation miscarried, though I thought I had an excellent meridian altitude. My eyes trouble me very much.

"*Thursday*, *11th April.*—Tried my hand for the first time in taking lunars. It is a little difficult without any assistance, but with practice I must and shall succeed. Pity my eyes and general health are so bad. After the exertion of to-day and yesterday, and exposure to the sun, I feel very poorly. Axel fortunately is a little better, thank God! but the rest won't move during the livelong day from their recumbent position. A Damara is an annoying and miserable being when sick; but indeed, this seems to be generally the case with the natives of South Africa. Livingstone reports similarly of the Bakwains. Had the curiosity to count the number of seeds in ears of the small sort of grain cultivated by the Ovampo; in one I found 2,140, and in another 2,200, and these were only average sized ones. I am sure I have seen ears quite twice as large.

"*Friday, 12th April.*—Utterly unfit for work; feel as if bruised all over. My legs won't carry me; headache, etc.; all clearly fever symptoms. Began this morning cutting out a pair of leather ox saddle-bags. Don't know what to do for hides and reins. I now regret having parted with mine to Pereira. Clouds rise toward noon, but disappear before sunset.

"*Saturday, 13th April.*—Very poorly; Jacob sinking; no improvement with the Damaras, speaking generally. Axel continues pretty well, but weak.

"*Sunday, 14th April.*—Sat up till two o'clock this morning practising lunars and latitudes; weather begins to be chilly at night. Fear I shall suffer after such unusual exertions in my weak state.

"*Monday, 15th April.*—Unable to accomplish much work, still I strive hard to do a little every day. Poor Jacob! I have now very little hope of his recovery; the last emetic does not seem to have done him the slightest good, and I dare not proceed farther. The lad is so weak, and he eats nothing. Chykongo is about to go elephant-hunting.

"*Tuesday, 16th April.*—Overtasked my strength

altogether to-day; have made a light travelling mattress out of the old one; it will serve as a kind of cushion for a pack-ox, and thus not be in the way. That rascal Joseph has not responded to my call, and I myself must now do the whole work of preparation for the journey.

"Chykongo came past with a large hunting party. I only observed about twenty guns. It seems the chief utterly discards the Portuguese fire-arms, having lost all faith in them since the introduction by the European hunters of superior rifles. Very poorly; head and neck ache, and that dreadful pain in my stomach, which has now continued for more than three weeks. What can it be? Is the liver out of order? At times agonizing pain in chest. Not doctor enough to prescribe for myself; am afraid of aperients and purgatives; instead of lowering the system I require tonics. Poor Jacob continues terribly weak; I dare do no more for the lad. The old woman and the children continue in the same state. What is to be done with these people when I leave? I cannot wait for their recovery; as it is, I fancy I am risking my own life by remaining here; Chykongo will never know the sacrifice I have made in delaying so long. Weather cloudy and close. Shall we have a little more rain?

"*Wednesday*, 18*th April.*—Continue wretchedly weak, and that troublesome flatulency continues. Jacob eating a little to-day; but still I have no hopes of the poor lad.

"*Thursday*, 19*th April.*—Spent a very bad night; the little giblet soup I partook of last evening distended my stomach till it resembled a drum-head, and the pain in consequence was very severe. I had, in addition, slight attacks of ague and fever. Oh! when will this end? This morning I tried cold dripping wet sheets, and the wearing of a wet stomach-pack. Thermometer at noon, in the shade, 81 degs.

"*Friday, 20th April.*—Very bad night; pain in the stomach continues unabated. Felt quite faint from want of food, and, disregarding all consequences, partook of an ounce or two of boiled lean mutton and a plate of soup. Notwithstanding my indisposition, I got through a good deal of work. The big pair of pack-saddles are nearly ready, and those for the donkeys quite. Jacob remains in the same state, but eats heartily; what am I to do without him—the only interpreter I have? Thermometer inside the house, 81°. Continue slowly the perusal of Livingstone; it is a wonderful book, and the author a still more wonderful man. What a mass of information he possesses on various subjects; and then his fortitude and perseverance under the most trying circumstance are truly marvellous. Poor Venus! my best dog, died suddenly yesterday afternoon. Axel thinks she has been sick some time. What beasts those Ovampo are! I had scarcely turned my back on the carcass before some lads, who were near, whipped it up and devoured it.

"*Saturday, 21st April.*—Acted the cobbler to-day; my last 'sick' boot* has long been ailing, and as it is pretty comfortable, I have done my best to make a neat job of it. I have, moreover, attended to sundry other little matters in relation to the journey; but I generally pay dearly for my exertions. I am 'as weak as a rat,' and very much afraid that the acidity in the

* One of a peculiar form for Andersson's crippled leg.

stomach will end in dysentery, which God forbid! Poor Jacob! by this disease he has been reduced to a shadow. Fancy I have at length discovered the family to which that curious bird *Eforema* belongs. If I am not mistaken it is allied to the Abyssinian horn-bill, or it may be identical with it. Thermometer hardly reached 80° to-day, and yet it has felt very close in consequence of the thunder and lightning that is in the air.

"*Sunday, 22d April.* — Very poorly, and even weaker than usual. As yet the cold dripping sheets and wet body bandages have wrought no improvement in my health. Jacob as usual; the rest of my people in the same state as for some time past. Getting hard up for eatables, have repeatedly sent to Chykongo, but can get nothing from him. One of his wives, however, on my applying to her, brought a basket of beans of both kinds, and some meat. Thermometer under veranda at one P. M., 85°; cloudy, with thunder and lightning, but very little rain.

"*Monday, 23d April.* — Enjoyed a pretty good night, though troubled with dreams. Thought, consequently, to find myself stronger, but scarcely had I got over my cold bath before excessive faintness took possession of me; forced myself for awhile to work, but at last was glad to take to my bed. Thermometer under veranda from noon to three P. M., about 87°, at sunset 80°.

"*Tuesday, 24th April.*—O God! what a night I have spent! This indigestion, flatulency, or whatever it may be, will kill me if it continues much longer. I can hardly hold the pen, and my breathing comes so labored; pulse nearly 90°. Generally feeble. Goliath down with fever; Jacob's appetite increasing wonderfully. I have just managed to finish Livingstone; like the book far better this time than on my first perusal of it. He is certainly a most remarkable man.

" *Wednesday*, 25*th April*.—Another dreadful night. With desperate effort I mounted my horse for a little fresh air and exercise; could only walk him about. Counted a good-sized ear of Holcus Sorghum, and found close on fifteen hundred grains in it; another ear, now lying before me, is apparently twice its size. Thermometer at sunrise 60°, at noon 87½°, sunset 80°; wind northerly.

" *Thursday*, 26*th April*.—Spent another bad night; it is now nearly three days since I ate anything. Had a fowl killed and broiled; I sadly want meat, but it may not agree with me. There is something so very painful about my stomach as at times to amount to agony; I, moreover, feel so weak occasionally as hardly to be able to rise from my bed. Fancy the cold body bandage does me harm, and I shall, therefore, discontinue it for awhile; too weak to sponge my body. Averse as I am to medicine, I would give much to have a skilful doctor's advice and attendance. Jacob looks miserable, poor fellow; he spent the night at the quarters of Chykongo's chief wife, where he was made to partake of some doctor's stuff. Rumor says the Bushmen have killed a large male elephant; I hope it is true. Thermometer at sunrise, 56½°: noon to three P. M., 88°; sunset, 80°, Weather feels very oppressive; a few clouds about, but I fancy we have done with the rains for this season. Goliath very poorly.

"*Friday, 27th April.*—Again a bad night, though not quite to the extent of the two or three preceding ones. I am consumed with thirst; but everything I drink, be it water, toast and water, or what not, is instantly converted into gas. Took my usual horse exercise this morning, but felt very weak after it; always suffer most toward evening and during the night. Jacob decidedly getting better, but still very feeble. Thermometer at sunrise, 59°; noon, 89°; one o'clock P.M., 90°; sunset 81°.

"*Saturday, 28th April.*—Horse lost last night, and, as a consequence, no ride for this morning. It is too bad of Chykongo's people not to look better after the stallion, as he it is that draws away the mares. Thermometer at sunrise, 56°; noon, 87°; one o'clock, 89°; and at three, 90°; sunset, 82°.

"*Sunday, 29th April.*—Very ill last night; about midnight obliged to get up and take a few drops of morphia, which relieved me somewhat, but banished sleep. Took half-an-hour's exercise, and thought myself the better for it. Actually able to give myself a good washing, and to eat a tolerable breakfast. In the afternoon again became very much troubled with wind, which caused me great pain; feel sleepy. The country begins to wear an autumnal appearance; the grain has turned yellow, except patches here and there of *Holcus Sorghum*, which still lingers in its spring dress. The grass is turning whitish, and drooping, and some trees are losing their leaves. Thermometer at sunrise, 56°; noon, 87°; one o'clock, 88°.

"*Monday, 30th April.*—Another dreadful night; the gasses seem to be most commonly generated toward nightfall, ending in terrible pain in the pit of the stomach, or on each or both sides of it. Took my morning ride with less pain than usual. The air is so pleasant that one fancies it is impossible not to be benefited by it; but somehow I returned home weaker than I departed. Jacob seems poorly to-day. Thermometer at sunrise 53°, noon 87°, one o'clock 88°, sunset 82°.

"*Tuesday, 1st May.* — Night even worse than the preceding: compelled to rise from my bed about midnight, and administer to myself five or six drops of morphia, which afforded a slight relief; but am afraid it constipates the bowels. The quantity of gas in my stomach this morning was so great as to compel me to take a dose of salts, which had the desired effect, though without decomposing the gasses, which are what really trouble me. I don't know whether I act judiciously in taking any kind of medicine in my extremely debilitated condition, but what am I to do? I tried long enough without medicines; God help me now! I feel that if there is not soon some change for the better, my constitution cannot possibly hold out much longer; I try strenuously, as I have always done, to bear up under all kinds of illnesses: but I am now at times so weak as to be unable to rise up from my chair or bed.

"Thermometer at sunrise 54°, noon 88°, one o'clock 89°, three o'clock 90°, sunset 83°.

"Axel killed a fine large pau (*Otis Kori*). Poor fellow! he is very proud of his performance. The bird is in excellent condition, but weighs only twenty-two and a-half pounds.

"*Wednesday, 2d May.*—Managed the night pretty well by sticking to the small opiates lately begun; took also a small dose of calomel, and somehow fancied I was the better for it almost immediately afterward. I also indulged freely in drinking water obtained from crushed wheat, which at first I thought pleasant, but subsequently suffered severely from. Well, I must drink. Day dreadfully close and sultry. At sunrise the thermometer stood at about 60°, noon 89°, at three o'clock 91°, and at sunrise 82°.

"Chykongo returned last night, and his people to-day; quite empty-handed, I am told. These Ovampos only frighten the elephants and make them savage.

"*Thursday, 3d May.* — Terrible night; for once, morphia had not the desired effect; went out on horseback; had not had a gun in my hand before for several weeks. Had a fair chance at an Eforema, but this bird cares not a straw for No. 4. I will never go out again without having one barrel loaded with buck-shot.

"Very close last night; sky overcast as if it was about to rain. Thermometer at sunrise 63°, noon 88°.

"Killed an ox lately bought from Chykongo's son, which must at the time have been suffering from lung-sickness; sent the chief the neck and hide, the rest of the carcass we have carefully jerked, and it must last us a long while.

"*Friday, 4th May.*—Tolerably easy last night, with a single dose of morphia, and a small one of calomel toward morning; but tongue looks very bad. Rather chilly before sunrise, when the thermometer stood 54°; noon, 84°; sunset, 80°. The mornings are just bearable, but after twelve o'clock it is just the reverse. Have indulged to-day in a glass and a half of milk, and a sip or two of beer, neither of which, I suspect, has done me much good.

"Chykongo with me; he has promised to get things ready for my journey; but it seems doubtful whether Chykongo will be able to accompany me; if not it will be a serious disappointment.

"*Saturday, 5th May.*—A bad night, attributable in some measure I believe to my having taken a few drops too many of morphia, which constipated the bowels. Poor Jacob! down with a raging fever. Well, I must now give up all hopes of taking him to the Cunené, though it will be hard for me to be without an interpreter. Atmosphere chilly this morning; thermometer down to 49°, half-an-hour before sunrise; at noon, 88°; one o'clock, 88°; sunset, 82°. Caught Chykongo's son in the act of abstracting a pound of fine gunpowder from the packed saddle-bags. I can stand it no longer, and will complain to his father.

"*Sunday, 6th May.*—Bad night; ate a little arrowroot late, and fancy it was too much for the stomach. Thermometer, sunrise, 52°; noon, 88°; sunset, 83°.

"*Monday, 7th May.*—Rather uncomfortable night; took a large draught of buttermilk, it looked so tempting. Closed my letters of yesterday to Mr. H——, Een, Palgrave, Hartley, and wife. It is still with difficulty I can guide the pen for five minutes together. Cloudy and close. Thermometer from noon to three o'clock, 88° to 91°, according as the sky was bright or overcast. Jacob excessively low; have now no expectation of being able to take him on the journey; if I did, it would only remain to leave him where he might be worse than here. Should he get better he could join me in the Ovaquenjana by-and-by.

"*Tuesday, 8th May.*—Oh, horrors! the letters sent for the hunters nearly two months ago were returned to me last night. This is a great misfortune, as one of them related to my wagon, which was to meet me here on its return from Otjimbingue, about August. Again Chykongo sent to say he could only supply me with one pack-ox. This is really too bad, having preferred my wants to him nearly two months ago. I can't get anything from him. Have sent for the old gentleman this morning. Jacob has a lucid interval, and I might have a fair opportunity of explaining everything.

"*Wednesday, 9th May.*—Rode up to the chief's werft, but though I waited there a long time he did not show himself. Left word I expected him at home at once, where I soon afterward had the satisfaction of seeing him. Poor Jacob! so weak as hardly to be able to articulate, much less to interpret properly. Altogether it was the most languid and unsatisfactory interview that I had had with the chief. There is evidently something wrong; he seems to be careless of my reproaches. However, he says the people shall be ready to-morrow morning, when he will himself come down and see me off. May he keep his word. Declares that Joseph has absolutely refused to accompany me. Really such a scoundrel deserves severe chastisement, and I hope to live to see it inflicted; the man is without feeling thus to leave me in the lurch.

"Thermometer at sunrise, 50°; at one o'clock P. M., 84°; and at sunset, 76°."

CHAPTER XVIII.

Start for the River Cunené—Arrival at Nauma's werft—Ugly women—Extraordinary spectacle—Author's life endangered—Singular hair-dressing—Hyenas troublesome—The iron mine—Typandeka's hospitality— A great misfortune—Reach the Cunené—Altercation with ferry-men.

AS will be gathered from the last chapter, Andersson's health was at the time in a most precarious state, whence one would have supposed he would never have ventured on the journey he was about to undertake; but on the contrary, that he would have lost no time in heading back to his quarters at Otjimbingue, where medicine, proper food, etc., of which the poor fellow stood so much in need, were obtainable; but though quite aware of the desperate risk he ran, his indomitable spirit determined him to carry out his long cherished purpose of proceeding to the Portuguese settlement of Benguela, which, in fact, he all but accomplished, though, as the reader will presently learn, at the sacrifice of his life.—ED.]

JOURNAL.—*From Ondonga to the Cunené.*

" *Thursday, 10th May*, 1867.—Chykongo proved true to his word, though he arrived with his men very late. However, we effected a start from his place about 10.45. But my outfit, so to say, was a very sorry one; having, as I have said, sent the wagons and the greater part of my people in advance, it merely consisted of a few pack and slaughter-oxen, some milk goats, and a riding horse for myself. A good many natives, whom the chief had placed at my disposition, accompanied me. Off-saddled at 2.15. Quite one and a half hour's delay. Stood my first day's exertion exceedingly well, considering that prior to setting off I had to work hard to get things ready, besides half packing the oxen.

"*Friday*, 11*th May*.—Left bivouac at 7.40; reached Kombonde's werft at 10.5. Not more than five minutes' delay. Course about 305°. Thermometer at sunrise, 54°. Well received by the hereditary chief of Ondonga, who is said to be very stingy. Asked for a slaughter goat, but could only succeed in exchanging four of my dry milk goats for three supposed to be in milk, and one ram. Left Kombonde's werft in the afternoon (2.40 P. M.); bivouacked at 5.5. Perhaps five minutes' delay, but travelled slowly (Goliath taken ill); course about 306° or 307°. The night promises to be very cloudy. We are now in the wedge of Ondonga. Palgrave, ——, and others lay here for some time. Observed a troop of 'Ahem' cranes, consisting of ten.

"*Saturday*, 12*th May*.—Very cloudy and close night. Thermometer about half an hour before sunrise, 78°. Horse not recovered for nearly an hour after we had packed. Nevertheless, effected a start at 6.30 A. M. Entered at once the bush that divides Ondonga from Ovaquambi. It consists chiefly of oxonlati, and is exceedingly monotonous. A couple of months ago, the greater part of this country was under water, and now not a drop is to be seen. Halted at 9.30. Travelled well; course winding from 296° to 315°, average perhaps 305°. Off again at one P. M. Passed a couple of small vleys in half-an-hour. Filled our 'vabye,' and proceeded till 3.40, when we camped for the night, the men looking very tired. About twenty-five minutes, delay. Road very winding; course perhaps 315°. The bush not changed in character.

"*Sunday, 13th May.*—Cloudy first part of night, but it cleared up after midnight. Thermometer at sunrise, 50°. Left bivouac at 7.7; reached first village (rather cluster of villages) of Ovaquambi at 11.15. About half-an-hour's delay; course perhaps 215° (220°). The approach to the country is very beautiful, consisting of fine grass savannas, here and there dotted with lovely island-like clusters of trees. Presented with two young cattle, one of which I slaughtered for my own people and for our new-found friends. Nauma keeps up his name for hospitality and friendliness for Europeans. Loaded with dishes of porridge. There seems a great number of hamlets clustered together at this point. Can there be any particular object in this arrangement, or is it simply that the soil is universally favorable? Very sick.

"*Monday, 14th May.*—Though exceedingly ill, I tried hard to get an observation last night, but finding the sky obstinately cloudy, I unfortunately desisted, as toward midnight it cleared up beautifully. Thermometer a little before sunrise, 54°. Left bivouac about 5.3 A. M.; reached Nauma's werft at 11.35. Some twenty minutes' delay; course about 350°; too long in the saddle. Found Nauma nearly as he had been represented to me. But what surprises me most is his physiognomy, which is so different from that of his people. He reminds me exactly of old April at Otjimbi. He was dressed in a blue-striped shirt, moleskin trousers, and "veld" shoes, with a small wideawake hat on his head. Clothing does not misbecome him. Unlike other African chiefs, he did not let me wait for his arrival, but came up before I had off-saddled. We shook hands. Scarcely had we off-packed when he presented me with two sheep and a pig. Got also a can of honey from him; the very thing I have so much longed for. Ate some of it at once, but it disagreed with me, though I hope it will ultimately act as a laxative, my chief object in partaking of it. Can get no milk; all the cows have been sent away, the calves having died of lung-sickness. Must try to buy a few goats in milk. Found my old servant Africa just risen from his bed after a long attack of fever; very weak and hardly able to move about; willing enough to accompany me. While on the road here, it struck me it would be a good thing to get the loan of Nauma's cart, I dare say he will let me have it to the Ovaquamyama. Several Ombranderas were pointed out to me. This, I believe, is a tribe lately attacked by the Ovampo and the Ovangandyera. It is one of those tribes who have no chiefs.

"This country and Ondonga are almost fac-similes; but there seems to me to be a trifling difference, viz., the cultivated portions run in parallel ridges with something like well-defined 'omurambas' between, which portions must be more or less under water during the wet season. The ridges are covered with clusters of palm and other wild fruit-trees, but nowhere so plentiful as in Ondonga. The ground on these elevations is exceedingly well cultivated. The corn lands are much closer than in Ondonga. The latter has been represented as much larger than Waguarambi, but I question it. There seem plenty of people about. Africa tells me that the country extends considerably to the northward, but less to westward. Nauma keeps a bodyguard of some thirty or forty young men, who sleep in a shed abutting on his werft. These are ordered about on all sorts of occasions and business. Poor fellows; they are not allowed to grease themselves, which in this boiling climate must be a great privation. When the chief gives an order, the men are expected to run.

"*Tuesday, 15th May.*—Tried to have a little talk with Nauma, but it is hopeless, with such interpreters as I have. Has kindly lent me his cart and oxen; the pole of the former is broken, but being well lashed with supports, I am in hopes it may carry us safely to the Ovaquamyama. It will be a great comfort to have the vehicle, though small; it is a sort of house. Have presented Nauma with my double-barrelled two-grooved rifle, in which I have no particular confidence, and hope he will give me some cattle in return.

"*Wednesday, 16th May.*—Sat up till twelve o'clock last night taking observations, but, most strange to say, north and south differ some eight miles. Can the sextant have got injured? The meridian altitude of the sun gives also a widely different result. Took no medicine last night, for the first time for many weeks past. The honey does some good, though the stomach continues to feel frightfully distended. Left a bag of powder with Nauma for twenty milk goats and fifteen kids that he brought me. Asked the price of the rifle; but told him it was a present. Has promised to supply me with a herd. Sent half my party back to Ondonga. I have some suspicion that the rest will decamp ere long. Have treated them exceedingly well. On looking more closely at the pole of the cart I found it quite broken off, and consequently advisable to get a new one. Luckily Nauma has a piece or two of wood prepared in the rough. Had nearly finished it by sunset.

"*Thursday, 17th May.*—My Ovampo received a message last night from Nauma ordering them to sleep at a distance, on the plea that he and Chykongo were enemies. Confound such fancies! I will not stand it, and will tell him so. It put the men in a great fright, and they feared to go to sleep. What a strange state these tribes stand in toward each other; they never seem to be quite at peace. Luckily, their mutual wants compel them to keep open communication with each other, and thus trade and barter flourish in spite of the enmity of the rulers. Tried hard again last night to get north and south observations to come closer; but no. The several sets came out beautifully, differing only a few seconds from each other; but there is a difference of more than five seconds between north and south. What on earth can cause this? It is also the case with my little sextant, and I don't understand how to correct it. I am much chagrined at this, as I had reckoned so much on being able to take lunars. However, I don't despair of getting over the difficulty. Nauma did not visit our camp, because, he said, the Ovampos were there, and yet he came to us daily before. Went to him in the afternoon and represented to him how unfair and capricious was his conduct. Made a fresh arrange ment with him—viz., I am to let the Ovampos return to their homes, he supplying me with the necessary complement of men in their stead. He insists upon it that the Ondonga people are no friends of the Ovaquamyama, as they are always shooting them off. This is contrary to Chykongo's statement, who assured me that they were great friends. I am quite at a loss to understand the motives and feelings of these people. There was Chykongo, for instance, declaring that he had sent twice to Nauma to make inquiries about the man who had run away with some cattle; but that chief denied such being the case. In fact no man had absconded. Africa, however, declares that the man is now living close to Kombonde.

"*Friday*, 18*th. May*—Therm., sunrise, 52°; sunset, 78°. Did not effect a start till 8.30; waiting all the time for Nauma to bring some vegetables, according to promise, and after all I found we were to get the supply at some village ahead. Came to a halt at 9.40, course 55°. Here we got a few small baskets of meal and a couple of baskets of beans. This is shabby of Nauma, after the handsome present I made him; the more so as I have only received from him a couple of cows and one slaughter-ox. Left again at 12.45. No more corn-fields in this direction. At two o'clock entered the bush; bivouacked at 3.50; have experienced very great trouble with the people. Nauma has sent me the whole of his body-guard, besides a number of other men. These fellows are accustomed to be tyrannized over by their master, and now that they find themselves masterless they show their devilish nature to perfection; a greater set of scoundrels I never had to deal with. What on earth possessed Nauma to send them? If he had given me three or four men it would have been quite sufficient, and I feel certain I should have got my work done properly. Now, if I issue an order, there is a general stare, and then a burst of laughter. One fellow had actually the insolence to imitate my poor limping gait. It is very unprofitable and undignified to be running after these fellows with a stick. We all know how troublesome it is to change servants; but when servants are every time to be taught their duties afresh it becomes a heart-rending affair.

"*Saturday, 19th May.*—Thermometer, half-hour before sunrise, 58°. Off again at 6.50 A. M.; came to a halt at eleven. Road frightfully winding; hardly know what course to put down; say 65°. Left again at 2.29; till 4.5 course about 25°; till 5.10, when we bivouacked, 45°. Plenty of water on this 'treck;' great dearth of birds and game; observed, however, some 'spoor.' The only quadrupeds hitherto met with were a few zebras, two gnus, and a steinbok. Sun burned very much in the afternoon.

"*Sunday, 20th May.*—Thermometer about an hour before sunrise, 43°; afternoon, 79°. Thank God! we are quit of the greater part of our escort. What is left don't promise much; I never was more disappointed in my life. Left bivouac at 6.40; came to halt at 10.10 A.M. For the first two-and-a-half hours course about 20°; afternoon, 85°. Road very winding. Water boils here at (defective thermometer) 206°; best, 206°; atmosphere five minutes previously, 79½°. If correct, this gives a fall of 1,000 feet since leaving Ovaguambi.

Hardly possible, and yet I cannot be mistaken. The fall and drainage of the Omurambas are directly northward to the Cunené. We have only just entered the Ovaquamyama country, and can, therefore, hardly judge of its appearance. Left again at 2.50; came abruptly to a standstill as early as 3.40, because a fellow says something about having to conduct us to the chief to-morrow. What a nuisance. Course about 85° or 90°. Thus far I rather like the country; it is a great change from Ondonga and Waguambi. You cannot see a hamlet here till close upon it, being invariable buried, in or rather, perhaps, surrounded with, trees or bushes, and the whole, often several miles in circuit, encompassed by a stout hedge of thorns. There are plenty of fruit trees, besides the ordinary forest trees, but only one palm as yet. I have great hopes of making a good collection of specimens of natural history, should Typandeka, the chief we are about to visit, prove favorable to us. The Omurambas have plenty of water and water-fowl. Observed large numbers of Sabini. The specimens of women hitherto seen are exceedingly ugly and unwomanly in appearance. They wear large skins clumsily arranged behind, and the hair is outrageously dressed.

"*Monday, 21st May.*—Treated last night night by the chief with maggot-filled beans for supper. It would seem as if the natives could not keep this vegetable from one harvest to another without its being quite destroyed by worms. However, to them, I dare say it is of no consequence, nay, perhaps an advantage, since, when in the state described, the beans serve for both meat and bread. Treated to an extraordinary spectacle this morning. A number of women suddenly made their appearance, their whole bodies, the crown of the head excepted, being covered with ashes, giving them the most hideous appearance; and, to heighten the disfigurement, they had strings of decayed corn-stalks slung across their shoulders, which produced a rattling sound when moving. They were without ornaments of any kind, the skins being attached to the waist by strips of bark.

"What can be the object of this hideous disfigurement? They began a kind of chant (one woman only in the first instance) terminating in a general shrill chorus, with a shout at the end of it. Could it have been as a compliment to us? We were just intending to 'unspan,' when the chief insisted on our awaiting the return of the messenger from Typandeka, who soon afterward arrived, telling us we must wait three days before that chief could receive us. I felt sure this was an imposition, but said nothing. An hour afterward another messenger made his appearance, who informed us we might 'treck' to the chief's werft the next day at noon. I must, however, try to get off early to-morrow morning, as I cannot stand the sun. Axel out shooting, but obtained only a few ducks and some common small birds; says he saw some *Lamprotonies* of a new species, but from the description he gave of them, I suspect they were *Talacoma Retsi.* One of the men accompanying Axel was treacherously shot in the eye by an arrow. The poor fellow's companion tried to catch the intended murderer, but the bush favored his escape. The shaft was poisoned, and, in extracting it the eye was pulled out of the socket. Thermometer at sunrise, 64°; noon, 84°; and 74° at sunset.

"*Tuesday, 22d May.*—Thermometer at day-break 46°. The people told me not to 'treck' until the sun got warm, but conceiving this to be merely a ruse for their own convenience, I effected a start at 7.19; and when they saw me resolved, no opposition was attempted. At first our course was nearly 330°, afterward the route wound about so very greatly that I am unable to determine it, perhaps 3c, 350°. About twenty minutes' delay; off again at 2.48 P. M. Arrived at Typandeka's at 5.45; no delay, the road dreadfully circuitous. For the first hour we steered, I imagine 340°. Afterward between N. and 45°. Average perhaps 15°.

"Compelled to strike one of the Ovaquamyama fellows for utter disregard to my orders, upon which the scoundrel had the audacity to level an arrow at me; seeing however that I did not flinch, he thought better of it; he being worse than useless to me I got rid of him forthwith. The rest, though bad enough, I can get on with.

"What reception shall I meet with from Typandeka? The success of my future efforts depends entirely on his good-will. The sight of a white man and his accompaniments are still a curiosity. Troops of men, women, and children are following us for hours. The cart seems chiefly to occupy their attention. The men, so far as I have seen, are fine-looking fellows, while the women, on the contrary, are frequently hideous; in great part, however, owing to their attire. The way the hair is dressed is remarkable for both variety and ugliness; it defies all description, with some it is made up in such a manner as to look like great coils of snakes.

" Astonishing number of wild fruit trees about the hamlets ; but the palm is not quite so frequently seen as in Ondonga. The baobab is rather common, but quite small. The fruit is just ripe, I forgot that it was eatable till I saw my fellows partaking of it ; it has a pleasant taste, and contains a good deal of yellowish white pulp, with softish kernels, and longitudinally disposed thread-like veins which greatly interfere with the extraction of the eatable portion.

" I have seen the redoubtable Typandeka, and was very well received. He even took me to his werft, which is very similar to Chykongo's, but more lightly constructed. The palisading is higher. After walking through several open spaces, we entered the long avenue, at the end of which we began to zig-zag. Counted ten doublings ere we came to the *sanctum sanctorum*, which was a fine large space surrounded with three or four huts, evidently his sleeping apartments. A woman covered with ornaments entered during our *tête-à-tête*, and on asking him if that was his wife, I understood him to say she was a dowager of his predecessor, but I am not sure. Before leaving the chief I witnessed some dancing of both sexes (they were held apart). The women clapped their hands to some words pronounced by one of them, the rest joining in chorus after each burst. The men kept jingling two sticks together, individuals occasionally springing out a few paces, as if in pursuit of something. On the whole it was more interesting than the dancing at Ondonga.

" Typandeka very curious to know who was the greatest chief. Of course there was but one answer, and in this instance quite truthful. Presented me with a fine slaughter ox. The chief's head was ornamented with a great many (say from twenty to thirty) of the large white shells so much valued by African savages. He had also several about each arm, near the shoulder. Round his waist he wore an enormous stiff leathern girdle, quite eighteen inches in breadth. To this was attached four immense bunches of finely and evenly cut reims, arranged one behind and three in front, two of the latter being situated a little higher than the centre one. All these bunches are dyed jet black, while the girdle is smeared and greased with some red stuff. The effect is good. The figure of the chief is somewhat gawky, and he walks badly. The ornaments just named are worn by comparatively few. Can they be a sign of rank?

" *Wednesday*, 23*d May*.—Took excellent southern star observations last night, but only one northern, and that was evidently just past the meridian. If not much out, the difference was little more than two minutes; am anxious to get a few more to certify or disprove this approximation to correctness.

" Slaughtered Typandeka's ox, which yielded excellent meat, but little or no inside fat. The Ovaquamyama are getting worse and worse; am half distracted as to what is to be done with them. I am afraid to touch them; must try and send home the worst. Typandeka paid me a visit in the afternoon, brought me an enormous basket of meal; talks of buying my flint-guns, powder, etc. asked him what he would like to have, should my wagon return this way from Otjimbingue, but could get no decisive answer. Everything shown to him he would buy; this I much doubt.

"Weather rather close to-day, though the thermometer only ranged at sunrise, 55°; noon, 81°; sunset, 75°. The sun scorches very much in the afternoon; troubled with head and neck ache; very poorly; Goliath ill; Africa improving, I think. Finished my letter to the Portuguese authorities, in English, Dutch, and Swedish. The Hollandish gave me the only trouble, never having previously indited half-a-dozen epistles in that language, and those were addressed to people who understood not good Dutch.

"Axel out shooting, but met with no success; great scarcity of birds. No water, and consequently no waders. This is a great disappointment, as it may compel me to move ahead to the neighborhood of the river, which I should like to visit first. I have a mind, instead of requesting Typandeka to furnish me with men, to proceed with letter to the commandant at Humbi, that he would allow some of his people to accompany me to the Cunené, and the black chief of the Ongombi tribe, who I don't think trusts the Portuguese. Spoke to the Ovaquamyama last night about their disobedience, and said that I would require three of them to stay with me; they appeared satisfied; but would they take their departure, and leave those I have pointed out? I will not trust them.

"*Thursday, 24th May.*—Thermometer at sunrise, 51°; noon, 81°; sunset, 75°. The Ovaquamyama have not yet faced homeward as ordered; urge they must first be told by Typandeka that they are to do so. Well, if they choose to stay I will not feed them.

"Sun scorchingly hot in the afternoon, suffered dreadfully to-day; toward evening the pain became almost unbearable, so weak as hardly to be able to hold up my head. When I think of what I am about to undertake in my present debilitated condition, the matter looks desperate, but I must not be disheartened ; I have overcome worse difficulties. Quite at a loss to know what course to pursue, whether to attempt reaching Humbi first by going there on horseback, or trying to take the cart as far as the river? The latter course would be preferable, as I don't see how I am to divide my sick and weak party. On inquiring from our Ovaquamyama guide as to the nature of the country in advance, he declared it was too bushy for a wagon, but I would risk that, as we could make slow and short journeys.

"*Friday, 25th May.*—In vain I tried my sextant last night with fresh corrections to index glass ; the result remains the same. Curiously enough, the meridian altitude of sun gives the same result as the average of the N. and S., and S°. Took a dose of morphia last night, which helped me very much, and made me feel less heavy in the morning. In the afternoon the pain returned in all its force. Visited Typandeka at his request. There was great banqueting going on ; no men, however, except such as entered from time to time for orders, seemed to be allowed in his own 'Kotla,' only some of his wives and children. Saw the drummers for the first time ; they hold the drum between the legs, just above the knee, and then stoop forward, applying chiefly the palms of their hands to the parchment. In the middle of the latter is a large black patch of some gluey substance, which is constantly applied to. One purpose is evidently for stopping up the places that have got windy. Made a rough sketch of the chief's wife; not her features, for she could not sit still a moment, but her dress and ornaments I got pretty well. The decorations on the heads of some of the women consisted of huge plaits of artificial hair, set closely with cowrie shell, the whole weighing certainly not less than thirty or forty pounds. The women thus decked are compelled always to support the hair with their hands. It strikes me that after awhile the whole is cut off, for many women have quite short crops, with a few beads or other trifling ornament attached. I saw one with three hair-pins, the top forming a cross of ivory stuck upright at the back of the head, and the effect was not bad. I find some of the women wear a leathern girdle, with huge tassels attached, in like manner as the men. Thermometer, sunrise, 51½°; noon, 80°; sunset, 75°.

"*Saturday, 26th May.*—Spent a wretched night; am afraid I have to thank Typandeka's beer for that. Poor Axel continues to suffer from toothache, and Africa is in bed. Thus not one of us in health. Night quite close and very cloudy. Thermometer, at sunrise, 62°; noon, 81°; sunset, 72°. Typandeka has presented me with a tusk (ivory) of about forty-five pounds' weight, and a cow and a calf. He certainly behaves well toward me; better, I fancy, than any other.

"*Sunday, 27th May.*—Hyenas and jackals exceedingly troublesome at night; the dogs are very watchful, but keep a safe distance from the first-named brutes. Without dogs, however, one could not rest in safety, exposed as we are. To set a spring-gun would be of no use, as the jackals would spoil all. Typandeka with me; spoke to him about ordering such of the Ovaquamyama as I did not require to return to their homes. He seemed but half inclined to undertake the task. At all events I am determined henceforth only to supply three of them with food. Made the chief a present of two pounds of coarse powder, and five pounds of common beads. I find only certain kinds of the iatter are bought for ivory, the rest cattle. He promised me two or three samples of the former. Rallied him about making me wait a day behind on first entering his country, to which he replied, that the werft was sickly at the time, and that it was needful to purify it before I could be seen. Of course this is all stuff. Told him to treat white men well, as it was by so doing that Chykongo had become the great man he was. 'With what shall I make my peace with them?' he inquired. 'Oh, nothing in particular,' I rejoined; 'only behave well to them, and don't deny their reasonable requests; if, for instance, they wish to hunt elephants in your country, or to visit the rivers, give them men and let them go.' He seemed pleased at hearing this, as my request appeared rather to startle him.

"*Monday, 28th May.*—The hyenas continue to infest the neighborhood during the night, but all the dogs being then at large, we are well guarded. Were I well I would endeavor to kill some of them. The glands at the back of my throat are now swollen to such an extent that it is with the utmost difficülty and pain, I can swallow anything, even though it be only a little liquid. The ailment has assumed a more serious form than at Ondonga, where I had the white sore throat badly enough; it now affects my whole head, and I have difficulty in pronouncing a few words. May it all end for the best! But may it please Thee, Almighty God, to afford me some relief, as in my present weak condition I cannot well withstand such a complication of disorders. Poor Axel's teeth continue to give him much pain, and Goliath is helpless with his aching leg. Truly we are a piteous gathering. The Ovaquamyama have at length taken themselves off, leaving me only two boys, which is just one too few for my purpose. I thought at one time that every soul of them had deserted. Another basket of meal; but we are getting too much, as, do what we will, that which we already possess is spoiling. Thermometer at sunrise, 53°; noon, 80°.

"*Tuesday, 29th May.*—Thank God! the swelling in my throat has burst, and a quantity of disagreeable matter came away, which afforded instant relief; and, so far as the infliction in question is concerned, I now entertain hopes of a speedy recovery. Very ill in the afternoon, arising in great measure, I doubt not, from indulging in a cup of sour milk during the last two days. It is clear I must stick to solids as much as possible. The coldest day we have yet had; the thermometer not rising to 80°; at sunrise, 48°; noon to two o'clock, 79°; sunset, 72°.

"*Wednesday, 30th May.*—Typandeka sent to say he was sick, and wished me to come to him; but I had neither horse nor man at command. Very ill the whole afternoon; the nights and mornings are just bearable; the rest of the day I am so weak that it is with difficulty I can rise from my seat. Toward nightfall, moreover, headache and pains in the back of the neck set in with great severity. Africa very poorly; Axel obliged to lie down for awhile owing to toothache and cold shiverings, but toward evening was much better. I quite dread his falling ill, as he is now the only one I have to depend on. Read in Smollett to-day how the Duke of Buckingham (Villiers) debauched the Countess of Shrewsbury, and then published her shame; and not content with this, he so repeatedly taunted her husband that the poor fellow was at last compelled to send him a challenge, which proved at once fatal to him. The same day the brutal Duke proceeded to the deceased's seat, where he lay with his wife, having previously shown her the blood of her husband on his sword. I am afraid I shall never get this terrible tale out of my head, and I fervently thank God I don't live in an age when brutality and force were the only qualities that ennobled a man. Good God! that such crimes should really be overlooked, and the man who committed them actually honored with the first place in the king's regards.

"*Thursday*, 31*st May.*—Typandeka with me; asked him as to the situation of the iron mine, which he says is not far distant, and within his own country. As regards the last point, I have my doubts, being inclined to think it lies in some district impoverished by his invasions. Promised to procure me a specimen of the ore. He declares that, with the exception of a few tusks of cow-elephants scattered about his werft, he has no ivory whatever; if so, he must then have sold it to the Portuguese since Een was here. Promised me a basket and a copper-sheathed knife.

"*Friday*, 1*st June.*—The chief sent me as a present a four-pound tusk. Axel taken ill with fever during the night. Went out shooting myself, but the horse having walked from me, I was compelled to foot it home. Fortunately I was equal to the task; but had the same thing happened in the afternoon instead of the morning, I must have been left in the veldt. Killed a fine handsome specimen of what I fancy is to be a new species of *Lamprotonies*. In the afternoon very ill; Africa also weak, and unable to do any kind of work. It is strange we should all be attacked with low fever. Can there be anything in Typandeka's assertion that our camp is too cold. I have no doubt there is water beneath us, for I find the natives often digging at the root of fig-trees.

"*Saturday, 2d June.*—Axel so much better as to be able to go about his ordinary business. As for myself I am wretched; my bowels must be terribly out of order. One of the Ovaquamyama lads sulky, and has actually run away. I must try to catch the scoundrel, and, at all risks, give him a good flogging. Thermometer at sunrise, 48°; noon 78°; sunset, 74°.

"*Sunday, 3d June.*—Very poorly, my stomach is becoming almost as disorded as when at Ondonga. I must take more exercise; but it hurts me, the head being always more or less affected thereby. Typandeka sent word he would visit me, and that some ivory would be forthcoming for the guns. Informed him in reply that I myself was very ill, which, as he did not make his appearance, probably prevented his coming. Thermometer at sunrise, 42°; noon, 79°; sunset, 72°.

"*Monday, 4th June.*—Spent a dreadful night, and thinking greater exercise might do me good, took a long ride in a new direction. Swallowed a dose of salts this morning, as I am perfectly constipated. Africa continues weak. Typandeka with me; told him of my desire to visit the Cunené and Humbi. To my proceeding to the river he had no objection to make, but said it was useless for me to go to Humbi, as the people there were unfriendly. This is all nonsense. In my very helpless state, however, I can do nothing but bide events, and some lucky incident may yet enable me to put myself in communication with the Portuguese. If not, I shall probably retrace my steps to Ondonga, as soon as possible, and from thence to Damaraland. My health will never hold out another year without medical aid. Asked Typandeka to send one of the Bangara traders to me. Thermometer at sunrise, 41°; noon, 74°; sunset, 68°. This is one of the coldest days we have had. A northerly breeze, which is quite unusual, has been blowing.

"*Tuesday, 5th June.*—Thermometer at sunrise, 40°; noon, 74°. Out shooting; both the Ovaquamyama boys hiding away in the bush; have sent to the chief, requesting him to furnish me with others in their stead. Trust he will grant my request, for this is quite distressing.

"*Wednesday, 6th June.*—The lads just spoken of appeared by the cattle in the course of the morning; gave them no food last night, which acted better than a flogging, for there was no trouble with them to-day, but how long will it last? Typandeka sent for me in the afternoon; but being very unwell I felt half inclined to refuse the invitation; went, however, to his werft, where I was kept waiting a full hour, and when I saw him he seemed half drunk. He offered me some Portuguese brandy, which I refused with disgust; he also proffered me two kinds of beer, one of them so full of meal that it might be said to contain both food and drink.

"*Thursday, 7th June.*—The chief made his appearance about 9 o'clock, with some men; at 11.30 A.M., I succeeded in making a start. Axel played me a thoughtless trick at the outset, which nearly put an end to the day's journey; but luckily all terminated satisfactorily at the expense of some twenty minutes' delay. Proceeded till 4.40 P. M., when I off-saddled; the guides wanted to go farther, but I was quite done up; course at first pretty steady at 155°, but varied; afterward between 155° and 140°, the last half hour we even went 120°; nevertheless the average will probably be 150°. Travelled at a good pace

"As far as we have thus come there would be no difficulty about bringing a wagon; we only passed two insignificant bushes. In traversing the last wood, which offered no impediment to our vehicle, I observed the singular fact that nearly every tree of a certain species was all but destroyed, little more than the trunk itself, and sometimes not even that, remaining. It must be a very brittle wood and easily injured; no other tree seemed to have suffered any damage.

"*Friday, 8th June.*—Thermometer at sunrise, 44°. Left bivouac at 7.30 A. M.; road frightfully winding. For the two-and-a-half hours I was at a loss to put down a course, say 140°. Came to a halt at 11.10; nearly an hour's delay, and slow, irregular travelling.

"Up to this point villages very numerous, and there seemed more corn, which grows to great perfection.

Observed no jungle forest, but immense number of baobabs. Off again at two o'clock. Find our halting place is really the end of the inhabited portion of the country to the westward. Came to a halt after what I fancied must have been two-and-half hours' smart travelling, but cannot tell exactly, as my watch got one of her fits to stop. Passed several vleys, but not a water-bird to be seen. Regular Waguambi bush and forest; hitherto there have been no particular obstacles for a wagon. Deadly ill; drink large quantities of icy-cold water. I dare say it does me no good, but I cannot help it. Got large reinforcement of men to our original outfit, some thirty in all now. I suppose they are afraid to visit the river in small parties. Course nearly 140°.

"*Saturday, 9th June.*—Left bivouac at 5.55 A. M.; came to a halt at 9.35; two minutes' delay. Course most variable; for the first two hours perhaps 130°, afterward as much as 150°, if not more northerly. I never travelled with any natives who understood moving on a straight line so little. Every five minutes we are off at an angle of 45°.

"Saw one wild pig and an ostrich. Axel fired unsuccessfully at the former. I fancy the lad got frightened, as the pig was coming toward him, probably with a view of seeing what object it could be. The country seems very destitute of game, but there are spoors of elands, giraffes, and gemsboks. Off again at twelve; bivouacked at three o'clock; course for the first two hours nearly north, or about 170°, afterward, perhaps 140°. The people, who have now become utterly unmanageable, move about in the most disorderly manner. They chase squirrels the whole day. Observed a troop of hartebeest, and another of elands. Country quite open for wagons; I am inclined to think the people are taking us a circuitous route, but for what purpose heaven only knows.

"*Sunday*, 10*th June*.—Thermometer at sunrise 50°. Left bivouac at 6.18 A. M.; came to a halt at 9.18, perhaps ten minutes' delay; course nearly north. Suddenly abandoned this morning, not only by the two Ovaquamyama lads, but by all Typandeka's people, the guide included. What can be the meaning of such villainous conduct? Surely the chief never meant us to be conveyed into a perfect desert, and there left to shift for ourselves? However, if they thought that by leaving us they would cause us to turn back, they will find themselves egregiously mistaken. It is not the first time I have been thus treacherously dealt with; but then I had my own men in sufficient numbers. Now there are but two left to me, one of whom must carry a heavy burden, and he, moreover, is weak and ailing in his leg; but what I most dread is the want of water. Of food we have as yet enough, but the precious liquid seems scarce. I was very thankful therefore, when I found a fine vley after three hours' travel. Observed bustard, gemsboks, wild pigs, and a troop of elands. Axel had a shot at one of the latter, and says he wounded it. Off again at 1.50 P. M.; bivouacked at 4.30. Course nearly 160°; travelled steadily and without delay. Saw much game, both four-footed and feathered; as also the recent tracks of others. Francolins, of more than one kind, were very abundant. Our Otjimbingue friend killed an individual which I at first took to be new to me, but it may be *Fr. S.*, only it is so small. Was fortunate enough to find a fine vley of water, by which we bivouac. Thus one day of our forlorn condition is happily ended.

"*Monday*, 11*th June.*—Thermometer at sunrise, 45°. Left camp at 5.53; came to a halt at seven, in consequence of Axel having a violent attack of tooth-ache. This is a great drawback, as one does not know when he will get better of it. Lions about during the night and this morning. Axel's ox ran away with and threw him, breaking girths, nose-rein, etc. Have had the great misfortune to lose my watch keys; and, as ill-luck will have it, I have no pinchers or tongs small enough to serve as substitutes. Got a real fright; for a couple of hours both horse and cattle were lost to us, having strayed to a distance; their disappearance for good would have been tantamount to the sacrifice of my own life, at least, since I can hardly walk a distance of one hundred paces.

"*Tuesday*, 12*th June.*—Thermometer at day-break, 45°. Left bivouac some twenty minutes before sunrise; and after, as nearly as I can guess, two and a-half hours' travel, reached the Cunené, or rather its overflowings, for no stream was visible to the eye, all that was to be seen being an immense expanse of reeds and rushes, where we again came to a halt. Both Axel and Goliath seemed much gratified that I had brought them thus far in safety.

"On the way from our last bivouac, we observed some giraffes, and Axel, who by this time had recovered from his tooth-ache, shot a duiker, and in the reeds now before us we noticed some antelopes, and an abundance of water-fowl. The forest, moreover, swarming with birds. Water boils here at 107½° ; atmosphere shortly before 88°. No, it was next to impossible to read off the true thermometer, it having become so blackened ; the defective one, however, reads about the same. In the afternoon, while debating as to the likelihood of our soonest reaching the river by following the reeds in question in an eastern or western direction, some seven or eight natives, a few of them armed with the old Portuguese musket, suddenly made their appearance, and that without showing signs either of surprise or apprehension. I gave them some Cavendish tobacco and meat, with which they seemed mightily pleased; fortunately, they understood the Damara language so well that Goliath was enabled to converse with them pretty fairly. Told us they belonged to Humbi, or Gombe, as it was pronounced in these parts, and that we were not far from thence ; that we must follow the banks of the river, and then an Omuramba, which would lead us to the ferry, where we had only to shout to be heard by the ferry-men on the other side, and to be responded to. The commandant, they said, would be delighted to see us. May all this prove true ; as to the river itself they described it as small. How can this be? All Europeans who have been favored with a sight of the Cunené, have described it as a glorious river, with magnifient scenery on its banks. The only explanation I can give is that, from the country hereabouts being so flat, the side-flowings absorb so much of the main stream. In some parts the vegetation reminds one of the Okavango and the Teoughe. Evidently much game hereabouts. Axel had a couple of shots at pallahs, and says he saw two dark brown antelopes without either *horns or tails!* What on earth could they have been?

"*Wednesday, 13th June.*—Could hardly shut my eyes last night, from thinking of the pack-oxen, which managed to elude our attention just before tying-up time. As soon as it was light enough, I set out, with Goliath and Axel, in search of the animals, hoping to find them close to our camp; but in this I was wofully disappointed; had the utmost difficulty in discovering and following their 'spoor,' which was lost dozens of times, I accompanied the lads to near our former bivouac when I returned to camp, giving them strict injunctions not to show themselves without the cattle. It seems these had touched and drunk at the vley, and then, without stopping to feed, had pursued their course for Ovaquamyama; however, they were overtaken before they had gone far, and were safely brought back in the afternoon. Now, suppose they had been lost in earnest, our lot would have been a miserable one. I have not enough people to attend to everything, and feel sure that the brutes will continue to give us trouble and anxiety as we proceed. Lions about during the night. It is a great mercy they did not come across the strayed cattle. Thermometer at sunrise, $43\frac{1}{2}°$; noon, 88°; and in the sun, 105°. Having lost so much time, I packed up in the afternoon; but it was a foolish thing to do, as both men and beasts were fagged. The sun, moreover, is frightfully scorching. Goliath suffers so much from his leg that he is unable to walk, and stands with difficulty. After more than an hour's languid travelling, we bivouacked on the bank of the river, which we can now fairly see for the first time ; but it is as yet an insignificant stream. Excessively poorly.

"*Thursday*, 14*th June*.—Goliath managed to assist in packing the oxen ; gave him one to ride, while Axel carried the sextant, etc. After about one and a half hours' travel we came to a place where many paths met, and where people had been sleeping ; thought it best to pack-off and shout. The Gombe men spoken of, said the ferry was not far off, and I am afraid of passing it, the more so as the road ahead does not look near so well beaten. After an immense deal of shouting and bawling, we were at length answered, and in the afternoon five men made their appearance ; treated them to snuff and a little meat, and sent them up to inform the Commandment at Humbi of my arrival. Gave them a copy of my passports, and a short note to their chief; trust they will safely deliver the little packet, which they took charge of with considerable distrust.

"*Friday*, 15*th June*.—Thermometer at sunrise, 43½° ; and at mid-day, 87°. In the afternoon the men to whom I had intrusted my letter returned with it unopened, and of course unread. This made me at once suspect they had never delivered it. Nor could we make head or tale of their statements, which were mere rigmarole. However, they said the white men were awaiting us, and that we had better cross over ; the werft, they added, was not far off. I did not much like following their advice, but, seeing no better alternative, we saddled up and went down to the river, where, after taking the things from off the cattle, we were told we must pay before proceeding further. This at once confirmed my suspicions as to their never having informed the Portuguese of our arrival. I was taken a little aback, and told them that I did not know that it was customary to pay beforehand, but that, nevertheless, I would do what was reasonable. 'What would be the payment? I inquired. 'Beads, a coat, calico, or the like,' was the reply. I had neither the one nor the other to spare, but promised to procure the needful from the Portuguese as soon as we arrived at their station. 'No,' said they, 'we will first go home, but return early to-morrow.' 'If such be the case,' I said, in rejoinder, 'you will not find us here.' But they remained deaf to my remonstrances, probably never dreaming that I would keep my word, and departed the way they came. When they were gone, we returned to our bivouac, which, though only a few hundred yards distant, I was hardly able to reach from weakness, and where, after vomiting a great quantity of water, I all but swooned away.

"*Saturday, 16th June.*—So ill for a few hours last night that I almost despaired of my life; another such attack or two would, I feel certain, prove fatal. It seems to me that life at times hangs on an elastic string, which an unusual tension will instantly sever. If it were not for the few drops of morphia that I take nightly, I should never be able to resist these repeated attacks of excessive weakness. At times I think it a little hard never more to see the faces of the beloved ones, but then I resign myself to God's will.

"Left bivouac at sunrise; got back to our old sleeping place in good time. Observed numerous pallahs, and had I been provided with a rifle could easily have brought down a couple. Succeed at last in securing the new craterope, that I have observed since our arrival on the river.

"Just at dusk Axel succeeded in knocking over a large male water-buck (*Aigocerus Ellipsiprymnus*), probably an adult. I wish it had been a pallah instead, as its flesh is reported to be most unpalatable; however, it is meat, and we are now safe from starvation. But we can only carry a small portion with us; it is to be hoped, however, the natives will come, when we might exchange as much as we don't require for vegetables, etc.

"*Sunday, 17th June.*—The meat of the water-buck answers to its ill-repute, being excessively tough and unsavory; even the heart and liver are barely eatable. In the afternoon a number of Humbi men made their appearance; treated them to meat and tobacco, and offered to exchange some of the former for meal, beans, etc.; said they were willing, and would return to-morrow with the needful; hope they will keep their word, as Axel, my store-keeper, is now without the former, and his beans are all but gone also. Excessively ill myself; had a sharp attack of ague.

"*Monday, 18th June.*—Axel came full upon a large male lion this morning as he was seeking for a wounded bird; this is the second time he has been lucky enough to fall in with one of those beasts. He says it took not the slightest notice of him, and to the report of his gun was equally indifferent."

CHAPTER XIX.

Premonitions of death—Axel Ericson's account of Andersson's last days—Extreme sufferings—Death of the traveller—Notice of his career and death in the "Cape Town Mail"—General regret in Sweden—Recognition of his merits as a Discoverer—In Memoriam.

ON the 16th of June, as shown by Andersson's Journal, he retraced his steps to his former encampments, where he remained until the 18th; when, worn-out with his manifold sufferings, and chagrined at the treatment he had met with at the hands of the ferrymen, he turned his back on the Cunené, and set off on his return to Ondonga, and this under no very favorable auspices; as to say nothing of his most miserable state of health, his whole escort, so to speak, consisted merely of the two lads, Axel and Goliath, the rest of his people, as recently shown, having deserted him.

But this his retrograde movement was made too late, for the hand of death was then upon him, and though he lingered a short time longer, in which his sufferings would appear to have been dreadful; yet, with the exception of a letter to one of his people regarding his worldly affairs, and a most affectionate one to his poor wife,* both of which were penned only a

* After speaking of some private matters, he goes on to say:

"I wanted to have told you a long time ago of my approaching death, but had not the courage to do so; and now I find it is nearly too day or two before his dissolution, he does not appear to have been capable of any exertion whatever. We are, therefore, indebted for what is known of his last days to his faithful follower, Axel Ericson, who, in a letter to poor Mrs. Andersson, says:

"Not hearing further from the Bangarris, and no other course being left to him, Mr. Andersson, then worn out with illness, determined on retracing his steps to Ondonga. On the fourth day, we reached the first of the Ovaquamyama werfts, but the people refused to show us the way to the chief's residence, and we were therefore necessitated to find it out as best we could by the aid of the compass. At length, on the sixth day, we arrived at Typandeka's abode, Mr. Andersson being then quite exhausted, when I immediately made his bed in the cart, and from this bed he was never able to rise without my assistance.

"One of the head men, shortly after our arrival, came over to visit Mr. Andersson, who requested to see Typandeka himself, with whom, as he told the man, he

late, as I am dying fast from the united effects of extreme debility, dysentery, etc. I have been senseless more than once during the last few days, but have at last roused myself to this last effort.

"Oh! blessed wife, we shall never meet in this life again, but surely in the next. I had thoughts of turning this journey to such good account for my poor family: and though it may have cost me my life, it is to be hoped it will bring something to your home, poor wife! I can see you so overwhelmed with grief when these lines reach you, and that you learn my bones are bleaching in this distant wilderness.

"I feel ill-prepared to leave this world; but I trust in God's mercy, and, above all, in His immeasurable love in sacrificing His only Son in order to redeem a wicked mankind. I very much want Divine consolation and support. A good honest clergyman would be a boon in my poor forlorn condition; but I too weak to write more."

was greatly displeased. But not until eight days afterward did the chief make his appearance, and then he looked afraid, and would not venture in the vicinity of the tree where we had encamped, but sat down at some little distance. I had to lay some skins and karosses on the ground near to the chief, and thence to carry my poor master, the tears flowing from my eyes while I bore him like a child in my arms. All he said to Typandeka was: 'Behold what your people have done. I shall let Nauma, Ochikongo, and Kamaherero know of it.' After this he requested me to carry him back again to the cart.

"The third day after our arrival at Typandeka's werft, he said to me, 'Axel, my last day is near'; and on the following one, June 27, he called me, and afterward wrote his last letter to his wife. He then named to me the prices of some articles for sale, and cautioned me not to leave Damaraland until the hunters went west.

"The day after Typandeka's visit we set out; but first I tried to make Andersson's bed in the cart as comfortable as possible, notwithstanding which he, at the least jolting of the vehicle, would cry out with the agony it caused him.

"Early on the third day, as I was assisting him in his bed, something seemed to break in his stomach, and he suddenly grew worse, and a kind of green slime came running from his mouth. He said, 'Now, Axel, it is all over with me.' He then requested me to read some Psalms suitable for a dying person, which I did; and having read them over twice, he remarked, 'How beautiful is the Swedish Psalm-book!' and continued, 'Greet

Een, and tell him how sorry I am not to see him again'; and added, 'I am now satisfied to die, I suffer so fearfully.'

"The next day he appeared a little better, and on the following one, the 4th of July, we left the last of the Ovaquamyama werfts, early in the morning, but were necessitated to make two trecks to enable us to reach the water. In the afternoon, Mr. Andersson became very sick, and the whole of that night and the following day the slime aforementioned was constantly running from his mouth; his weakness had now reached its extreme point. In the afternoon he, however, asked for a piece of fried liver, which I immediately prepared, and some of which he ate, but scarcely a quarter of an hour elapsed ere he died.

"As I could not bury Mr. Andersson's remains in a place where I might not afterward be enabled to find them, I inspanned, and made a moonlight treck; and next day, about noon, arrived at the first werft of the Ovaquambi. Here I decided on making my master's grave; but the chief Nauma would not consent to his remains being interred so near to him, and I was therefore compelled to retrace my way back about a quarter of an hour; and there, between two trees on the right of the road, I found for them a resting-place. I had only an axe and a tin dish with which to make the grave, and this was in hard, clayey soil.

"When I afterward asked Nauma why he should order me to bury his friend so far away in the bush, he wanted to send people back to reopen the grave; but this I of course would not permit."

Thus miserably perished in the flower of his age

(he was only forty-two), Charles John Andersson, adding another to the long list of enterprising men who have left their bones to whiten in the African wilderness.

On its being known at Cape Town that he had been thus prematurely cut off, the newspapers and periodicals were filled with panegyrics on the poor fellow, and regrets for his death ; of which the following, from the "Advertiser and Mail," is a fair specimen ; and I quote it the rather as the extract contains a short biographical sketch of Andersson's early life :

"Year by year, and even month by month, it is our melancholy task to chronicle the decease of men who stood conspicuous among the benefactors of their country and fellow-countrymen ; and who, by their departure, leave blanks behind them which their successors find it difficult to replace. Another of these we have to announce to-day in the death of John Charles Andersson, one of the bravest of explorers, the most enthusiastic of sportsmen, the most observant of naturalists, and withal as gentle and modest in feeling and demeanor as intrepid and fearless when surrounded with the most appalling dangers.

"Mr. Andersson, though a Swede by birth, was half an Englishman by blood, and quite a South African by adoption. From his father, a gentleman connected with some of the best families in England, he inherited a passion for sport and for nature, even in her wildest and sternest moods. When quite a youth, for family reasons he adopted his mother's family and Swedish name of Andersson ; and at the age of twenty-two, in 1840, he visited England, and there met with Mr. Galton, who was then organizing an expedition for the exploration of South-Western Africa. Arrangements were made by which he was to accompany Mr. Galton on this adventurous trip ; and in the following year they reached Cape Town, and proceeded together to Walwich Bay, whence they penetrated through Damaraland to the then utterly unexplored country of Ovampoland as far as Ondonga—a densely populated locality where within some thirty miles there are something like twenty thousand inhabitants.

"Of this journey, a most graphic and interesting account was soon afterward published by Mr. Galton, in a work which at once stamped that gentleman as one of the most skilful of travellers and explorers. After their return, while Mr. Galton proceeded to England, Mr. Andersson set about organizing, in 1851 or 1852, an independent expedition of his own to Lake Ngami. In this he succeeded admirably, reached the Lake, and penetrated a considerable distance to the northward of it. The results of his observations and explorations on that expedition, as well as the previous one, he published in his well-known and admirable volume entitled 'Lake Ngami,' which was prepared under his own personal superintendence in London, 1856, and which attracted the attention and secured the applause of the most distinguished literary and scientific authorities at home, from the 'Athenæum' to the 'Quarterly Review.'

"We well remember our first meeting with him, then in London, in Bloomsbury Square, near the British Museum, and the hearty welcome he met with from the Museum authorities, who knew so well how to appreciate the rich and abundant stores of specimens he had brought home with him from the wilds of Africa.

"In the following year he returned to the Cape, and accepted an appointment as superintendent of the mining operations of the Walwich Bay Mining Company. These proving unsuccessful, the engagement was soon broken off, and Mr. Andersson, his passion for travel and adventure still strong upon him, resolved on another expedition into the Interior. His friend, Mr. Green, having failed in an attempt to reach the Cunené—the boundary river between Ovampoland and the Portuguese possessions—he determined to repeat the effort, and to trace the river to its supposed source eastward toward Lake Ngami. Instead of the Cunené, he struck upon the Okavango, a river flowing eastward; and here it was he encountered a ferocious rhinoceros, which thrust its horn into his thigh, inflicting a gashing wound, which kept him months a helpless cripple in his tent. On his return to Otjimbingue he wrote an account of his journey, which was soon afterward published in a handsome and most interesting volume, entitled 'The Okavango.' Shortly after this he arrived in Cape Town, and in 1861 married the sister of Mr. Atchison, the Secretary of the Post Office, and with her proceeded to Otjimbingue, in Damaraland, where he had accumulated a considerable amount of property, and where he intended settling down in lucrative trade, supplying the elephant-hunters with the stores they required, and forwarding cattle and ivory to Cape Town in return. For some time this went on successfully, and large herds of cattle were sent down to Namaqualand, and across the Orange river. Then came the unfortunate and miserable war between the Damaras and Namaquas, in which Mr. Andersson felt that the latter were the assailants, and in the wrong; and living as he did among the Damaras, with all the chivalry of his nature, he devoted himself to their cause, and finding them to be cowards as they were, he himself became their chief and leader in the war. The natural result was embittered hostility against him by the Namaquas; so that the herds of cattle which he was then forwarding through their country to the colony were stopped, seized, and confiscated. This was heavy loss enough, but worse followed.

"In an attack by the Namaquas upon his own station of Otjimbingue he led the repelling party; and in the heat of the conflict found himself deserted by the cowards for whom he had ventured all. He was shot down by a bullet, which smashed his leg, and it was almost by a miracle that he escaped with his life. By the careful attention of his devoted wife, and the missionaries, and though last, not least, Mr. Baines, the artist, who happened to be then at Otjimbingue, he survived this wound; but when he returned some nine months afterward to Cape Town, it was only to find himself pronounced, by the surgeons whom he consulted, a cripple for life. During his long stay as an invalid here, at the residence of his brother-in-law, he devoted the weary hours to the composition of a work which he fondly hoped would prove the crowning triumph of his career. This was an elaborate and scientific description of the Birds of South-West Africa, the materials for which in his possession were of the richest and most extensive character. His collection of birds—of which duplicates and triplicates were sent to the museums at home—was exceedingly varied; the colored illustrations of them, prepared by his friend Mr. Baines and himself, in Damaraland, were very superb, and as they were then exhibited at the Public Library (and may still be seen there) attracted the admiration of every one; while his MS. descriptions of them extended over very many volumes. Arrangements were made with Messrs. Day and Son, of London, to have the work published in the first style of art at a cost of £3,000, and a large number of subscribers were found over the colony to make up the guarantee required by the publishers.

"But, in the meantime, the energetic traveller, though a cripple in person, and by that disastrous Damara war utterly ruined in property, lost not a jot of effort or enterprise. Accordingly, in May of 1866 he left Cape Town and proceeded to Damara once more. His first ventures in trade were successful; but his ill-luck still attended him, for the stores of ivory, feathers, etc., which from the interior he had sent down to Walwich Bay were seized by Namaqua marauders and carried away. His next determination was to proceed northward through Ovampoland, and open up a trade between the white hunters of the south and the Portuguese possessions to the north of the Cunené. Mr. Smuts, who is now in Cape Town, informs us that when he last saw Mr. Andersson it was at Ondonga, and that then he seemed in miserable health, but still bent upon his northward venture. That was in May of last year. How he fared since then, and until he met his melancholy fate in July, is touchingly told in the tale forwarded by his faithful Swedish attendant to Mr. Frederick Green, which reached Cape Town only yesterday, and which will be found elsewhere in our columns to-day.

"And thus has poor Andersson gone, and left a devoted wife and four helpless children to lament their irreparable loss. But his name will long be remembered. It is marked ineffaceably on the map of Africa. What Livingstone has achieved for the East Coast, that has Charles J. Andersson done for the West; and his name and fame will be ranked with those of the Bruces and Parkes of earlier days, and the Livingstones, Spekes, Burtons, and Bakers of our own time."

In Sweden, his native country, his sad fate was greatly deplored, not only by his numerous friends and acquaintances, but by the public generally, as is to be inferred from articles that appeared in the press overflowing with his praises, and laments for his untimely end.

In conclusion, I would remark that Andersson, as an explorer in unknown lands, stood high in the estimation of the scientific world; for though his discoveries, as compared with those of some others, may sink, in a degree at least, into insignificance, they were still considerable, and as such were recognized by several learned bodies; among the rest by the Royal Geographical Society of London, which presented him with a valuable testimonial, and by the University of Lund, in Sweden, where he graduated, which conferred on him the dignity of Doctor of Philosophy — "a fitting acknowledgment for the services rendered to the cause of civilization and science." But the diploma, unfortunately, did not arrive in Africa until after Andersson had passed beyond the reach of earthly distinctions,

It may be proper to add that those in Sweden who held Andersson dear have caused a simple marble tablet to be placed in the parish church of Tunheim (near the town of Wenersborg), with an inscription in Swedish, which, translated, reads thus:

To the Memory of

CHARLES JOHN ANDERSSON,

THE AFRICAN TRAVELLER,

BORN IN WERMELAND (SWEDEN), 1827,

DIED IN THE OVAMPO WILDERNESS (SOUTH AFRICA), 1867.

"During life he feared God,
And, dying, trusted in His mercy."

THE END.

www.ingramcontent.com/pod-product-compliance
Lightning Source LLC
LaVergne TN
LVHW020215110826
845151LV00003B/727

* 9 7 8 1 4 2 5 5 3 3 6 6 3 *